ME, MYSELF, & I

To Lynn

Archibald D Hart

Me, Myself, & I

*How Far Should We Go in Our Search
for Self-Fulfillment?*

Dr. Archibald D. Hart

Servant Publications
Ann Arbor, Michigan

Figure 6, on page 234, is entitled "Hierarchy of Needs" and is taken
from *Motivation and Personality* by Abraham H. Maslow. Copyright 1954
by Harper & Row, Publishers, Inc. Copyright © 1970 by Abraham H.
Maslow. Reprinted by permission of HarperCollins Publishers.

The names and characterizations in this book are fictional, although
based on real events. Any similarity between the names and characterizations and real people is unintended and purely coincidental.

Vine Books is an imprint of Servant Publications especially
designed to serve evangelical Christians.

Published by Servant Publications
P.O. Box 8617
Ann Arbor, Michigan 48107

Cover design by Michael Andaloro

92 93 94 95 96 97 98 10 9 8 7 6 5 4 3 2 1

Printed in the United States of America

ISBN 0-89283-766-7

Library of Congress Cataloging-in-Publication Data

Hart, Archibald D.
   Me, myself, and I : how far should we go in our search for self-
fulfillment? / Archibald D. Hart.
      p.   cm.
Includes bibliographical references.
ISBN 0-89283-766-7
1. Self-actualization (Psychology)—Religious aspects—Christianity.
2. Self. 3. Psychology and religon. I. Title.
BV4598.2.H37   1992
233'.5—dc20   92-20657

Contents

Introduction

I N THE STEW OF OUR "ME GENERATION," I can-
not think of any ingredient more important than the topic of
the "self." My own thoughts about the self have been simmering
on the back burner of my mind for a long time. I now believe
they are ready to come to a boil.

As a Christian psychologist, I regard Scripture as my guide to
understanding the essential nature of human existence. But I
am constantly appalled to see how it is used to perpetuate false
beliefs and generate unhealthy believers. Many people are thoroughly confused about themselves. Much of this confusion stems
from some very distorted psychology along with a selective use of
Scripture. This book is my attempt to more properly relate
Christian theology to secular psychology.

Scripture has long been misused to support various pet theological fads. The Christian church has always had to contend
with heresy, but the false beliefs of our modern age seem to be
different. They are not gross distortions of the gospel, as we find
in gnosticism or universalism. Today's heresies are more subtle,
more personal. Masquerading as "spiritual ideas," they can do
even more damage than any classical heresy.

This misuse of Scripture has been nowhere more harmful

than in our understanding of the self. No other idea common to both Christian theology and psychology—except perhaps that of neurotic guilt—has been more distorted. No wonder, then, that many Christians are confused about how they ought to think about themselves.

Just the other day a pastor asked me, "What am I supposed to believe? On the one hand, I'm told that the 'self must die,' but I have a teenage son who is desperately trying to develop a little self-esteem and struggling to find himself. I just don't know what to tell him or how to help him overcome his problem. I am so confused about what the Bible teaches about the self and what I sense people, including my own son, need to hear. Sometimes I just want to throw in the towel."

This pastor is not alone in his confusion. Like so many others, he has been cautioned not to believe everything that modern-day psychology has to say. And rightly so. But neither have we given him anything better. In this vacuum, many Christians have developed a "theology of the self" that sees the self as a threat to the gospel. At the other extreme, the world has developed a "psychology of the self" that majors in selfism and is heavily centered in secular humanism.

What is a Christian to believe? Should a parent tell a child who feels worthless: "You are no good at the core, so just accept it"? These little ones have been entrusted to us as parents. Do we encourage and develop our children's best, or do we treat them as creatures whose will must be broken, esteem shattered, and fulfillment discouraged? Sadly, many believing parents have opted for the latter, believing such a faulty approach to be biblical. They may not say it in so many words, but this subtle suspicion of the self relentlessly drives their actions.

A significant part of the problem resides in our use of language. We are not always clear nor consistent in our use of the term "self." We simultaneously say that "the self must die" and "I must help to build my son's self-esteem." In fact, we are *not* talking about the same concept. The word "self" may be the same, but we mean two different realities. Vague and conflicting definitions account for a lot of our confusion.

The preacher who calls us to "deny our self" means something quite different from the counselor who tells a distraught mother of a wayward teenager to "be true to yourself." The preacher is calling us to set aside our self as the source of personal ambition or selfishness and to be open to the claims of Christ. The counselor is talking about the self as a set of convictions or beliefs. "Be true to your convictions and hold on to what you believe." The counselor hopes the mother will not be swayed by her teenager's pleas for freedoms the mother knows will only lead to catastrophe.

But the problem runs deeper than this. We cannot deny some fundamental conflicts between Christian theology and secular psychology. Such differences cannot be disposed of by simply redefining our terms. We desperately need the *insights* of psychology to help us *diagnose* our problems, coupled with the insights and *power* of Christianity to *solve* them.

As we attempt to develop a biblical understanding of the self, we need to be sure that we are not simply buying into secular notions of the self. Just because they are popular doesn't mean they are correct. Instead of being rooted in a thoroughly scientific process of discovery, many ideas in secular psychology are simply philosophical in origin. In other words, they are just someone's ideas about something. Much of what Christians take issue with flows from this realm of philosophical psychology. These influences need to be tested against Scripture.

One of my goals for this book is to identify these philosophically-based ideas in order to decide whether they square with Scripture. I do not intend to provide a philosophical or theological treatise on the topic of the self. Others are better equipped than I to write such a book. Instead, I have tried to make this a practical handbook on the self. Pastors as well as laypeople face the daily struggle of relating to their own selves or of helping others to understand the complex relationship between their emotional and human selves and their walk with God. Misleading ideas about the self—both psychological and theological—can cause a lot of unnecessary disruption and pain.

Christians walk a narrow spiritual path, one which often conflicts with the ideas and behaviors of non-Christian friends and neighbors. But no matter how spiritual we become, we never cease being flesh and blood. We have to contend with our own distorted psyches, with impure motives, and unstable feelings. We cannot ignore or bypass the basic givens of life. We can never totally transcend our humanness.

Our "self" is a reality that cannot be ignored. Whether you acknowledge it or not, your self cries out to be understood. Your ideas about it need to be informed by a biblical perspective. Then and then only will you be a healthy self.

Psychology is a science which studies the behavior of the mind and tries to understand how it learns, thinks, and motivates our behavior. Even while providing valuable insights into how the self operates, psychological understanding will always be limited. We will never discover everything there is to know about the self. Our minds need divine revelation to fill in the gaps.

Only God really knows our hearts, the innermost part of our selves. Only his Word can establish crucial boundaries for the self. We ignore these revelations to our peril. On the other hand, we also ignore to our peril some of the solid insights of psychology, those not at variance with God's revealed Word. I am constantly amazed by how congruent Scripture is with the essential truths we are discovering about the mind.

If we set aside those concepts which are simply conjectures or projections of someone's own mind, the essential discoveries of psychology very much harmonize with Scripture. If God created us, surely he knows how we operate spiritually *and* psychologically. God's Word, describing the human condition from a spiritual perspective, will not conflict with what we discover about the mind and the self from a psychological perspective. There will always be quacks and those who promote non- scientific assertions of psychology. Our job is to learn to discern true from false, to distinguish what is helpful and what is not.

This book explores this *harmony* between God's Word and our puny attempts to describe the human psyche. I have chosen to focus on the self because this central concept seems to cause more confusion than any other. Psychologists and theologians alike—especially the pop-theologians who write a lot of the books attacking the self—have grossly misunderstood it. How crucial that we "clean up" this confusion by clarifying what both Scripture and psychology have to say about the self.

This clarity is particularly important for those who engage in counseling or psychotherapy. Of all the branches of psychology, psychotherapy has been more influenced by philosophically-based ideas than any other. In recent times, we have made strides in correcting its underlying bias toward non-scientific ideas. But so many popular therapies lack validation from empirical research and depend entirely on the gullibility of hurting people for their success. Let's admit it. A lot of contemporary psychotherapy is mere "pseudoscience."

I don't mean to imply the absence of helpful therapy. We cannot throw out the baby with the bath water just because the water is dirty. We are still psychological beings who need help in understanding ourselves. The more we know about how we tick internally—including what God has revealed about our "selves" —the more we will be able to live the abundant and satisfying lives intended by our Creator.

I have three objectives in mind for this book. First, I would like *to clear up our persistent confusion over the nature of the self.* We cannot begin to understand how perfectly the Bible "fits" our human condition if we do not first understand the concept of the self. So much has already been written about self-esteem, self-actualization, and self-acceptance—both for and against— that the average believer is nothing if not confused. Too often the word "self" is used without clarifying what is meant.

Second, I want *to show how the gospel is essential to the healing of the self.* Secular psychology by itself cannot bring real salvation to any human being. We desperately need a Christian psychology that understands how God works through the Spirit in the innermost parts of the self. Without spiritual healing, wholeness in body and mind remains incomplete.

Third, I want *to provide resources for healing the self by using an integrated approach.* Certainly, God's work at the core of the self is essential to producing wholeness. But for many it is *only the beginning.* Deeply wounded people often face a lengthy struggle to overcome the damage already inflicted on the self by abuse, misinformation, and dysfunction. God intends us to be whole selves, and he has provided the resources for us to achieve this wholeness.

I invite you to set aside prejudices and preconceived ideas in order to explore with me the wonderful world inside your own self. If you do, you will discover how perfectly the gospel of our Lord Jesus Christ fits the human condition. Perhaps you will stand in awe, as I do, before your Creator as you realize the beauty of his loving design.

PART ONE

The Problem with the Self

1 Sick of Our Selves?

Beware lest any man spoil you through philosophy and vain deceit, after the tradition of men, after the rudiments of the world, and not after Christ. For in him dwelleth all the fulness of the Godhead bodily. And ye are complete in him.... **Col 2:8-10 KJV**

I REMEMBER HER as if it were yesterday. Dark hair, brown eyes, pretty, and only nineteen. Let me call her Sonja. With her sights set on becoming a school teacher, she had just arrived at the university. In my late twenties, I had just begun working toward a second career in psychology.

Also very active in Christian youth work along with my wife, I watched this vivacious young woman throw herself into the thick of things with enthusiasm. Sonja's solid biblical foundation had prepared her to teach in our Sunday School. Her extraordinary musical talent led to performing at youth rallies and helping to train our youth choir.

What impressed me most about her, however, was her self-confidence. Not that Sonja acted as if she felt superior to others. On the contrary, she seemed extremely understanding and considerate. She seemed self-possessed, serene, and assured. Without apparent defensiveness, she displayed the courage to be imperfect without feeling devastated.

In a word, Sonja struck me as healthy. If she made a mistake, she readily admitted it and tried to correct it. If she was criticized, she listened carefully to her critic, accepted feedback graciously, and never seemed to bear a grudge. Marked by a deep spiritual commitment and obvious love for her Savior, Sonja showed all the promise of becoming an outstanding school teacher.

But then something went wrong. Eager to become even more committed and to delve deeper into the Christian faith, she began attending a weekly meeting of another Christian group led by a former minister of one of the mainline churches. This man had become disenchanted with his church's theology and had started his own Christian retreat center just outside the city. Visitors could stay over and many local people attended the meetings as well.

The leader had attracted a strong following with his charismatic personality. At first he seemed to be preaching a legitimate gospel, with a strong emphasis on claiming a deeper, more victorious personal life. Sonja found the message appealing and was drawn in more and more, while still participating in our youth group. Slowly, I began to see a change. She often seemed depressed. Her vitality vanished. The brightness in her brown eyes faded. She even seemed to start dressing dowdily.

From our conversations together, I noticed increasing self-doubt. Listening to this man's preaching and attending private counseling sessions with him had begun to erode her self-confidence and undermine her esteem. The preacher told her she was "too full of herself," that no one deserved to be so happy.

This man's general ministry style entailed a frontal attack on the self. Adopting a literal interpretation of Galatians 2:20 ("I am crucified with Christ"), he preached that everyone had to "die" within themselves. He interpreted "good" feelings as sinful and enjoyable acts as wicked. One must hate oneself and be unhappy in order to be truly spiritual. He believed that human nature, even when redeemed, could not be trusted.

Slowly this minister began to manage people's lives, including Sonja's. We were powerless to stop him. He advised people to sell their farms and give the money to his center. He matched young people for marriage and told couples when they could procreate. He became a strict disciplinarian, all in the name of Christ.

Under this constant bombardment on her self, Sonja plunged downhill fast. One day I heard that she had been hospitalized in the state psychiatric hospital where I was doing my research. After a few weeks of intensive care, Sonja was discharged. But her pain seemed unbearable. She had come to believe that she was the most wicked, vile, debased, repulsive, demon-possessed, and depraved person that had ever walked on God's earth.

Early one morning, when she could no longer endure the emotional onslaught, Sonja left the center. She walked the half-mile to the railroad tracks and laid her head down on the steel rail. Death came quickly as the train rounded the bend. The inquest found no fault with the preacher. It did turn out to be the beginning of the end, however. Not long afterwards, public sentiment began to turn against this man and his message. The center eventually closed.

This true story illustrates just how destructive faulty theology can be. *True theology does not harm the self.* If anything, it repairs it, upbuilds it, and strengthens it. God's plan of salvation perfectly fulfills the needs of the self. When this plan is distorted and twisted to fit the warped minds of dysfunctional preachers and teachers, havoc ensues in the soul, making shipwreck of the self.

PREACHING A SICK THEOLOGY
IN THE NAME OF CHRIST

You may think this story is too far-fetched to be relevant to today's church. Unfortunately, I have encountered many such examples, right here in the United States. The same kind of personal harm is often perpetuated by well-meaning, but unwitting preachers of the gospel. *Sick pastors produce a sick theology that shapes a sick church to yield sick selves.*

Sometimes it's the sick theology that produces the sick pastor. I call such ministers "pathogenic agents" because they create pathology wherever they go. They may be ignorant of what they are doing or unenlightened in some understanding of the human self. They may be misguided by poor theology and a superficial understanding of language. Whatever the case, in the name of Christ they preach not salvation *for* the self, but an anti-self message that leads to psychological destruction, or at least severe damage. Christian parents, influenced by this message, then pass the damage on to their children and to their children's children.

What really lies behind this misguided anti-self propaganda? Is it merely a fear that too much sinfulness resides in the self, which must therefore be eradicated? Our common fear is that everything about the self—self-esteem, self-fulfillment, or even self-acceptance—smacks of selfism, an unhealthy preoccupation. Knowing how desperately people want to feel better about themselves, many pastors are unable to integrate this human need into sound biblical theology.

If preachers are confused, imagine how confused the average Christian believer can be. Adding to the confusion has been a flood of books that have attacked psychology, claiming it fosters false ideas about the self. Every suggestion of anything good in the human psyche is labeled "humanistic."

What are Christians to believe? What does the Bible really say about such topics as self-concept, self-image, self-esteem, self-fulfillment? How do old-fashioned but nevertheless legitimate ideas like self-denial, self-sacrifice, self-surrender, and death to self fit into these more modern ideas? Are these ideas really opposites? What does God really want us to do with our "selves"?

While I would not be so arrogant as to suggest I have the answers to these vexing questions, I can at least help you understand some of the issues. Perhaps, like myself, you have been exposed to a theology that has been very "down" on the self.

But is it any wonder that critics of the self abound? Clearly, the "self" has become a national obsession. Think about it. The advice of the sixties was "Do your own thing." The seventies pushed a preoccupation with ME, hence the "ME generation." In the eighties, the "New Age" movement pushed the self right over the top. It reigns as king or queen—or even as a god or goddess—over a realm that serves its every whim and fancy, demand and desire.

The nineties has brought increased demands for alternate lifestyles and for freedom to choose life or death for unborn babies or for the elderly. The self has become the sole arbiter of its own destiny. Our "culture of narcissism," as Christopher Lasch calls it, pervades all areas of life. As we approach a new millennium, this narcissism shows no sign of abating.

If any generation in the history of the world needs help understanding the self, certainly it is ours. We are lost, wandering in the wilderness of psychology, with no sure signposts to show the way. In fact, the psychological signposts we do have all seem to point in different directions.

But well-meaning critics of the self often contribute to our confusion. "Psychology-bashing" has become a popular evangelical sport. And though we need to think critically about psychological concepts, much of the current attack on psychology only tends to muddy the waters. Even so, more than a grain of truth can be found in what critics of the self have to say. Our task is to extract this truth and then synthesize it into a meaningful whole.

Critics of the self range from fundamentalist authors to secular sociologists and philosophers. Since my primary concern is centered on how the body of Christ understands and uses the notion of the self, I will focus exclusively on those who attempt to present a biblical critique. What do the critics of the self really have to say? Where is their criticism legitimate and where is it not? What should we believe and what should we reject? Let's take a look at the major antagonists of the self to discern the kernel of truth in their claims.

CRITICS OF THE SELF

The critics of the self from within the body of Christ fall mainly into two camps. The first criticize psychology itself.

Believing all notions about the self belong to the field of psychology, they reject such notions. They tend to ignore sociology, anthropology, and the other human sciences. They feel threatened by psychology's powerful insights and potential for undermining everything they teach. They fear that it threatens to become a religion in its own right.

This first camp of critics believes that Christians are abandoning spiritual resources in favor of purely human means to solve personal problems. They disagree with many of the solutions that psychology has suggested for enhancing the self, ideas like assertiveness, self-love, and self-actualization. They are right to feel threatened—up to a point. A Christian psychology *is* concerned about these very same issues.

Few of these critics have received any in-depth training in psychology and therefore do not adequately understand the concepts involved. They justifiably fear that pride will get the better of us, that too much dabbling in the self will lead us to become like gods ourselves. They perceive psychology and psychiatry as totally incompatible with the Christian faith. They believe the very term "psychology" (which literally means the study of the soul or psyche) is a misnomer, because the profession denies the very existence of the soul! Certainly, many of their concerns are valid. I hope to show, however, that these critics overgeneralize their arguments and literally throw the baby out with the bath water.

The second camp encompasses those who find fault with psychology's excessive preoccupation with the self. Some of these critics come from within the discipline of psychology itself and thus have been well trained in the area. This group voices the same essential concerns as those in the first camp. But their broader understanding of the issues renders their case more plausible and their arguments nearer the truth.

While accepting the value of psychology, this second camp criticizes it for some of the ways it has conceptualized the self. These critics, I believe, put psychology in its rightful place: subservient to the revealed word of Scripture. They perceive many flaws in how psychology both understands and tries to heal the self. I myself belong to this second camp of critics.

Of course, this second group is not homogeneous. Christian psychologists don't necessarily embrace a *Christian* psychology. They differ widely in just how much of psychology's understanding of the self they accept. Some may be too uncritical of psychology. Having been trained in a purely secular setting, some Christians fear that too much theology will contaminate their psychology. Thus, they tend to separate the two disciplines as much as possible. This sort of person keeps one foot in psychology and the other in their faith.

We need so much more than simply psychologists who are Christians. We desperately need a Christian psychology that understands the limitations of merely humanistic psychotherapy and how God works to bring healing to the self.

Let's review each of these camps in greater detail to enable us to develop a more balanced understanding of the self.

CAMP NUMBER ONE:
THERE'S NOTHING GOOD ABOUT PSYCHOLOGY

This first group of critics is totally opposed to everything that psychology stands for. Psychology, in their view, contradicts the gospel and is dangerous to the faith. While not dealing specifically with the concept of the self, these critics automatically demolish it as part of their argument against psychology.

In this limited space, I will confine my comments regarding this group to Dave Hunt, in his book *Beyond Seduction*[1] and John MacArthur, Jr., in his book *Our Sufficiency in Christ*.[2] No doubt many other authors deserve a response, but I will focus on these two as more or less representative of this first camp of critics.

Dave Hunt, a former CPA management consultant, has extensively researched Eastern mysticism, cults, the occult, and psychic phenomena. He exhibits a passion to see us return to a truly biblical foundation for Christian living. In *Beyond Seduction*, Hunt expands on his rejection of psychology as follows: "Christian psychology is one of the most alarming examples of a wrong approach to Scripture; it is based upon predetermined theories that are imposed upon the Bible." He goes on to assert that these ideas were not developed by sincere Christians, but are "contrivances of humanists hostile to God's Word, psychologists looking for solutions to human problems outside Scripture."[3]

Hunt's wholesale condemnation of psychology paints a black and white picture. It's an all or nothing, take it or leave it approach that confuses many Christians.

While it is true that a lot of *therapeutic* psychology derives from humanistic roots, not all of it does. We simply cannot afford to throw all psychology away just because some of it has gone astray. We still must reckon with the complexity of our minds and emotions. The study of the psychology of learning, perception, and personality is just as valid as the study of anatomy or surgery. But I have yet to hear Dave Hunt or anyone else clamoring for a "Christian theory of surgery."

One of the greatest errors many critics, including Hunt, make is that they fail to adequately distinguish between *general* psychology and *therapeutic* psychology. They say "psychology" when what they really mean to say is "psychotherapy." Psychology is more than psychotherapy. It involves studying such matters as how the brain learns, how we see and perceive, how the personality develops, and how emotions are affected by the endocrine glands. By studying such areas, we delve more deeply into how God has created the human body and brain. In this sense, the study of psychology is no different than the study of other medical sciences, which surely do not threaten the Christian faith nor undermine the Bible. If anything, these sciences can help us understand more clearly how perfectly the gospel fits our human existence.

So what, precisely, is the problem? Psychotherapy is what causes most of the commotion. Historically critical of the Christian faith, psychotherapy is a less scientific, more philosophically-based discipline which purports to define what is "normal" and "not normal." The assumptions which underlie psychotherapeutic approaches need to be critically evaluated. Dave Hunt is correct when he says that we have not yet developed a Christian psychology at the therapeutic level. I am sure he would agree that we desperately need a bibically sound approach that incorporates Christian values.

But let me be fair to Hunt. He quite rightly points out how easily our thinking about the self becomes self-centered and how this "selfism" has its roots in humanism.[4] Many Christian psychologists have, in fact, been heavily influenced by secular humanism. As a result, they often present a self-centered understanding of the self, and some of them attack the very idea of self-denial and self-sacrifice.

While Hunt is right in warning us to be careful about how we think about the self, I believe he unwittingly leaves the impression that a person can get along quite well without any self at all. Thus, self-denial becomes a matter of *doing away* with the self. I know that Dave Hunt has a self, that he feels about himself and has an attitude toward himself. This is what self-esteem is all about.

To label all self-esteem, self-worth, self-acceptance, and self-love evil "selfisms" overstates his case against psychology.[5] To insist that a person must not have feelings toward the self—from which esteem, love, and acceptance flow—is to describe a person who doesn't exist.

For good or ill, humans possess a self and need help in dealing with that self. The truth is that *Christ is the true answer for the self's problems.* Since the self is not innately good and tends to be overly concerned about itself, it must be subjected to the control of Christ. And as Christ enters in, he controls, shapes, and guides the self. He does not destroy it nor does he despise it.

Dr. John MacArthur is another prominent critic of psychology. By implication, he rejects the concept of the self in his book *Our Sufficiency in Christ.* MacArthur is pastor of Grace Community Church in Sun Valley, California, which experienced a very unfortunate lawsuit a few years ago. A young man took his life while being counseled there. Although the church was exonerated of liability, the experience raised several important issues for Dr. MacArthur.

He asserts that true psychology—"the study of the soul" as he terms it—can be done only by Christians, since they alone possess the resources for understanding and transforming the soul. "The secular discipline of psychology is only capable of dealing with people at the superficial level."[6] The self needs more than self-understanding to be made whole. And this deeper insight can only come out of a Christian perspective. I could not agree with him more.

MacArthur admits that certain techniques of psychology are useful in lessening trauma or dependency, or that certain emotional illnesses can have organic causes which require medication. And, he rightly points out that a lot of psychology cannot be regarded as a science.[7] His issue is with therapy, not psychology. Most counselors today are *not* using scientific psychology to guide their therapy. Most apply a mish-mash, hodge-podge, hit and run assortment of techniques, most of which have never been tested in a scientific laboratory. Where they have, few have proven effective.

The dependence of many Christian psychologists on "human therapies" is clearly a problem. But the mistake that MacArthur makes is to equate "Christian psychology" with Christian psychologists.[8] Just because someone is a Christian and a psychologist does not mean that one is practicing an authentic Christian psychology. Certainly, it is unfair to judge whether or not there *can* be a Christian psychology by whether or not a Christian psychologist is being true to biblical teaching.

In a chapter on "Psychological Sanctification," MacArthur comes closer to the issue of the self. He says that the worst that psychology can offer is to help you "look deep within," or "get in touch with your inner self." He goes on to say that "Scripture gives no such counsel. We are to *fix our eyes on Jesus*. There are no reliable answers within."[9]

MacArthur's argument goes like this: psychology wants you to look within. But there are no reliable answers within yourself. Therefore, we must not look within. Sounds reasonable, doesn't it? But here's the catch. If we never look inside ourselves, how will we be able to discover the *problems* of the self? We need to accurately diagnose the disease before we can find a treatment. Looking within helps locate the problem, though it doesn't supply a solution. MacArthur is correct when he asserts that the "right answers" are not in ourselves, but in Christ's gospel. But we would be less than human if we tried to be oblivious to what is going on inside ourselves. As fallen human beings, we often prefer to keep our sins and hurts hidden deep within us. Looking within provides a way of uncovering hidden hurts, unforgiven sins, barriers to God's spirit, areas of self-deception—precisely what a Christian psychology should uncover. How can you appropriate God's forgiveness and healing if you never explore the recesses of past hurts, fears, and traumas?

Paul explicitly advocates such an approach in the context of confession before partaking of the Lord's supper. "But let a man examine himself, and so let him eat of that bread and drink of that cup" (1 Cor 11:28). Self-examination is an aspect of "looking within." Jesus advocates it with regard to our motives in judging others (see Mt 7:5). Paul reiterates the point in order to test whether we are in the faith (2 Cor 13:5).

CAMP NUMBER TWO:
OUR PROBLEMS WITH THE SELF

Turning now to those critics of the self from within psychology, let's look at the arguments of Dr. Paul Vitz of New York University. His criticisms are fairly representative of those Christian psychologists at serious loggerheads with the secular humanist aspects of their discipline.

Dr. Vitz rightly draws attention to the immense popularity of selfism within the church itself.[10] He observes that with the rise of secular ideas and values, especially psychological theories, the basic Christian concept of the unique importance of the self was stripped of its theological justification. The notion of pride as the fundamental sin, along with greed and envy, gave way to the belief that our most basic sin is to be chaotic and unfocused.

Its importance having been enhanced by democracy, the individual self was provided the necessary "rationale" by selfist humanism. Self-realization soon replaced salvation.

Vitz's main discussion centers on five theses:

1. That psychology as religion exists.
2. Psychology as religion can be criticized on many grounds, not just religious.

3. Psychology as religion is deeply anti-Christian.
4. Psychology as religion is extensively supported by higher education.
5. Psychology as religion destroys individuals, families and communities.[11]

However, Vitz clearly states that he is talking about *psychotherapy* rather than general psychology. He specifically *excludes* experimental psychology (study of sensation, perception, cognition, memory etc.) which has little to do with humanistic self-psychology.[12] He also excludes behaviorism and psychoanalysis because these disciplines have other problems. I find this a pity because much of what Vitz has to say applies to these disciplines as well.

Our issue as Christians is with the therapeutic psychologies: counseling and psychotherapy, not with psychology in general. If we reject all psychology, we paint a picture of the human person as devoid of substance, a body with no mind, feelings, perceptions, memory, knowing, or even believing. It is psychotherapy that has become a "religion" in itself. This distinction is extremely important.

The essence of Vitz's book is that nearly all psychotherapies foster "selfism." This introverted preoccupation inevitably ends in a relentless and single-minded search for and glorification of the self.[13] Such *idolatry* of the self directly collides with the Christian injunction to *lose* the self. Humanistic selfism leaves no room for sin. In fact, it worships sin. Selfist love is in opposition to Christian love. The modern self is intrinsically self-destructive. Transcending the self will not cure our problems, but will only make them worse. The human self needs *repairing* before it can become *actualized*. We will deal with how one repairs the self in a later chapter, as well as how it can be damaged and disfigured by sin and trauma.

Vitz's criticisms are all valid. But the manner in which they are presented can leave the wrong impression. We begin to suspect everything that psychology has to offer because so much psychotherapy is "selfist" and humanistically based. Furthermore, since the self is central to humanistic psychology, we feel it necessary to reject all notions about the self.

No matter how unacceptable today's selfist psychologies may be, human beings are still left with a psyche or soul with which to contend. I am still a self, whatever anyone thinks about modern ideas, about self-esteem, self-awareness, or self-actualization. And since I am a self, I need to know what God's remedies are for its ailments. I need all the help I can get in understanding the truth about my self, its sinful nature, how it needs to be regenerated and filled with God's Spirit.

How can we ensure our protection from selfism and egotism? We must begin by adequately understanding what the self is all about. As Oswald Chambers, the author of *My Utmost for His Highest*, so eloquently says, "the teaching of our Lord and of the Apostle Paul continually centers around 'I,' yet there is no egotism about it."[14] This great biblical scholar and preacher then goes on to say that "everything in the Bible is related to man, to his salvation, to his sanctification, to his keeping."

Chambers distinguishes between *egotism*, which is a conceited insistence on "my particular ways, manners, and customs," and *egoism*, which is merely a way of thinking which makes human personality the center. Humans are the central focus of God's revelation. The self is the target of salvation and must be centered on God. My self is a human edifice in which God is to be glorified. This is why we are commanded to let the mind of Christ be in us, that is, in our selves (Phil 2:5).

How refreshing! In this very remarkable book, Oswald Chambers provides us with a clear description of the biblical importance of the individual self, uncluttered by humanism and its counter-critics. After all, he wrote it before 1917, before Freud had really made much impact, and before Carl Rogers could even talk.

Later, I will have more to say about how the self fits into God's plan for us. He created us to be selves, each unique and precious. Unfortunately, the word "self" has come to mean many things, but we must not forget that at root it is part of God's own image. He created us and breathed life into our nostrils. We became selves—not living gods, but living souls. Every corpuscle, every muscle, nerve, and sinew was infused with this divine image. Even the angels cannot reflect the glory of God as we can. As we proceed, I hope to clarify the structure of this God-given self.

CLEANING UP THE SELF

There is one important point I need to make before we proceed with understanding the true nature of the self. It is this: regardless of what psychology has discovered about the self and regardless of whether or not we believe there is such a thing as the self, we all have to live with the self within us. The problem is that this self is lost, hidden, concealed, suppressed, and even disguised from all of us. What will become very clear as we proceed is that the self is a lot easier to talk about than it is to expose, easier to discover in others than in yourself. In most of us, it is only an infant longing to grow to maturity.

This is the strange thing about the self. Most of us have never fully encountered it or made peace with it. We have lived with it for all these years, and yet we feel that we are living with a stranger within.

What's going on?

Whatever your opinion of the secular psychologies, you cannot avoid facing the common theme they nearly all agree on: that the "true" identity of the self in all of us has been obscured from our awareness by the layers of conditioning that our minds have received ever since childhood.[15]

Consider the recent rediscovery of the brilliant colors in Michelangelo's Sistine Chapel frescoes. Centuries of soot and dust had added thick layers of grime to the surface of these masterpieces. They had become so dark and colorless that people had come to believe that this was their original tone. With careful cleaning and restoration their true brilliance has been restored. The frescoes are not dingy and morbid in their tones, but vibrant and bright. Centuries of bad air and careless cleaning had perverted their true splendor.

What better illustration can there be for what happens to the self? Almost from birth, a conditioning process begins to conceal my true self. Oh, it's not intentional. No one is trying to harm me. It's the by-product of the normal process of social-ization and of sin. Gradually the self becomes concealed behind layers of muck and is robbed of its true glow. Poly-chromes become monochromes and brilliance is replaced by drabness. The true nature of my self is lost, awaiting the ulti-mate cleansing and restoration that only God's Spirit can bring. But even then, as we shall see, the true self may remain concealed. The years of conditioning, of being told to "do this," "not to do that," "feel this," "act that way," have left a bar-rier that continues to conceal the real self, even when God has cleansed us at the core. I may continue to be afraid of what people think if I reveal too much of who I really am. I may not be able to trust those who say they love me. And while I might have an inkling of what my real self is like, I cannot bring it into the light where it can be viewed by myself and others and received as acceptable.

This means that we retreat from our true selves and live behind facades, masks, and pretenses; that we don't have any sense of who we really are. We long to be able to speak our true mind, scream if necessary, let our feelings out or insist that someone keep a promise, but we are unable to do so because we aren't sure our selves can survive. So often I've wanted to follow a dream, risk a venture, or just go out and sit in the park and cry, and my self wouldn't allow it because it didn't know if it was permissible. The grime of learned expectations and the fear of ridicule and rejection have concealed my true heart.

Sometimes I feel that my world has told me what I should feel and what path I should follow to the degree that my self is no longer able (if it ever was) to truly decide anything. In moments of weakness I even question whether it is my own self that loves God or whether I am just trying to please someone else. Fortunately these moments are rare, but they do come.

So becoming a Christian doesn't necessarily reveal the true nature of my self. I may glimpse enough of my rottenness to beg for God's forgiveness and to surrender my will to him, but do I not still have much conditioning to undo? Each day I try to search my inner self for the presence of God and try to discern his guidance instead of searching the hearts of others. It's not that I care less about other people, but by listening to my own self, peeling away some of the dead varnish, I can begin to discover more about how God deals with my self, than in any other way.

PSYCHOLOGY AND SPIRITUALITY WORKING TOGETHER

Being a Christian involves growing into the likeness of Christ. True, this is a spiritual process. But it is also an emotional and psychological process. We need God's restorative grace, but we can also benefit from the understanding that psychology can provide. Many of us are handicapped in our spiritual lives by years of exposure to dysfunctional environments. We are plagued by our faulty selves. Thankfully God knows this. As our Creator, God understands how we are made, how we function, *and* how things go wrong—not just physically but also psychologically. He knows how we operate in both the psychological *and* spiritual realm. He also knows that we often need help overcoming psychological and emotional problems. He knows how our moods affect our worship, how dysfunction in relationships will breed grudges and anger, and how abuse can destroy hope and make it hard to have faith. *He knows this!* He doesn't bypass our feelings, thoughts, awarenesses, reactions or behaviors in pushing us to spiritual wholeness. He seeks to heal them as a part of his work in us. He helps us to become fully integrated persons. His call to spirituality and holy living is not a demand to deny our psyches. It is a call to *integrate who we are in our minds with what we are in our spirits.* So much of what is presented in contemporary Christianity is not a call to integrate our emotional and spiritual lives, but a call to deny who we are as whole persons. It is no wonder that many have become disillusioned and have given up the faith. They feel hypocritical. They are taught to "split" their personalities, to deny psychological reality in order to "transcend" their humanness.

It is true that more than anything else, we desperately need a renewal of God's Holy Spirit in the church today. But I would say that we also desperately need a vision of how we can be *healthy in our whole beings*—how spirituality and psychology can work together to make us more complete in Christ.

This working together is what *integration* is all about—it is the bringing together in total harmony of the various realms of our existence: physical, psychological, and spiritual.

In pleading for a greater integration of our psychological and spiritual selves I am in no way asserting that psychology is the superior way of knowing the self nor is it to be the supreme judge of truth. If anything, psychology has to be scrutinized by the standards of Scripture, not the other way around. But what I am asserting is that the *same God* who wrote the Scriptures is the *same God* who created us and who knows how we function in *all* aspects of our being. The God of the Bible is also the God of our minds. It is with confidence, then, that we can expect God to be a part of all we discover that is truthful about ourselves. This truth will not work against this gospel but alongside with it, ensuring that "he which hath begun a good work in you will perform it until the day of Jesus Christ" (Phil 1:6).

CHAPTER 2

Stuck with Our Selves

I AM A *PERSON*. I think, I feel, I experience, I'm happy, I believe, I obey. I am more than just a body, more than glands, chemistry, blood, and bones. I throb with energy, thrill to the cry of a newborn baby, and get goose bumps when I see an autumn sunset.

I can fall passionately in love with the girl of my dreams, dote on my children, and idolize my grandchildren. I can desire intimacy with my wife, closeness with my friends, and camaraderie with my work colleagues. I can admire beauty, yearn for foreign travel, and talk to a cherished pet as if it were a person.

I can be stubborn when told to do something, easily irritated by long lines, aggravated by egotistic bores, and devastated by failure. I like to have fun, learn new hobbies, sail boats, and ride a bicycle. One day I want to be able to paint in watercolors and learn to skate so that I can glide over ice as easily as the dancers on TV.

I am a *human person*. At times I am torn between loving and hating. I reproach myself for not living up to my expectations or being the best person I can be. Sometimes I feel content with who I am (usually when sitting on the beach in Hawaii and watching a sunset), but at other times I wish I could just erase everything and start over again. There are times I feel so much neurotic guilt I want to scream. At other times, ecstatic joy over-whelms me and I marvel at my capacity for bliss.

When I least expect it, my body aches all over. But this part of my self is never as painful as when my heart aches. Sadness and separation seem to go together in the self. When someone in my family has suffered a major setback, my chest throbs with a deep and indescribable ache. Anguish and ecstasy, agony and exalta-tion, these all seem to be an essential part of myself.

Because I am a human person, *I have a self.* It is by no means a perfect self. On the contrary, I am flawed, error-prone, stained by sin, and often selfish. In fact, it is a "fallen" self, and I will have a lot more to say about this in later chapters. *But I am nevertheless a self, the only self I can be.* God doesn't transplant a new self; he repairs the one he has already given me. I can no more change and be another self than I can fly to the moon. I am *stuck* with me, for better or worse. Is this a problem? It shouldn't be!

Despite my imperfection and incompleteness, in some myste-rious way, *my self bears God's image.* Contrary to what I deserve, my wretched self has been redeemed by amazing grace and given a special place in the kingdom of God. I am a joint heir with Christ.

The self is more than just who I am as a person. *The self is me knowing that I am a person.* Me being able to decide what sort of person I want to be. Me making a myriad of decisions every day and trying to shape my own future according to God's plan for my life. Me haunted by the memory of my history—where I've come from, the many mistakes I've made and failures I've expe-rienced—yet oriented to the future because of having been re-deemed and forgiven for all my failures.

I am a self precisely because I can *choose* to obey God and *decide* what course my life will take. My self is alert to myself, sen-sitive to the feelings of others, and aware of its presence in the world. *My self is a given.* I cannot deny that it exists. Even though there are many problems within myself, in some mysterious way God calls me to *relate* to myself—an aspect of selfhood that many psychologies have never fully understood.

I need to be aware of what I am doing, feeling, and thinking. God has given me this capacity, one which too often is unused. I have an opinion about myself and a desire to see my self grow as a person. It is my *self*—not my mind, brain, glands, or any other organ of my body—that responds to God's call and that has to come to believe that what God has told me of himself is true. It is the meeting of my self with God that leads to salvation.

OUR STRUGGLE WITH OUR SELVES

So if I am a self because this is how God has created me, why then do so many others try to make me feel guilty because I am only a person? Surely I'm not alone here. Don't you often find that people just can't accept the fact that your self is all too human, imperfect and prone to making mistakes?

People want us to be perfect. Often these people are not perfect themselves, but expect us to be. I can't tell you how often I just want to scream, "Please let me be an imperfect person! Let me make mistakes, fail, and be an ordinary human. If you help me develop the courage to be an imperfect person, I know that I will be a better person to you." Few of us seem to really believe this paradox.

I have not always been so convinced about who I am as a self. Ever since I started studying psychology more than thirty years ago, I have been vexed by what appeared to be a conflict between how psychology views the "self" and how theology (at least the particular brand of Christian teaching I had learned) views the self.

I became a Christian when I was eighteen years old... an old-fashioned, dramatic conversion in an evangelistic service. Many of my friends shared the same conversion experience, though few survived to become what I consider genuinely alive spiritually. Unable to secure an adequate foothold on the slippery slopes of their intellectual and personal mountains, they gradually fell away from the faith. A few of them gave up on their faith struggle for the same reasons that I felt so vexed. They couldn't quite integrate what they knew about themselves with what so many eager but often inadequately informed preachers were trying to tell them. So they threw in the spiritual towel.

Ambiguity between the help I tried to give hurting people from a spiritual point of view and the skills that were emerging in my formation as a Christian clinical psychologist tore me up for many years. Again and again I seemed to knock my head against theological brick walls. The theme of my personal struggle was always the same: issues surrounding that thing we call the "self." What was the nature of my personhood? *Who* am I? *What* am I?

I struggled to understand what my friends were trying to say when they preached about "dying to self." They quoted Matthew 16:24: "If any man will come after me, let him deny himself and take up his cross, and follow me." Others spoke of "crucifying the self" (Gal 2:20), "sacrificing the self" (Rom 12:1), and being "delivered from your self" (Lk 4:18).

The basic message was always the same: somehow you've got to get free of your self. The logic seemed to be, "Christ has died and now lives in you, so you don't have to live as a self anymore. If you have any problems with who you are as a person, it is because your self is getting in the way. There is basically nothing good in your 'self,' so you might as well throw it away."

But no one ever defined what this "self" was.

The topic became even hotter when the issue of *self-esteem* came up. How can "esteem" come from a self that is so rotten? How can a self pull itself up by its own rotten bootstraps? "Surely," these anti-self protagonists would argue, "any value that the self has comes entirely from Christ, so how can the self take any pride in it?"

Without realizing it, of course, they had switched phrases. "Esteem" had become equated with "pride." They saw self-esteem as an attempt to "deify" the self, to make it into its own god, or at least to attribute more value to it than it deserved. These same issues from my formative years as a Christian still abound today.

I have never espoused a secular humanistic framework for psychology. On the contrary, I have tried my best to remain true to an evangelical theological position, to give preeminence to Scripture as a source of truth, and to apply this truth to life's difficulties. But I became more and more confused. How could I be "true" to Scripture (or to the particular interpretation I had learned), yet give some credibility to the understanding of the human self emerging from legitimate psychology?

Was this just a paradoxical but inevitable tension between the gospel and the human sciences? Or merely a problem of semantics? Did some theological approaches actually misuse or even abuse the concept of the self, or were we really supposed to live a life of habitual self-denigration, ultimately achieving annihilation of the self? This felt awfully like masochism.

Am I never allowed to "assert" myself, even when I am defending someone else's rights? Do I not have any rights at all? Must I constantly berate myself because I have a thing called the "flesh" or the lower nature, like a wild animal trying to get out of its cramped cage? Was there a biblical understanding closer to God's plan for us?

Am I alone in struggling with these issues? Of course not. Almost every week or two, I sit in therapy with a pastor or devout Christian who struggles to make sense out of this same confusion.

A pastor I counseled recently was literally pressuring his wife into an early grave by laying his exaggerated expectations on her and forcing her to work part-time to help with the family finances. His salary was a mere pittance. His church had promised a review after the first year of service, already three years ago. This pastor kept waiting for the church elders to take the initiative to grant him a much needed and long overdue raise. But no one budged. Everyone avoided the issue.

To keep their finances afloat, the pastor asked his wife to increase her work hours and leave her two small children in a neighbor's care for almost the full day. She maintained the home, tended as best she could to her young children, and then earned the money needed to keep them alive. Her husband, of course, was also working long hours, never taking a day off to rest. Money matters seemed "unspiritual," so he said nothing.

Eventually his wife's health and mental stability snapped. She had reached a state of total exhaustion. When I asked this man why he had not talked to his board about the overdue raise, he responded, "But as a Christian pastor, I am called to sacrifice my rights. How can I ask for a raise? They'll think I'm too materialistic!"

Having heard this story too often for it to faze me, I hardly batted an eyelid. "What about your wife? Don't you have an obligation to protect her? And what effect is this having on your children? How much damage do you think your self-sacrificing has caused your loved ones?"

Finally I got through to him. This pastor was blaming the church for being insensitive to his needs and breaking their promises, when the real problem was that he himself was a coward. He could not speak the truth in love. Afraid to be honest, this man carried around a chest full of resentment and bitterness. Finally he spoke up, only to find that everyone was more than willing to grant the raise. He had not received it because he had not asked.

Unfortunately, such a sad tale is not an isolated incident. This pastor is not alone in his confusion about his "rights" as a self. I use the term knowing full well that many readers will immediately say, "But we have no *rights* as Christians. We are to be subject to God's control." Such a response really begs the question. Being subject to God's control is not at variance with what it means to be a true self. Quite the contrary: it is precisely because we *do* subject ourselves to God's control that we *can* become a true self.

FACING THE REAL ISSUES

Why make sure that what we believe about the nature of the self is correct? Some Christians would argue that we need be concerned only about God's side of the gospel's equation. True, his is the most important side. It is what *God* has done, not us, that makes salvation possible. But there *is* also a human side. We are free-will agents who can, and must, choose our own destiny.

This human aspect of the equation needs to be understood as thoroughly as possible. No preacher of any repute would tolerate theological nonsense. By the same token, psychological nonsense should be equally intolerable—not just by preachers, but by all those who passionately cling to the gospel as a word of healing and salvation to a lost world. Each of us needs to be concerned about what is preached, taught, and written about the self. The gospel has been tailored to fit the self perfectly. False beliefs about the self are obstacles to the gospel and handicaps to the development of whole, healthy, vital, and dynamic believers.

I would suggest at least three other reasons for clarifying what we believe about the self. The *first* has to do with *identity*. The dictum "Know thyself" has been variously attributed to Plato, Pythagoras, Thales, and Socrates. Modern psychotherapists continue to preach the same message.

Theorists insist that a sense of "identity" is more crucial in establishing mental health than almost any other issue. Of course, there is more to self-knowledge than just having a sense of identity. As amazing as it is, the human mind really lacks enough brain cells to know itself completely. Nevertheless, to be a fully functioning human being requires some measure of self-understanding. People must know what they think, what they feel, and what causes them to behave the way they do if they are to live in any meaningful sort of way. Such knowledge influences what they choose to do and what they expect from life. It also helps them grasp the meaning of their past and the potential of their future.

"Know thyself" is no mythological advice; it is plain common sense. Scripture advocates the very same idea in several important contexts. In Romans 12:3, the Apostle Paul, after warning us not to think of ourselves more highly than we ought, says, "but rather think of yourself with sober judgment, in accordance with the measure of faith God has given you" (NIV). A more complete translation would be, "think your way to a sober estimate [of yourself], based on the measure of faith that God has dealt to each of you" (NEB).

This reference to self-identity underlines the importance of knowing ourselves honestly and truthfully. As we will see, knowing ourselves is the very foundation upon which any healthy self-esteem must be built. The theme of self-examination is a common one in Scripture. The resulting understanding of one's self is always a prerequisite to turning back to God (Lam 3:20), as well as a necessary protection against hypocrisy (Mt 7:5). Not knowing our sin erects a barrier between us and God. Not knowing our own faults sets us up as a hypocrite every time we criticize someone else.

Self-deception is another theme often tied in Scripture to a lack of self-knowledge. It creates a distorted or prideful self-esteem (Ps 36:2; Gal 6:3), along with a spiritual bondage (Is 4:20) and poverty (Rv 3:17). One verse especially sums up the importance of honestly and truthfully knowing your own self: "The way of a fool is right in his own eyes, but a wise man listens to advice" (Prv 12:15). There is no fool like the one who is totally ignorant of his or her own motives, desires, weaknesses, and blind-spots. Such a person is to be pitied.

"Know thyself" is thoroughly consistent with a biblical perspective on the self. Furthermore, God has not left us to our own devices, but enables us in the journey toward better self-knowledge through his Spirit. Jesus promised: "Howbeit when he, the Spirit of truth, is come, he will guide you into all truth: for he shall not speak of himself..." (Jn 16:13). "All truth" here means not only doctrinal truth but also truth about our personhood.

The *second* reason we should seek to understand the self concerns *self-evaluation.* Many who travel the road to heaven through the wilderness of this world part ways at this juncture. They find it quite acceptable to "know yourself" in terms of our gutter qualities—the sort of knowledge which can lead to repentance and bring us to God through Christ. But what about how we *feel* toward ourselves, our self-evaluation? How and what sort of value are we to place on ourselves? Must it always be self-hatred... or can we even dare to "love" ourselves?

This issue has spawned heated debate. On the one hand are those who denounce "self-love," holding it to be a major flaw in character, even a sin. They quote Proverbs 16:18, "Pride goeth before destruction, and a haughty spirit before a fall." On the other hand are the champions of self-love who claim to be equally spiritual and biblical. They have their verses as well.

I will treat this topic more fully in a later chapter, but how we evaluate and value the self, along with what is the appropriate way to "love" or "esteem" it, is not a simple issue. The pervasive humanistic orientation has contaminated much of the church, eliciting a strong reaction from many Christians with very legitimate concerns. The ensuing confusion is all the more reason why we need a clearer understanding of how God sees the self and how we are to view it.

A *third* reason concerns the ways a *restricted self* damages people. Of all the components of our being, the self has the greatest potential to be harmed. Neurosis resides not in the brain, but in the self. Emotional dysfunction is not just a matter of conditioning certain neurotransmitters to respond in a certain way. It is rather a devastating impairment of the self, to its beliefs, feelings, desires, and dreams. Nathaniel Hawthorne vividly portrayed these painful shackles: "What other dungeon is so dark as one's own heart? What jailer as inexorable as one's self?"[1]

The self is inextricably bound to issues of health and emotional adjustment; it is also a vital factor in social interactions. We cannot ignore it. And we certainly need as complete an understanding of it as possible, both from a biblical and psychological perspective.

THE SELF IN SCRIPTURE

How does the Bible see the self? Even if the Scriptures concede its existence, do they advocate that we have nothing to do with the self or that we handle it with kid-gloves? I will devote a whole chapter to this topic later, but a brief statement about the centrality of the self to our life in Christ may be helpful at this point. Consider for a moment some of the statements in Scripture that have a bearing on the self:

- Ignorance of the self misleads and deceives (Is 44:20).
- We are to search the self (Lam 3:40).
- We are to be honest about ourselves (Mt 7:5).
- We are to examine ourselves (2 Cor 13:5).
- We are to control the self (Prv 16:32).
- We are not to be self-willed (Ti 1:7).
- There is a limit to what the self can do (Jn 5:30).
- The Christian doesn't judge the self (1 Cor 4:3).
- We are to deny ourselves (Mt 16:24).

- We are to humble ourselves (Mt 18:4).
- We are to think about ourselves honestly (Rom 12:3).
- We are not to please just ourselves (Rom 15:3).
- It is the self that is saved (1 Cor 3:15).
- The self is to walk as Jesus walked (1 Jn 2:6).
- We are to keep ourselves unspotted (Jas 1:27).
- We are never to forget ourselves (Jas 1:24).

While I have made no attempt to clarify the various meanings of the self as they are used in these verses, Scripture clearly accepts the self as a given. God's bringing me into existence includes the creation of my self.

Sometimes a part of the self—albeit a major part—is referred to as *the heart*. Scripture does not refer to it as just the pump that circulates blood, but as the human soul or core of our being, the center of our feelings and motives. The Apostle Paul says, "With the heart man believeth unto righteousness" (Rom 10:10). His words imply that faith is not a matter of intellectual knowledge, but of a deeper belief involving all the emotion and experience one can bring to bear.

Scripture refers to the heart as the *core* of the self, the seat of our *affections*. But the self also embraces thinking or, as psychologists prefer to call it, *cognitions*. The self embraces *volitions*, the use of the will. I can choose to act in a certain way; I can decide what to do or what not to do. The self is the *totality* of what and who I am as a person. More accurately, it is what I am beyond my glands, biochemistry, corpuscles, and muscles. It is the non-physical part of me.

J. Bronowski makes an interesting observation in his little book, *The Identity of Man*. He states that living things are made from the same atoms as dead things, but are not ruled by the same laws.[2] The atoms that make up my body are exactly the same the moment before I die as they are right after I have taken my last breath. What makes the difference? Setting aside the issue of the soul and its departure, what constitutes who I am beyond the conglomeration of atoms that make up the physical me? The difference is my "self." It includes my soul, but is more than my soul. It resides in my body, but is more than my body. It is I myself.

THE RECEDING HORIZON

We've talked a lot about the self without attempting to define it or even to describe it. What do we mean when we say "I am a self"? The self is the essence of what it means to be a human being. It includes all the attributes of the person: physical, mental, spiritual, moral, and social. The self is the totality of the person.

The self is extremely difficult to define because it is like the horizon. You never quite get to it no matter how far you travel. I remember going on family trips across the flat lands of the Transvaal in Africa. No mountains, just miles and miles of road. In the distance was the horizon. "How far is it to the horizon?" I would ask my dad. "You can never get to it," he would respond teasingly. "It moves back just as fast as you move toward it." His words sounded awfully profound. The horizon isn't a thing at all. It's just the point where the earth stops being visible.

The self is like the horizon. It's the furthest point you can see inside. And the nearer you think you are getting to it, the further back it recedes. You can never quite grab it, hold it in your hands, and say "Here's my self," as if it were a fish you had just caught.

What then is the self? It is the essence of what it means to be me. *It is the total person.* But how does the self fit in with my body? How is the self related to my personality? My soul? My spirit? And how does the Bible understand the self? All very important questions that I will explore in the next few sections.

According to some philosophers like Socrates, the self is not identical with the body. The self is nonphysical and nonchemical. It is housed in and somehow connected to the body, but it is certainly not identical with the body in which it lives. Our bodies do not make decisions. Our bodies don't feel pity when we see a starving child. It is our *selves* who feel these things. So, traditionally, that aspect or part of a person which ponders, decides, and initiates changes in the body, is what we call the "self." [3]

Not only is the self not identical with the body, it is also not identical with one's mind. Now here it gets a little tricky. Just where does the body end and the mind (which is housed in that part of the body we call the brain) begin? Philosophers spit venom when it comes to such discussions. But a little reflection should clarify this point.

My self (the "I") can will, decide, love, hate, and believe. In a sense, it controls these processes of the mind. But it needs the body and the mind in order to exist. The self "possesses" them just as the president of a company "possesses" the company. The president decides, directs, and controls what goes on. He or she is not the machinery that manufactures something, nor the product which is manufactured. But the person in charge is *in* all of it. This is the self.

Many of us find our innermost selves unfathomable. While the self is a given, we can't know all we want to know about it. Indeed, knowing too much can be hazardous to one's health. Too much self-knowledge has driven some people crazy. Most of us could probably not survive the total revelation of our true selves without God being present to correct our vision, counter our despair, and offer us his forgiveness. Only God can know the human self totally: "Can any hide himself in secret places that I shall not see him? saith the Lord. Do not I fill heaven and earth? saith the Lord" (Jer 23:24). Only God can make it possible for us to face up to this self-knowledge.

To say "I am a self" implies many things. For instance, I am *uniquely different* from other selves. Not only are my genes different from yours but I even aspire to be different from you. Not superior or inferior, but different. If we were all the same, we would be nothing more than fleshly robots. But no two of us are identical. What constitutes this difference is called the "self."

We are a self because we are so *unpredictable* (a consequence of having free will). Computerized robots governed by sheer logic do exactly what they are told to do. They are actually quite dumb, or at least only as intelligent as their inventor. On the contrary, I am not predictable, at least not totally. My habits may offer a high degree of probability about some behaviors. For example, you may predict that I would not be able to pass by a specialty ice cream store without buying a little something for the road. But on an off day, I might turn up my nose at the stuff. This element of surprise is what makes me a self. I can sometimes be arbitrary, ornery, strong-willed, and insist on "doing it my way." My ways may not always be nice, but they are what makes me a self.

We can't really say that animals are selves for this very reason. A bad-tempered dog is not the same as a strong-willed child. The dog does not want to be free to be himself, but is just doing what instinct and bad training have programmed him to do. Children of a certain age, however, are beginning to feel the pull of individuation. They are starting to discover that they have a self, one that strangely longs to be free. Unfortunately, they don't yet know how to discipline this self and so need to be held in check. Only humans have been created with this awesome capacity.

"I am a self" also implies that I am *free from other selves*. Not that the peak of selfdom is to be rid of all constraints, moral or social, as some would suggest. To totally ignore all rules and do everything our own way is sociopathy, not selfhood. It is not zig-zagging our way through life that makes us free, but having the freedom to choose our own path with dignity. Free will is part of selfhood.

I dabble a bit with statistics on my computer. It has the ability to generate "random" numbers, ones that come in a purely chance order. Because no two are ever alike, random sequences are often used in research to avoid biasing. Is this freedom? Absolutely not. To be a self, I must also have a *degree of consistency*. A large part of who I am was there yesterday, is here now, and will be somewhere tomorrow. If I were to wake up tomorrow and not be the same general person I am today, life would be impossibly unpredictable. I would not be a self.

Having some limit to my unpredictability may seem a little contradictory, but it really is not. A football game can take the form of many different plays. To the uninformed spectator, the various formations may seem random and unpredictable. But certain boundaries proscribe the game of football. Chalk lines clearly mark the playing area. Time limits and rules are enforced by the officials, even though some of their close calls face inevitable disputes. Overall, we can see enough consistency between games to recognize each one as football. But we watch each game precisely because of its tremendous unpredictability. Who will win and how is sometimes not decided until the very last second.

The game of life is somewhat the same. Human beings are

bound by certain limitations in terms of time and consequences. In fact, we get into a lot of trouble when we fail to recognize our personal boundaries and become too enmeshed with others. Certain rules may be imposed on each of us by our boss or by our bank. Traffic cops referee the streets to keep us from crashing into one another. One day the clock will expire for each one of us. Death is very predictable. But we keep watching the game day by day to see how it's going to turn out.

Lastly, to say "I am a self" implies one other important fact: I have the ability to *transcend my self.* I am not the helpless victim of the various forces within me. I am not a machine programmed to perform certain functions, no matter how brilliant. I am not just an animal that obeys the laws of instinct and of nature. I am a self precisely because I can rise above my self. I can see what I am doing and choose to change it.

Let's say I am devastated by grief over the death of someone I dearly loved. I can reflect on my very real feelings and choose to rise above them. I can walk outside of the funeral home to smell a rose and experience the most wonderful of sensations, or imagine the radiant colors of a sunset as if it were actually happening. I can laugh at a funny gesture or dream of flying as if I have wings. I can soar above myself and make everything, myself included, the object of my experience. I have a capacity for life unlike any other creature. God has given me a self.

WHAT THE SELF IS NOT

We may further clarify the self by considering what it is not. In an example of semantic sloppiness, several other terms are often used interchangeably. Let's examine how each one differs.

The self is different from the *ego,* a psychoanalytical term denoting that part of the psyche which experiences the external world through the senses, organizes the thought processes rationally, and governs action. The ego also, supposedly, acts to mediate between the impulses of the *id*—that part of us that is the reservoir of all instinctual drives and which pursues pleasure— and the *superego,* the conscience that enforces moral standards.

While the ego which perceives, thinks, and acts is central to our personality, it is actually unknowable.

While some psychologists use the term ego as synonymous with self, I prefer not to. One can suffer impaired ego functions, but still never be without a self. I can "know" my self; I cannot "know" my ego. The ego represents only a *limited* part of the self. It may in some ways represent the self, but it is not the self. The ego is not a person, place, or thing. It is a passionless entity, useful but emotionally meaningless in itself.[4] It is an abstraction denoting a set of functions and nothing more.[5] The self exists because I exist. It is not the same as the ego.

The self is also different from *personhood*, by which we mean the state, quality, or condition of being a person. To be a person is to be a human being as distinguished from a thing or a lower animal. A person is a man or a woman, a child or an adult. Personhood says nothing about who the self is, how it feels, thinks, acts, lives, or dies. It is a neutral term that describes a whole class of selves. It doesn't describe you or me in our uniqueness.

The self is also not the same as *personality*, by which we mean the habitual patterns and qualities of behavior of any individual expressed by physical and mental activities and attitudes. Your personality best describes you, distinguishes you from others, and most impresses you upon others. Again, it may say nothing about the inner you. Your personality might be introverted or extroverted, passive or aggressive, choleric or sanguine, but this still doesn't begin to dive beneath the surface of who you are as a self.

Describing your personality may say nothing about your character, identity, or essential qualities. It is only a fraction of your true self, the tip of the iceberg visible above the water. You cannot ever discover or reveal all that comprises everything still hidden beneath the surface. No test will ever be devised that can capture it, let alone measure it. The self is too vast, too complex, and gloriously unique to even think that it can be put into categories and catalogued like personality.

Our sense of self is very private. The self exists only for me and can be known fully only by God. The only time I lose this sense of self is if I become psychotic. Psychotics are confused about where they end and others begin, just as they are confused about where reality ends and fantasy begins. The chemical disruption of their brain confuses their thinking and they lose the awareness of themselves as a self. But every normal person is aware of his or her self and must come to live at peace with it.

DIVING BENEATH THE ICEBERG

Each one of us possesses a self crying out to be known and understood. How can we dive beneath the surface and discover the riches below? Our ultimate goal is not just to better understand the self, but more particularly to understand how to mold it according to God's plan for each one of us.

While we may be fully "aware" of ourselves, we often shut off this awareness for reasons we don't always understand. There is that part of me that "knows." But there is also that part that "is known." Both the part that knows and the part that is known makes up the whole *me*. At times I am more involved in trying to know than I am clearly known, but we cannot separate the two. The goal of maturity is to bring the two together in greater balance.

Too much preoccupation with self-knowledge leads to the danger of *introspection*. Sometimes we stare inward at our thoughts, feelings, and motives without any constructive agenda, but simply because we find ourselves fascinating. Uncontrolled introspection can make us morbid and melancholic. When we inevitably find something we don't like inside, we can muse too much in the deep recesses of our selves.

Can you know your self too much? Yes and no. The problem lies not so much with *how much* we know about ourselves, but *how we come by* this knowledge. That we should know ourselves to some degree goes without saying. Paul's call to self-examination whenever we partake of the Lord's Supper is to prevent us from eating it unworthily (1 Cor 11:27-28). Clearly the injunction here is to examine the self for sin so that it can be confessed and cleansed before eating the bread and drinking the wine.

Paul later advocates a more thorough self-examination: "Examine yourselves to see whether you are in the faith; test yourselves. Do you not realize that Christ Jesus is in you—unless, of course, you fail the test?" (2 Cor 13:5, NIV). As a way of discovering where the self stands in relation to faith in God, self-examination is an important *spiritual discipline.*

But should this self-examination go beyond the discovery of sin and the testing of faith? I believe we are given such a mandate in Matthew 7:3-5 (NIV) where Jesus challenges us to examine our uncharitableness. He is essentially challenging us to examine our motives in judging and condemning others and our own self-deceptions: "Why do you look at the speck of sawdust in your brother's eye and pay no attention to the plank in your own eye? How can you say to your brother, 'Let me take the speck out of your eye,' when all the time there is a plank in your own eye? You hypocrite, first take the plank out of your own eye, and then you will see clearly to remove the speck from your brother's eye."

If self-deception is the basis for all hypocrisy, then searching one's heart and soul is the antidote. The more we know about our deep motives toward others, the more we protect ourselves from false goodness, sanctimony, and pretense. Chicanery, double-dealing, underhandedness, and deceit are kept at bay. We are, to put it simply, a nicer person the more fully we know our selves. God is already fully acquainted with our inmost secrets. We can pray with the psalmist, "Test me, O Lord, and try me, examine my heart and my mind; for your love is ever before me, and I walk continually in your truth. I do not sit with deceitful men, nor do I consort with hypocrites" (Ps 26:2-4, NIV).

No, we can never know our selves too well. But *how* we come to know our inner selves is crucial in determining whether we will use this knowledge properly. When is self-discovery a problem? Let me suggest five ways in which self-discovery can be a problem:

1. *When the discovery is too fast.* The inner sanctum of the self often fails to contain a lot of good news. What we discover there is not always palatable; it is neither pleasant nor agreeable. Uncovering

our inner realities will not bring delight and cause to celebrate. Our true motives are often selfish. Our love is far from perfect— probably downright selfish. We discover a lot more hate than charity.

Uncovering the self too quickly then can awaken dread and terror. The discovery may need to be taken in small doses so that we can recover and adjust to a truer picture. Too much, too fast is self-defeating. It has driven many people crazy, especially when not accompanied by a healing process. Once we have pulled back the cover to reveal some aspect of our true nature, there is no going back. Unless God is present to us at that instant, receiving such a dismal disclosure will do more damage than good. This means that God should always be a part of any attempt to really discover yourself. Only he can repair the ugliness we find within.

2. *When the discovery leaves no room for forgiveness.* The real inner self is not sterilized and free of contamination. Sin always leaves behind an infection. Since we are born with sin, it shapes and corrupts the self as it develops through the formative years—soiling, defiling, tainting, and polluting at every opportunity. No one has a self that is pure, virtuous, innocent, simple, or just plain decent. We are all adulterated. As we discover the self's true character, we will inevitably feel blameworthy.

The only forgiveness that can operate in the deep recesses of the self is the forgiveness of God. Without this companion on the road to finding out more about our selves, our confidence will be shattered and our hope lost. Awareness of who we really are should turn us toward God, not drive us despairingly away from the only salvation available to us. Be open, therefore, to God's forgiveness. Be generous in giving it to others (God requires this of us) but also grant yourself this same generous forgiveness.

3. *When the discovery relinquishes self-acceptance.* Forgiveness from God precedes self-acceptance. Those who are totally self-accepting don't perceive any need for God's forgiveness unless the self-acceptance is based on the acceptance of God. But forgiveness is

only the first step. Nothing is more pathetic than a self that has been forgiven for all its imperfections, but then refuses to accept itself. This self begins to hate itself. It repudiates its true value and denies the truth of God's Word. In spurning the Spirit's overtures, it is almost guaranteed to remain an immature self.

4. *When the discovery is untruthful.* Not everyone's search to know the self is totally honest. Some people are selective. They notice the perfections and ignore the imperfections. They highlight that which seems ideal and turn the light away from dark corners. They see what they want to see, a little bit of generosity here and some competence there. And then they exaggerate their few good points. They expand on their good qualities, falsify a motive, color a minor sacrifice, and embroider a little praise-garment for themselves.

As people proceed down this false trail, they travel further and further away from the truth about themselves, creating only a distorted self-image with which they can live. The self they think they know doesn't really exist. It is merely a fabrication of their mind. They are discovering only a fantasy, and this knowledge is worthless.

God wants us to be totally honest in our self-discovery. Only then can he provide the healing we need. Furthermore, the more honest we are the more complete will be our healing.

5. *When the discovery is without humility.* The great pitfall of discovering an unreal self—especially when the distortion veers toward self-aggrandizement—is the risk of becoming narcissistic. The narcissist is self-centered, but the self here is grossly exaggerated. It is egotistic, puffed up, vain, smug, and self-serving. It looks out for number one, wraps itself in its self, loves only its own self, and consequently lives in disharmony with those around.

What keeps us from becoming narcissistic? Plain, old-fashioned, ordinary humility. Not humiliation. Not hurt pride or a feeling of contemptibility. Humiliation is not acquainted with forgiveness, but humility knows a lot about forgiveness. Not a false humility that tests to see if anyone protests our putting ourselves down. But a genuine realization of one's own real self, with all its flaws and imperfections, that keeps us from judging others and thinking we are better.

The word humble is similar to *humus,* which means soil or earth, the common origin of all life. A genuine humility keeps us at this level, near the absolute grounding of our existence. From this position, we know where we have fallen from, but we also know we can rise to the heights that God calls us to. Common dirt, yet an heir to the King. A self centered on God can be protected against narcissism, no matter what it discovers about itself.

Now what I have just said about self-discovery should begin to give you an inkling of what it means that God has created us in his image and that, as believers, we are to cooperate with God as he remakes us in the image of his Son. In a later chapter, I will examine more carefully the idea that we are created in God's image. What is important to grasp at this point is that we are not stuck with the self we currently have. Life would be hopeless if our selves could not be shaped into something more meaningful and beautiful. The New Testament teaches very clearly that God went to a lot of trouble to make it possible for the self to be reborn, or re-created, through union with Christ. Because of this union we can begin to recover or restore the divine image in our entire being. When we become Christians we "put on the new man, which is renewed in knowledge after the image of him that created him" (Col 3:10). As God's image is restored in us, he will begin to remake the self, and we will be called on to collaborate with God in the process of our sanctification. It is important to realize that God can accomplish his work in us even if we do not fully grasp this self-understanding. God works in response to faith and self-surrender, not just to knowledge. He calls "come unto me," and we respond with "here I am, Lord." Whether or not we understand it, God works his miracles.

CHAPTER	Four Mistakes
3	Christians Make
	about the Self

But I know this, that in the last days perilous
times will come: For men will be lovers of them-
selves, lovers of money, boasters, proud.

2 Tm 3:1-2 NKJ

I KNEW I WAS IN TROUBLE the moment I saw
him. Don't ask me how, I just knew. Per-
haps it was his eyes. They were cold, unblinking, and fixed on
me. Perhaps it was the way he fidgeted or stood so impatiently,
waiting for me to finish with the lady ahead of him.

He seemed about fifty years old, tall, well-dressed, with a
prominent and powerful chin. He came right to the point.

"I'm Dr. Smith, and I'm here to tell you that you are wrong."

Thanks pal. Nothing like a direct approach! It's not that I
don't want to learn. I just don't like being forced to learn. I
sensed that Dr. Smith was going to force me to learn something.
He was going to stay there until I had learned. He was right, I
was wrong. It was that simple. He was a man with a mission.

I had just finished teaching an adult Sunday School class at a
large, affluent, suburban church. The people were intelligent,

responsive, and deeply interested in spiritual matters. Afterward, a woman had asked me a question about self-esteem. I hadn't even addressed the topic in my talk, but I tried to give a brief answer.

I explained that I had problems with the labels "high self-esteem" and "low self-esteem." The phrase "low self-esteem" is a contradiction in terms. How can esteem be "low?" Esteem is esteem. Besides, high self-esteem sounds like a commodity one can go shopping for, like designer clothes. But we were stuck with these terms, I said. I prefer the phrase "self-acceptance" to "self-esteem." Self-acceptance is merely the absence of self-hate. It fosters self-transparency not self-preoccupation. Low self-esteem is better described as "self-hate." I closed by offering to come back at a later time to present a more thorough, biblically-based understanding of this important topic.

Now, Dr. Smith stood scowling at me, and I guessed that he had trouble with my answer to that woman's question. "Self-esteem is all hogwash," he said. "Jesus doesn't tell us to love ourselves, he tells us to deny ourselves and take up his cross and follow him. Everything to do with the self is evil. Why can't we just accept that every human problem has to do with sin, and stop preaching this self-esteem stuff."

For a moment I was relieved. I actually agreed with part of his mini-sermon.

And then he came out with the clanger.

"You psychologists are all the same. You have your own gospel to preach."

Uh, oh. Now we had reached the crux of the matter. "You psychologists..." Who can argue against prejudice and prejudged attitudes? I politely told Dr. Smith that I actually agreed with much of what he was saying, but I suggested that he may not have been listening carefully to my response to the questioning lady. Perhaps, if he got a copy of the tape that had been recorded, he could try listening to it again to verify what I was saying. I moved on to the next person wanting to talk to me.

Later, I found out that Dr. Smith is not really a "doctor" of anything. He had bought his degree from a diploma mill and had a reputation for being a "heresy hunter," a person whose self-esteem is kept aloft by criticizing everyone else in sight. I felt sorry for him. People with closed minds are seldom happy!

Unfortunately, there are many Dr. Smiths in the church. I don't mean the bigoted, judgmental, closed-minded Dr. Smiths, but the ordinary Mr. and Mrs. Smiths who are confused by the critics and caught in the debate over the self. In fact, the very next person in line was a thirty-eight-year-old mother of a teenage daughter who was intensely preoccupied with how she looked and morbidly afraid of being fat.

"I know my daughter's problem is a problem of self-esteem," said the mother. "But I don't have the slightest idea how to help her. My husband walked out on us years ago, and I did my best to raise her. She's a Christian and deeply spiritual. But she still has a problem. Why do miracles never happen to me like they do in all the books I read about people getting healed?"

Like this mother, many Christians are confused and hurting. With them in mind, I want to challenge and clarify many of the false ideas that have arisen about the self. These ideas have developed in reaction to secular humanistic teachings that glorify the self and advocate a self-centered lifestyle. But this reaction has gone too far, and is creating serious damage in its own right. The truth is often hard to find when you are in reaction. Instead, you tend to fall into opposite errors from the ones you are trying to avoid.

Let's take a look at four of the most damaging ideas Christians have about the self.

POPULAR IDEA #1: YOU MUST DENY YOURSELF

Jesus, himself, tells us, "If any man will come after me, let him deny himself, and take up his cross, and follow me" (Mt 16:24).

The next verse reminds us that saving your life means losing it, and the parallel Scripture in Luke 14:26-27 links "denying" with hating father, mother, wife, children, brothers, sisters, and your own life, to be Christ's disciple. Our Lord places our love for himself far above our love for our family. The word "hate" is used simply to contrast the love we must have for him against the love of others.

"And anyone who does not carry his cross and follow me cannot be my disciple" (Lk 14:27, NIV). This last verse gets at the heart of the matter and explains precisely what Jesus means. Denying yourself means being willing to follow Jesus, carrying your own cross. Christ has just told his disciples that he must suffer. He is pointing them toward his crucifixion. Now he tells the disciples that they must suffer too. They must be willing to quit everything dear to them and deny all other loyalties.

Did Christ mean we should act hatefully toward our loved ones and never be loving toward them? Of course not! Rather, our love for God must transcend our love for those we hold dear. Our duty is *first* to Christ, and only then to others. *This is denying yourself.* We must love Christ more than our own selves. But this is not a mandate to hate ourselves in the sense of being self-rejecting and self-punishing.

Too many Christians unwittingly believe that denying the self means:

- You must deny yourself because it is sinful to do anything that gives you pleasure.
- Others must be allowed to take advantage of you, because being a Christian means you must let other people walk all over you.
- You must never think of yourself, because this is selfish.
- You must always take care of others first and put yourself last.
- You are not allowed to think for yourself.
- You must never have fun, only do your duty.
- Whenever possible, do something to humiliate yourself.
- You don't have any rights.
- Your self is vulgar and should be hated.
- Don't trust yourself.
- Nobody really loves you, so you will have to work extra hard to win their approval.
- Never try to aspire to anything; you do not deserve anything good in life.

Sometimes "deny your self" is also taken to mean "deny that you have a self." Clearly this is an impossibility. It's like saying to someone "deny that you are a person or that you are alive." The self exists whether or not we acknowledge its existence. Scripture never commands us to "deny the self," to discount the existence of the self. Instead, it commands us to re-order our commitments. "Self" here really means "priorities." Denying them involves rearranging them to fit God's priorities. Self-denial is a call to be patient in our sufferings. It is a call to holiness and obedience, a call to put our suffering, especially our sufferings for Christ, in the context of the cross. Christ bore the heavy end of the cross so that we could bear the lighter.

We trivialize Christ's call to die to ourselves when we think it simply means letting someone get the better of us or preventing ourselves from having any fun. Some of us combine self-denial with masochism—we actually derive pleasure from self-deprivation. Self-denial is not a matter of saying no to things we want or yes to something we hate just because we think there is something spiritual in robbing ourselves of pleasure.

Self-denial is often confused with self-discipline.[1] This idea suggests that we ought to say no to certain foods we tend to overeat, just because denying ourselves is good for us. It's not self-denial to refrain from overeating, it's just common sense. We ought to watch less television and resist certain sexual temptations. These are common-sense self-controls everyone should practice. Self-denial is much more than self-discipline. It involves saying yes to Christ and no to the natural inclinations of our inner selves. It is choosing to do something *better* than we would have done if Christ hadn't challenged us. But notice, it is still the self that does the choosing.

Whatever helps us to live our faith to the fullest, including the denial of alternative styles of life, will help us to be true to ourselves. Matthew Henry says it as follows: "We must deny ourselves comparatively; we must deny ourselves *for* Christ; we must deny ourselves *for* our brethren, and *for* their good; and we must deny ourselves *for* ourselves, deny the appetites of the body *for* the benefit of the soul."[2]

Self-denial, then, is an essential and fundamental law of becoming like Christ. It facilitates the bonding of our self to Christ. Our self becomes "hid with Christ in God" (Col 3:3), not abandoned or cast out. Self-denial is a grateful response to a loving God who calls us to find ourselves by losing ourselves to him.

POPULAR IDEA #2: YOU MUST DIE TO SELF

This idea runs a close second to "Popular Idea #1." It is closely linked to self-denial. In fact some people refer to these concepts interchangeably.

A pastor's wife once told me "I died to self—and my self nearly died." She was speaking of her confusion about what it means to "die to self." She had always thought it meant to give herself to others until it really hurt. She tried so hard to serve people that she neglected herself, becoming exhausted and then sick. She wasn't sleeping or eating very well and was even neglecting her own children. She really believed that this was what it meant to "die to self."

Others take "dying to self" to mean some sort of self-devaluation. They accept the fact that nothing actually "dies" in the sense that it stops existing. Dying to self, however, means that the self must be devalued, reduced to its true, unsavory nature and then starved of life.

Self-devaluation is a very clear and pervasive tendency among some groups of Protestant Christians. Many of us raise our guilt consciousness by being preoccupied with everything that's wrong with us. But this is nothing more than a form of self-righteousness—to keep one's consciousness of sin constantly at the boil. It sees the self as the source of all evil and tries to forcibly substitute a "pure" or "righteous" self in place of the human self. Some even preach a sort of "bypassing" of the natural self, believing that you can substitute another self that is purely "spiritual" in its place.

This idea traps us in self-alienation and forces us into a rigid split between a "human self" and a "spiritual self." It suggests that the human self has to be put to death so that the spiritual self can live. This is an erroneous and very damaging idea. The self that God indwells by his spirit is the *same self* that has feelings, watches sunsets, and cries when a child is sick or dies. *We do not have two selves.* We are in danger, sometimes, of encouraging the idea of multiple personalities when we try to split up the self like this. Yes, we have a dark side, a sinful side to the self. But this self is reborn, rejuvenated, regenerated, made anew when we come to Christ. How can it be put to death again?

Recognizing the presence of a self and its intrinsic worth does not jeopardize our awareness of sin. In fact, it is a prerequisite to conversion. I must know I am a self, that this self is sinful, and that God has redeemed it by paying the penalty for my sin through Christ. This is the beginning of faith. It is this same sinful self that is then regenerated in conversion. Thereafter, then, its task is to live for Christ, not die for him. He is our Messiah, we are not his.

You may be surprised to discover that Scripture never commands us to "die to self." Where does this idea come from then? Some beautiful verses in Scripture mention dying, but none of them can be interpreted as a command for the self to die. For instance, Paul says, "I die daily" (1 Cor 15:31) but the context is very clear: The end is near (v. 24), Christ has conquered death (v. 26), and Paul is threatened with death every hour (v. 30). So he says "I die daily" (v. 31). This is not a reference to the self dying but an acknowledgment that Paul's end is near. In fact, the end is so near that it is as if he is dying daily.

Again in Romans 14:8, Paul says: "For whether we live, we live unto the Lord; and whether we die, we die unto the Lord. Whether we live therefore, or die, we are the Lord's."

Again, this is not a reference to the self dying. If anything, Paul's emphasis was more on living than on dying: "For me to live is Christ, and to die is gain" (Phil 1:21). It mattered little to Paul whether he lived or died.

Where, then, does the idea of "dying to self," as it is popularly understood, come from? It came, I believe, mainly out of the Keswick movement, a pietistic movement that started in England earlier this century and stressed holiness in living and "victorious life" theology. I appreciate many of the ideals of this movement. I grew up under its influence and think its message is greatly needed today. Christ has given us the victory, and he enables us to live out his call to righteousness. But the movement also spawned ideas that were misleading if taken too literally or out of context. One of these ideas was "dying to self." Many hymns on this theme were popularized. Today, of course, we take this phrase out of the context of its original teaching and distort its meaning. Originally it was meant to be a call to a more complete self-surrender. Today it has become a call to self-destruction. There are Christians today who actually believe that a part of them has to be put to death. They're not sure what part, but they subject themselves to a form of "self-abuse" in the name of Christ as a way of keeping their "evil" self under control.

Of course, sin must be dealt with. But it makes all the difference, as we will see later, whether we are attacking the sin or the self. Christ came to liberate us from the sin that controls and holds the self captive. This frees the self to become what God wants it to be. If I work at killing my self I may have nothing to give to God.

"But what about Galatians 2:20 and Colossians 2:20 and 21?" some may ask. "Don't these passages speak of dying to the self?" Let us briefly look at each of these portions of Scripture.

First, Galations 2:20:

> I am crucified with Christ: nevertheless I live; yet not I, but Christ liveth in me: and the life which I now live in the flesh I live by the faith of the Son of God, who loved me, and gave himself for me.

Consider the context. Paul is discussing the glorious theme of justification by faith (v. 16). The Jewish Christians were puzzled: how does justification by faith square with the works of the law? He warns of the danger of reverting to Judaism (v. 18) and declares that we are now "dead" to the law (the old covenant) so that we can "live unto God" (v. 19). In effect, he is telling these Jewish Christians that they no longer need their sacrifices. They were part of the law. Then he comes to verse 20: "I am crucified with Christ." What does he mean? Many Christians conjure up images of their "self" being nailed to a cross and dying along with Jesus, but this is not what Paul is saying. Christ offered himself up as the ultimate sacrifice for all of us. By so doing he made us *dead to the law*. But Christ's death not only made us dead to the law, (meaning that we are no longer dependent on it for access to God), but it also made us *alive unto God*. Christ is crucified, yet he lives. In Christ I was also crucified, and I also live. *My self is not dead, it is fully alive.* My self doesn't die in this death transaction, it is made alive: "and the life which I now live in the flesh I live by the faith of the Son of God" (v. 20).

Hallelujah! Let us not frustrate the grace of God by trying to crucify the self all over again.

Second, let us examine the Scripture found in Colossians 2:20 and 21.

> Since you died with Christ to the basic principles of this world, why, as though you still belonged to it, do you submit to its rules: "Do not handle! Do not taste! Do not touch!" NIV

Again, consider the context. Paul is warning against certain teachings (v. 16). They are only "shadows," Christ is the substance (v. 17). He tells his readers not to worship angels (v. 18) and to remember that pride is at the root of many errors (v. 19). And then he reminds his readers that since they died, as it were, with Christ "this has set you free from following the world's ideas of how to be saved — by doing good and obeying various rules" (v. 20, LB).

Paul's message here is clear. Christ's death, not ritual observance of the law, is your salvation. Christ mediated your salvation, not angels. Be subject only to Christ, not to human teachings. There is nothing here about the self dying. Again, it reminds me that I (the self) have been made alive through the death of Christ.

So what do we mean when we encourage believers to "die to self," or to let the "self die"? We mean that to be fully alive in Christ takes a surrender of your will. Dying to self is not a matter of putting our personhood to death—this only happens when I physically die. It is a call to commitment, or, as the Apostle Paul so clearly and beautifully puts it in Romans 12, an invitation to be a "living sacrifice":

> Therefore, I urge you, brothers, in view of God's mercy, to offer your bodies as living sacrifices, holy and pleasing to God—this is your spiritual act of worship. Rom 12:1, NIV

The "body" here is the whole self. It includes both body and spirit. A "living sacrifice" is a dedication of the whole self to the service of God so that you can become an instrument of righteousness (Rom 6:13).

POPULAR IDEA #3: YOU MUST LOVE YOURSELF BEFORE YOU CAN LOVE OTHERS

You hear it in seminars. You hear it in counseling rooms. You hear it even from the pulpit. But is it true? "You must love yourself first before you can begin to love others."

Variations go like this: "If you hate yourself you will hate others" or "self-love is the beginning of love for all people." It has even become popular to present self-love as a Christian virtue. But both the word "self" and the word "love" remain inadequately defined. As a result, many biblical scholars have rightly taken issue with the popular notion that you must first love yourself before you love someone else, which they believe is a psychological idea, not a biblical one.

It is true that we all have feelings toward ourselves. God has given us the capacity to stand back and reflect on our inner selves, our motives and actions. And, as we reflect on our selves, we are certain to form feelings regarding those selves. The important question is: *What* are appropriate feelings about ourselves? What is healthy and what isn't? And, most important of all, what does God want us to feel about ourselves?

Let me begin by clarifying what is popularly meant when we say "you must first love yourself before you can love others." Contrary to what you might think, self-love is not the same as self-esteem.

"But the Bible tells us to love ourselves," many will object. "It says so, right there in Matthew 22:39." But does it? Let us look at this Scripture more carefully.

Jesus was responding to a question posed by a lawyer: "Which is the great commandment of the law?" (v. 36). He replies that it is to "love God with all your heart" (v. 37). But then he goes on to say that there is a second commandment that is like it and that flows out of the first (v. 38): "Thou shalt love thy neighbor as thyself" (v. 39).

How are we to interpret this verse? Is it a commandment to love yourself first before you can go and love others? No. It is a commandment to love your neighbor. Jesus assumes that you already love yourself, perhaps even too much. Many biblical scholars tell us that the correct interpretation of this verse goes like this: "You already love yourself so much, now go and love your neighbor *as yourself.*"

This reverses the priority and certainly changes the meaning of this text, and although it doesn't give explicit support or negation for self-love, it focuses on the need for us to love our neighbor. If you examine the other parallel references to this commandment (Lk 10:27, Rom 13:9, Gal 5:16, Js 2:18) you will also find they emphasize "love to neighbor," not "love to self." But even if we assume that Jesus gives us permission to be self-loving, what sort of love is this to be? A further, and equally important, issue is at stake here. It has to do with our use of the term "love." When most people think of love, they conjure up a rather sloppy, self-serving warm feeling. When they apply this to the idea of self-love, they invariably come up with a confused mishmash of self-feelings that border on narcissism. I have encountered Christians who genuinely believe that they should be generating feelings of tender affection or devotion toward themselves, which will then enable them to be loving toward others. Obviously, they misunderstand the true meaning of love. The love spoken of in the New Testament is *not* a special kind of feeling one should have, but a special kind of service that we should give to each other.

In the biblical sense, then, the self-love of which Jesus speaks refers to the natural protection we give ourselves. We feed, defend, shelter, preserve, support, and care for ourselves. *This* is what Jesus assumes. And *this* is what Jesus calls us to give to others also. Modern day notions of love are too sentimental and sloppy to be applied to the idea of self-love.

Yes, we do need to have a natural love or regard for ourselves. This means we ought to give due regard to the dignity of our own natures and to the welfare of our own souls and bodies. But just as we must not wrong and injure ourselves, we should not wrong and injure others. As we have opportunity we must do good to all—and this may mean sacrificing something we want for the good of another.

Telling people to "first love themselves before they can love others" can easily be bad advice, unless it qualifies the nature of that love. If it suggests a form of love that is self-serving, that seeks its own interests at all costs and over all other interests, it will foster a narcissistic self-preoccupation that turns people inward, not outward. Jesus simply was not advocating this form of selfism.

But by the same token, neither was he advocating self-hate as the way of enhancing our love for others. Loving others does not mean we debase ourselves. Humans are highly susceptible to self-hate, despite what the critics of psychology say, and they need little encouragement to fall into this habit. We are much more likely to remember our failures than our successes and to negate our accomplishments. Self-hate encourages humiliation not humility, self-degradation not self-surrender, and self-devaluing not self-honesty. When you surrender your self to the love of Christ you no longer need to hate your self.

POPULAR IDEA #4: YOU MUST SACRIFICE YOURSELF

There is no doubt in my mind that there is a sense in which we as Christians are called to "sacrifice ourselves." Notice, I didn't say "sacrifice our selves." This means something quite different. Again let me stress, one cannot "sacrifice" the self. We certainly cannot "sacrifice" the self as some act of propitiation or worship—yet I have encountered Christian groups who, without fully realizing it, believe that in "sacrificing" their rights or privileges they are performing a ritual sacrifice, similar to the animal sacrifice practiced in the Old Covenant. This leads to a very distorted understanding of the self and some very unhealthy practices.

Christian theology does not believe in any sort of offering or sacrifice to appease God. Christ was the ultimate and final sacrifice. No other thing or person can take his place. We usurp the work of the cross if we try to "sacrifice" our selves to God.

But we do sacrifice "ourselves" and here the meaning is different and connotes very clearly a *submission of our own desires for some greater good.* We don't sacrifice ourselves so that we can suffer deprivation and then present that suffering to God as atonement or as an attempt to win his affirmation. We "sacrifice" because it is a way of achieving something better, for ourselves or others.

Herein lies the potential for misunderstanding. Many Christians think they should always take second place, allow others to dominate them, give others the advantage. This "sacrificing" of themselves, they believe, is received by God with pleasure, just as if it were an actual sacrifice. This belief harkens back to an Old Covenant mentality. This isn't "grace," it is "works." We don't "sacrifice" ourselves in order to appease God. We do it as an expression of our love toward him and toward others. The difference is crucial.

What does it mean to "sacrifice oneself"? It means to surrender your rights. But we must be careful of both the context and the qualifiers in this surrender. We surrender our rights *when it serves God's purposes*. We don't surrender our rights just because someone says we must. There is no value in just throwing them away. The qualifier is that we sacrifice what is rightfully ours *when* it is appropriate for us to do it.

For instance, a father doesn't come home from work and say to his family: "My paycheck has fifty dollars more in it than we really need this week, so I 'sacrificed' it. I was driving through a ghetto and threw the extra cash out of the window. Hopefully someone who needs it will find it."

This isn't sacrificing anything. This is irresponsible, crazy behavior. It is selfishness of a different sort—seeking the pleasure of altruistic acts without regard for others. Sacrificing oneself *must* serve a purpose, or it is not a sacrifice at all. If the father had proposed to his family that they give fifty dollars to an elderly neighbor-lady who has no family and desperately needs help, this would be a "sacrifice." If they gave it when they couldn't afford to give it, it would be an even greater sacrifice. Sacrificing oneself, then is simply *love in action*. Don't expect God to give you extra marks for your pain when you sacrifice yourself stupidly.

We miss the boat on this "sacrificing" stuff at several other points also. The following, for instance, are not "sacrifices":

- If we surrender some right and then continue to resent it. This is not "sacrificing" anything. We feel robbed and become angry. It is not a free-will giving up of our rights.

- If we surrender something that wasn't ours to give in the first place. For instance, I don't think the father, by himself, has the right to decide what of the family's finances he can give away. It should be a family decision. Taking money from his family to give to someone else is not a sacrifice—it is robbery.

- If we surrender something out of cowardice. Sometimes we "give up" a right because we feel intimidated or bullied. We are cowards—then we rationalize our behavior as "self-sacrificing" and hope that God has noticed. We might even draw his attention to our sacrifice in our prayers before we go to bed. This leads to a lot of unhealthy under-assertiveness. Allowing yourself to be bullied is probably just as repugnant to God as always insisting on your rights.

Self-sacrifice, and by this I mean the surrendering of your rights and benefits, is an important Christian principle. It helps protect us from selfishness and it fosters a spirit of love. Philippians 2:4 is the clearest injunction I know: "Each of you should look not only to your own interests, but also to the interests of others" (NIV). This injunction, however, also has its context: "Do nothing out of selfish ambition or vain conceit, but in humility consider others better than yourselves" (v. 3).

Self-sacrifice, then, is an essential feature of the life of the believer, but it must be placed in the right context. The unrelenting giving away of belongings to others, or giving in to the will of others, is *not* what we mean by self-sacrifice. Self-sacrifice is an essential element in Christian love. Dr. Don Browning of the University of Chicago sees self-sacrifice as the "balancing" force in Christian love.[3] Because we live in a broken world, neither an excessive "giving in" to others nor excessive focusing on our own needs is desirable. Self-sacrifice serves as a "balancing weight" to even up injustices and to ensure that we are not selfishly concerned about our own well-being to the detriment of others. Self-sacrifice, then, rightly understood, benefits the larger community. It can be the antidote for selfism and the beacon light that makes the Christ-life attractive to others. After all, self-sacrifice is anything but natural. Our fallen nature much prefers to be selfish. But when the self is born anew it finds itself drawn to a strange new set of desires: it is drawn irresistibly to love others and is empowered to become unselfish.

4 | Beneath the Tip of the Iceberg

DEEP WITHIN EACH OF US IS A PLACE we call the self. It is a secluded place at the very center of our being, to which only God and we have the key. Few outsiders get to know this secret place which we keep hidden from probing questions and inquisitive eyes. It is a place where we dream our dreams and cherish our hopes. It is the place of feelings, where we can privately cry if we are hurt, lick our wounds if we are betrayed, and celebrate our joy when someone really loves us. It is the place of feelings.

The self is also a place of mystery, a profound place in which I hide my dark side. All the skeletons of shame and embarrassment are kept hidden there. It is a place of contradictions, problems, and often inner turmoil. Sometimes it feels as though a Trojan horse lurks in the shadows, like an enemy within. I myself often get lost in this maze called self. So much is hidden there that I am often afraid to delve into it. What if I should expose something I don't want to know? So much of it is hidden beneath the obvious, like a giant iceberg in my heart. So much of it puzzles me. It seems inscrutable, mysterious, unfathomable. This is my self.

We all harbor such a place. Even Jesus had a self, though he acknowledged that it was utterly rooted in God. "I can of mine own self do nothing.... I seek not mine own will, but the will of the Father which hath sent me" (Jn 5:30). It was Jesus' self that was obedient to God.

To be a person is to have a self. Some say that there is no central consciousness. The self is just our illusion. We are nothing more than a big computer. One day we will have robots that think and feel like us. But if this is true, they will only *seem* to have a self. A computer will never be able to love. To have a heart that sends blood throbbing through your body is to have a self. It is your being as a person—as someone who thinks, believes, feels, and who can be hurt—that makes you a self. It is your self that is obedient to God. I cannot conceive of my dog or cat or any other living thing having a self. Only human beings have selves, each gloriously complex in the super abundance of God. Animals do not have minds capable of doing the things that a self can do.

I am not talking about our spirit, our soul. I will try to clarify what I mean by those labels in a later chapter. I am talking about that eerie awareness we all have that we exist and that we can watch ourselves as we exist. Yet there is nothing mysterious or enigmatic about the notion of the self. It is not mystical, mythical, or fictitious. It is a fact. I have a self. It is who I am and what I am.

Psychology did not invent the self; God made it. We didn't just discover it in recent times; the self has been around since creation as part and parcel of what it means to be human. We are so wonderfully made that we have a mind that can reflect upon itself. The essence of this concept is that we actually know that we exist. Without this self-knowing or self-consciousness, the self doesn't exist. Only the object we call the body would remain.

So why do we have a problem with the self? I don't want to jump ahead of my argument, but I am sure that many readers are already suspicious about any discussion of the self. They have been indoctrinated with an "anti-self" fear. A few opening comments may be helpful in overcoming this barrier.

Frankly, I believe we have problems with this notion because secular psychology has presented too idealistic a picture of the human self. To put it in a nutshell, secular psychology, particularly its humanistic branch, has tried to portray the human self as innately good within itself and full of potential to become god-like. This view opposes what Scripture says, as well as what most people intuitively feel about themselves.

As we will examine in the chapters to come, the human self is on its own devoid of the potential for god-likeness. In the self can be found all varieties of imperfections, which makes us anything but god-like. But sin is a reality that psychology has not come to terms with, and no complete understanding of the self can be developed that ignores a biblical understanding of sin. Sin cannot be *discovered* by any scientific method. It must be *revealed* and *defined.* And the only resource we have for defining sin in this age of compromise and moral vacillation is God who has spoken his last word to us on the matter through his Word.

But even though the self is contaminated by sin, we still have a self. We cannot throw it out; all we can do is understand it better. And the better we understand it, the more effective we will be in helping ourselves and others come to the place where we can say with Jesus, "I can of mine own self do nothing.... I seek not mine own will but the will of the Father which hath sent me."

COMMON HURDLES

Of all the topics that draw students to the study of human behavior, none is more compelling than the study of the self. This preoccupation is born partly out of self-interest. People want to be better people. Hurting people want to minimize their pain and maximize their pleasure. Confused people want to understand what's going on within. After all, everyone is concerned about who and what they are. So the study of the self is for many a quest for self-understanding.

But this can hardly be enough of a reason for those of us who claim to be followers of Christ. We know about the dark side of the self and how it can be made whole again. We can receive forgiveness by responding to the gospel. We can find a new identity in Christ. As we learn to graft ourselves onto the true vine, we begin to live our lives to the fullest. Self-fulfillment becomes Christ-fulfillment. Self-esteem is grounded in the esteem Christ has for us and self-sacrifice becomes the ultimate gift we can give to others.

But Christians face other legitimate reasons for trying to understand the self. *First,* it is the source of many difficulties. Most people don't find it that easy to just "fully surrender their selves" to Christ in a way that miraculously heals their minds or enables them to become whole and free of emotional problems.

Second, it is a fragile thing, easily hurt and distorted. The sense of self is formed during the vulnerable years of childhood and early adolescence. Since the parents who shape this childhood self are themselves imperfect, they easily pass on this damage. The world is a hostile and dangerous place, definitely not "user friendly" to the self. As a result, we *all* suffer from some damage to the self.

Third, the self needs repairing. The better we understand the self, the more effective we can be in helping people turn to God's remedy for the damaged self. We live in an age when people are dubious about evangelism. They are "gospel shy." They've seen the abuses of TV evangelism, the hypocrisy of many public evangelists, and even the duplicity of overly ambitious pastors. When cloaked in religiosity, human nature can seem even more hideous. My response, then, has been to focus on the self's needs and to point people directly to God himself as the healer of souls. The better we understand the self and how it can be damaged, the more effective we are as a herald of the gospel.

But many conservative Christians have turned the self into a battleground. We are confused. Let's admit it! Just recently I spoke to a large gathering of pastors and spouses, more than one thousand of them. I briefly touched on the topic of the self and stated our desperate need for a "theology of the self." We needed a clearer, healthier, more thoroughly biblical understanding of what we mean when we talk about the self in relation to the gospel.

After my talk, I was immediately flooded with questions. It seems I had touched a sensitive nerve. One pastor asked: "When you talk about the 'self,' do you mean the same thing as human nature?" Another said, "I am confused. I preach about 'self-denial' a lot. I also preach about the importance of 'self-love.' But I've never quite got these two ideas together. How does 'self-denial' fit together with 'self-love'?" Yet a third pastor remarked, "I've always stayed away from preaching about the 'self' or any idea similar to it. I've been too afraid of being labeled a 'humanist' if I try to talk about the self."

No issue is more important for Christian psychology than the proper understanding of the self. Every other issue concerning our personhood depends on this one. Whether we are dealing with self-esteem or self-hate, self-actualization or self-sacrifice, we must be clear about the "self" part. Every question I can possibly imagine about myself is connected to this thing I call a self.

The question *"Who* am I?" can be handled quite easily—unless I'm suffering from amnesia. I can tell you my name, rank, and social security number. I can tell you where I live, what I do, and where I'm going. But suppose you ask a sort of non-physical question like, "Who am *I?"* I might begin to stumble. Answers are more bewildering, even haunting. I'm probing my self, shining lights in dark corners, and searching for some comprehension of what I find. I am being searchingly introspective and trying to find out who I *really* am, at this moment in time. This search-light is called *self-awareness.*

Now a funny thing happens. The more I probe and search the self, the more elusive and perplexing it becomes. This is because while a self can see, feel, and comprehend itself clearly at the physical level, the more it probes the non-physical, the more it fails to find itself. Eerie isn't it? It's like looking at your reflection in a mirror that is in turn reflecting your reflection in another mirror. You look deeper and deeper into more and more mirrors that stretch on for infinity. It's the self looking at itself. It cannot find the end.

THE MIRROR OF SELF-AWARENESS

I have said that the self is the essence of who I am as a person. But what makes it possible for me to know I am a self? Only human beings have these mirrors. Of all God's creation, we are the only ones who have the ability to "know" our selves, to observe them, think about them, and reflect on what they are doing. We know what we are doing within ourselves, and we know that we know we are doing so. It goes on indefinitely, like the reflection of a mirror in a mirror—one image after another going back into infinity.

This is the phenomenon of *self-awareness,* also called *self-consciousness.* The whole concept of the self is made possible by this self-awareness. God has created our minds with this awesome capability. It's as if we can stand outside ourselves and look back at who we are. I can look at me. I can judge my motives. I am aware of me and I am aware that I am aware of me. Can you grasp this phenomenal ability?

Of course, a corresponding responsibility goes along with this ability: God will hold me accountable for what I do precisely because I am capable of being aware of my actions. I can foresee the consequences of my behavior. We don't put *dogs* on trial for killing a farmer's sheep. We put the dog's *owner* on trial. Why? The person didn't attack the sheep, nor even command the dog to attack the sheep. The dog did it by himself. But the dog has no self-awareness. He just does what he is programmed to do by instinct: attack for food.

Humans are *not* programmed by instinct. They have brains so superior to any other form of life that they can transcend and override basic instincts. Most of what we do as humans must be *learned.* We can't even have sex by instinct like animals. We must be taught about it.

This idea of *self-awareness* is central to the notion of the self. The self is *not* a thing, a place, or a person. It is us knowing ourselves. The nature of this "self" or "I" is not absolutely clear. But what is clear is the undeniable existence of self-awareness.

Under certain conditions, self-awareness declines and even vanishes, for all practical purposes. Have you ever known someone who has become brain damaged through an accident, or watched the progressive deterioration of Alzheimer's disease? Then you will know what I mean. Our capacity for self-awareness is absolutely dependent upon our brain. It is the brain that gives it to us, not the soul or any other dimension. When our brain dies, even if the heart goes on beating, we are no longer self-aware and no longer responsible. That's just how it is. God understands.

For a certain part of every day, we lose our self-awareness. Sleep relieves us of responsibility. This is why sleep is often used for relief by those in intense emotional pain. "I long just to go to bed and fall asleep so that I can escape my problems," one lady told me. "But when I wake up I feel so disappointed, because all my problems are still there, staring me in the face."

Self-awareness doesn't force me to deal with my self, but it does force me to deal with reality. So the self and reality are inextricably linked. You can't have one without the other. The better I understand my self, the better I am able to deal with reality. This, alone, is enough of a reason for why I must come to terms with my interior landscape. It is the interface between me and the world in which I must live, the arena in which I live out my life. If my self-awareness diminishes—and some psychological defenses produce this effect, not just brain damage—I am no longer living life. I am just existing.

Furthermore, self-awareness is essential to a proper understanding of the gospel. Those who attack self-awareness as a psychological concept that has no place in the Christian's belief system do not grasp how essential it is to the understanding of sin. Self-awareness was there at creation, but with the fall came a profound state of sinfulness. Adam *knew* he was naked. This knowledge can only come through self-awareness.

The ability to know what is right comes from creation. The content of this knowing, that he was "naked," came from the fall. My cat is naked, but he is neither aware, nor does he care. He doesn't even know what naked is. Every evangelist who preaches the gospel speaks directly to this self-awareness. It is the only way God can access the soul and bring it to salvation.

While the self exists because we have the capacity for self-awareness, we can identify a certain "structure" to the self. Throughout this book you will find that I easily and frequently skip from talking about my "self" to talking about "myself." I do so quite deliberately, because I don't want to give the impression that there is another entity called the "self" that exists inside me quite autonomously. I think that is one of the mistakes many make.

For instance, when thinking about the Freudian idea of the "ego," many think that it actually exists as an entity. It doesn't! It is merely a useful concept in describing how a part of us functions psychologically. The "self" does not exist as such. It is not a person within a person. The self *is* the person. I am, you are, that person. There is no other entity within us.

But we have been created with such a fantastic brain that we have the capacity to be a self because we can observe ourselves from without. In other words, because I have this remarkable gift of "self-awareness," I can observe myself and think about the various states my self is in. I can talk about what I am experiencing, feeling, thinking, and doing. Self-awareness gives me the capacity to stand outside myself and *observe* what it is I am doing and feeling. And I am not suggesting that there is a "homunculus" inside all of us. Homunculus was the tiny dwarf supposedly created in the alchemist's test tube. Self-awareness is not a self within the self. It is just a capacity that we have for self-knowing.

It is precisely because I can *know* myself, *reflect* on my self, and *choose* whether or not I want to continue doing, thinking, and feeling, that I am who God has created me to be. Without this self-consciousness God could not hold me responsible for my behavior. There could be no sin! Furthermore, it is this capacity of myself to know the deep inner working of myself that God holds accountable. It is what makes me a "freewill" agent. I can choose to do right or to do wrong, to believe in God or not believe in him. But then, I am held accountable for these choices.

Another way of trying to understand this idea of a self within myself is to further consider the analogy of a mirror. Just a plain, ordinary looking glass helps you shave, brush your hair, or apply make-up. Yet think about what a remarkable instrument it is, apart from the fact that a mirror reverses the image so that how you see yourself is the opposite of how others see you. The wonder of it is that you see a whole duplicate world inside that mirror. Your world seems to exists all over again behind that pane of glass. You are there, your furniture is there, anyone else who enters the bathroom is there. Well, they're not exactly there, but to your brain it certainly seems as if they are.

Self-awareness is just like the mirror. I, myself, exist in reality on this side of the mirror. On the other side is my self. My mind and brain can help me to stand outside of myself and observe my self, its thoughts, feelings, and actions. In the mirror, I can see my hand come up to my face, even though I cannot see the same action in reality until my hand is almost at my face. In just the same way, there are many things I can see in my self that I am not always aware of in reality. I have to stop and observe myself, and reflect on the reflection, before I am fully aware of what I am doing.

Although I can see myself in the mirror identically, as if I really existed there, in fact I don't exist there. I am merely looking at a *reflected* image. So the self doesn't exist except as a reflection of what I am observing about myself. But this reflection is still very helpful to me. Without a real mirror I couldn't shave, brush my hair, or be sure I look presentable. Without the knowledge that my self gives me, I could be equally unpresentable to the world.

In summary, then, the concept of the self is vitally important. It is not something that exists in reality, but is a reflection of myself that I can see in my own mind. However, because I have a God-given capacity to see my self, *it is a part of my psychological system.*

But observations of one's self by oneself has its limits. Mirrors can become distorted. The presence of others may enhance or diminish one's feelings about the self. The experience of oneself is not always pleasurable or even tolerable. What makes for self-experience that is gratifying, wholesome, or just plain tolerable? What can we do about distorted or dirty mirrors? Where does one go to "clean up" a self that has been sullied by sin or aggrieved by abuse? That is what the rest of this book is about.

THE SCAFFOLDS OF THE SELF

Obviously the self is not just one single phenomenon, but is made up of many minor images. Psychology commonly talks about three aspects of the self: the *actual self,* the *ideal self,* and the *ought self.* Brief comments about these three aspects will help us to see how the gospel fits humans so perfectly.

The actual self. The term "actual self" means exactly what it says: who and what we actually are, what is real about us, and how we exist at the present time. This is quite easy to say, but can we really know this actual or real self? Not fully. We might have a bodily sense and something of an identity, but I doubt whether our own minds can fully discern or even comprehend our actual selves.

We would need a lot of other people who really know us to describe who we actually are, and even then they wouldn't have much of an inkling as to who we are inside ourselves. And as far as our insides are concerned, most of us have great difficulty grasping our self-images, figuring out our motives, understanding our feelings, or grasping how evil we can be. That's why we turn to psychotherapy—we hope to come to know our actual selves a little better.

But even the most brilliant therapist in all the world would not be able to help us discover our real selves completely. This is why we need help from outside of our humanness. A revelation from the One who has created us is necessary to show us aspects of our actual self that we could not discover on our own.

How else could we know the depravity of the human soul without such wisdom as Jeremiah 17:9: "The heart is deceitful above all things and desperately wicked: Who can know it?" How would we learn there is only one road to salvation without Romans 10:9: "That if thou shalt confess with thy mouth the Lord Jesus, and shalt believe in thine heart that God hath raised him from the dead, thou shalt be saved." Yes, we have an *actual* self, but we need help from outside our humanness to know it.

The ideal self. The term "ideal self" is much more personal, a reference to who you would like to be. It incorporates many positive qualities you admire in others and discards negative characteristics that you would not like to see in yourself. It is a mental picture of the perfect "you."

What happens when the actual or real self is perceived to be at odds with the ideal or perfect self? Trouble! One of the ways in which psychologists try to measure the difference between the actual self and the ideal self is called a "Q-Sort,"[1] in which a large number of statements such as the following are presented to a subject:

- I am satisfied with myself.
- I have a satisfying relationship with others.
- I trust (or don't trust) my emotions.

These statements are printed on cards which the subject sorts into two categories: "least like me" and "most like me" under either "my real self" or "my ideal self." The difference between the two categories is called the *self/ideal discrepancy*. The greater the discrepancy, the greater the supposed level of maladjustment. The closer your perceived real self is to your ideal self, the healthier and happier you are likely to be.

But pause with me for a moment and consider what a Catch-22 this all presents. First, we can't really know our actual selves that accurately to begin with. Are we not likely to present a distorted picture? Second, how can we know that the ideal we have conjured up in our mind is an adequately healthy or desirable ideal?

Suppose I am a gang member in a Los Angeles ghetto surrounded by those I admire. Their macho, anti-social skills and their ability to "knock-off" their rivals are likely to become my ideals. If I become like my peers, my actual and ideal selves will be pretty close together. By all psychological definitions I should be pretty healthy! But am I really all that healthy just because my actual and ideal selves are concordant? My ideal self is defined by my environment. What if my environment is very sick?

Many readers may not be able to identify with my gang member analogy, so let's come a little closer to home. Are your ideals shaped by your business associates, teammates, bridge-playing partners, school friends, or fellow workers? Are our own surroundings distorted in some significant way? Are we influenced by gross materialism or strong competitiveness? Our ideal selves merely reflect our environment and influences. They are the product of our values and what we desire, more than the product of absolutely trustworthy standards.

Before we try to reduce the gap between our real selves and what we would like to become, we should first examine our "ideals" and ensure that they are really all that ideal. How can we do this? If a pig wants to be clean, he cannot look at other pigs to find out what clean is. They are likely to be just as contaminated by the filth of the pigpen as he is. Again, we have to look *outside* our human frame of reference to reach satisfactory conclusions about what an ideal self should be.

Fortunately we have not been left to our own devices here. Recently I was reading a personal response paper from one of my Doctor of Ministry students. Let's call him Mario. Now serving in a very influential chaplain's position, he described how he had grown up in a "barrio" in California. All through his childhood, Mario's parents had told him he would never amount to anything, that he was worthless. Around him he saw nothing that he would like to become. The only models available to him were shaped by poverty, hatred, thievery, and hopelessness. His mother constantly threw things at him. His father was drunk a lot and often hit him.

What sort of "ideal" self does such a child begin to develop? Mario looked at his peers and older kids and naturally thought, "I would like to be like them. They're tough and can take anything." So he began to behave like them. He stole a little, threw rocks and broke windows a little, and started to develop his macho image as the only ideal he knew.

But at about twelve years of age, Mario was invited by a friend to go to Sunday School. Week by week Mario was exposed to sound Bible teaching by a godly man who really loved these barrio children. He began to discover a new set of ideals that would change the direction of his future. He began to long for a better life and to see that he was specially loved by a heavenly Father.

Slowly Mario's sense of worthlessness was replaced by a deep realization that God loved him. The boy came to passionately love God in return. In junior high he joined a Youth for Christ club, eventually becoming its president. He had broken out of his childhood prison and had found a new sense of value in himself. Mario now believed he could accomplish something worthwhile, that God could make something beautiful out of his life. His ideal self had been reshaped by an encounter with his Creator.

Do only the children of the barrio need to find an ideal self shaped by God and Scripture? Of course not.

Adrian grew up in an affluent home. Surrounded by high-achievers, he was driven at an early age to excel at everything. His ideal self was shaped by success. Whatever he did, he felt compelled to succeed at it. Because he couldn't always match up to his parent's expectations, Adrian found himself feeling worthless a lot of the time. The models around him were different from Mario's, but they were just as powerful in shaping this boy's internalized ideal. As a man, Adrian felt pushed to be "tough" in business. The dreams forced on him were those of great wealth, power, and influence. Perhaps Adrian would succeed where his father felt he had failed.

Adrian was also invited to go to a Sunday School in his affluent neighborhood. The message was the same as in the barrio. The same Christ, the same challenge, the same values were presented by another dedicated teacher. The gospel transcends social status and can appeal to every level of society. Slowly, with godly instruction, Adrian's ideal self became more balanced. He joined a Young Life Club and became one of its leaders.

Isn't it mind-boggling how the gospel can shape healthy selves from any sort of clay? Mario and Adrian would one day become the closest of friends because God called them both into ministry. Their "real" selves would take on the shape of their "ideal" selves. And because their "ideal" selves were God-centered, their lives would become rich with meaning and happiness.

The ought self. Finally, there is the "ought self." The ideal self refers to what *we would like to be*, a blueprint that we have designed for ourselves to become. The ought self is what we believe others want us to be. It is the attributes and behaviors that we believe are our obligations or duty to possess.[2]

Close friends and even grandparents are very influential in

shaping our "ought" self, but the main influence is our parents. Not only do they tell us what we "ought" to be, do, think and even feel, but we often take on the belief that we "ought" to be like them. This doesn't always motivate us to model ourselves after them—quite the opposite. We rebel and work hard at being the exact opposite. But this is still an "ought"—except it says "I ought not to be like my parents"!

Unfortunately, the ought self can easily become neurotic. It can adopt so many expectations from others that it becomes confused or over-controlling. We lose a sense of being in control of our own lives and become the victims of other people's control over us or what we perceive they want us to be.

Our *ought self* may be very much at odds with both our *actual self* and our *ideal self*. The greater this discrepancy, the greater our discomfort and distress is likely to be. For instance, suppose you have become deeply indoctrinated with the idea that you must be just like your father to be a successful person. If you feel that you are not anything like him, this discrepancy will cause you a lot of pain. Most of us are just not aware of our ought selves, so we never challenge it. We allow it to determine our unhappiness without even thinking about it.

Too strong an ought self can be a real problem. To be defined by others is never helpful. When these "others" are domineering, it can be downright hell. It completely stifles differentiation—the capacity of a family member to define his or her own life's goals and values (the *ideal self*). The pressure to conform to your surroundings is too great to foster individual growth. Since you cannot take maximum responsibility for your own destiny, you become too dependent on others to make decisions.

Murray is a perfect example. The oldest son in a close-knit family, it was determined at a very early stage of his life that he would follow in his father's footsteps. The oldest son always became what his father had tried to become. Like a long relay race, sons carried the baton until all had been accomplished. But Murray began to rebel at about age fourteen. His issue wasn't just with his father. His mother had become overinvested in perpetuating the father also. She conspired to develop a strong "ought self" in Murray, just to keep the family peace. In fact, that word "ought" became the most hated of all words to Murray.

"You ought to do what your father tells you to do," she would say as she served him his breakfast. "You ought to show more respect to your father," would accompany her parting kiss as he left for school. "You ought to tell your father how much you admire what he does," would greet him as he came home from school.

"Ought, ought, ought, ought... that's all I ever heard from her," Murray would tell me. It took a long time to work through his deep anger and resentment toward his parents for the damage they had done to his need to be his own self. Fortunately this family sought help soon after Murray began to rebel. After he got into trouble with the law several times, they realized that his acting out had deeper roots.

But scores of people proceed into adulthood with a highly developed and possibly neurotic "ought self." The potential for our ought self to be an ogre is pretty great. It can undermine our self-confidence and rob us of any sense of accomplishment. No matter what we achieve, it isn't good enough. No matter what we become, we "ought" to be someone else.

The problem with a highly developed ought self is that it gives others the power to determine who we become. Only God "ought" to have this power over us. If we are not watchful, this sense of being driven by our internalized "oughts" can become a form of self-imposed slavery. We begin to obey a false set of ideals, to seek the approval of others, and to erect an arbitrary set of laws. This isn't freedom. It's a form of enslavement. And it is the self that is enslaved. Thank God he can free us from this prison.

A TROJAN HORSE

Dr. James Masterson describes one other aspect of the self: the *false self*.[3] Approaching it from an offshoot of psychoanalysis called "Object-Relations Theory," Masterson defines the "false self" as a self that is constantly being sabotaged by self-destructive behavior.

Such a person has internalized many infantile fantasies that serve as defenses against reality. We all collect a kaleidoscope of self-images, like pieces of colored glass that form themselves into shapes, patterns, and designs. When these patterns don't fit together in any meaningful way, the light that falls through them is chaotic rather than organized, constructive, or pretty.

What is the effect of being a *false self*? A disorganized life that doesn't seem to be going anywhere. Consider a thirty-five-year-old actress who is quite attractive but who can't manage to form any meaningful relationships. She sabotages every date by "acting" instead of being real. Since she can't handle rejection, at the first sign of trouble, she rejects her date and storms out.

Perhaps a college freshman who daydreams excessively can't concentrate on getting any work done. He escapes from reality through alcohol and constantly fantasizes that somehow he will make it through life by being "rescued" by some wealthy relative. It could be a mother in her late twenties who uses food as a tranquilizer. She is riddled with worry and fear. She clings possessively to her children, won't even let a babysitter take care of them, and suffers constant nightmares about the day they will grow up and leave her. So she eats, and eats, and eats. Everything in sight. Food helps to soothe the anxiety. But to get rid of the calories, she forces herself to throw up. Her bulimia is well advanced.

These are examples of people with "false" selves.

A *real self* is made up of healthier images. The kaleidoscope is more symmetrical, producing varied, but integrated and attractive patterns which lead to constructive steps. Reality becomes easier to deal with because the internalized images of the real self are derived from reality rather than fantasy. A real self can deal with disappointment because it can see life from a larger perspective. A real self can handle failure because it can see the value of "missing the mark" and teach us to simply readjust our sights.

This distinction between a false and a real self is helpful, but it seems to me that these are not really two separate selves. They comingle within the one and only self we have. In fact, we all have a part of us that is "false," prone to self-sabotage like an enemy spy within our own ranks. But we also have a part of us that is "real," one that longs to be healthy, effective, productive, and successful. Most of us have more of the false self and less of the real self. Our task is to turn this around and increase the percentage of our selves that is "real."

One final thought: a self that is not centered on Christ cannot be anything but "false." It is founded on shaky ground. But claiming to have your life founded on Christ doesn't guarantee that all of your self is "real" either. Becoming a real self is a process that begins by being grounded on Christ, the sure foundation, and then grows through an ongoing experience of this Christ. Sadly, many believers have taken care of the foundation, but have done little to develop the real part of their selves.

—

PART TWO

—

Probing the Self

CHAPTER 5

The Damage-Prone Self

So I find this law at work: When I want to do good, evil is right there with me. For in my inner being I delight in God's law; but I see another law at work in the members of my body, waging war against the law of my mind and making me a prisoner of the law of sin at work within my members. What a wretched man I am! Who will rescue me from this body of death? Thanks be to God— through Jesus Christ our Lord!

Rom 7:21-25 NIV

I WILL ALWAYS REMEMBER THE DAY my world changed forever. Shortly after my twelfth birthday, I heard the dreaded news from my mother. I often wonder how my life would have been different if it had never happened. I went to bed one day as a certain self, and woke up the next day a different self. Having chosen bedtime to tell us, Mom had asked us to go to bed earlier than usual. My young mind immediately became a little suspicious.

She waited until my younger brother and I were all tucked in and then said, "Tomorrow we are leaving. I'm going to get a divorce. I can't stand it anymore."

Those few words completely changed my life—not for the better, but for the worse. The impact of that decision would damage my emerging and vulnerable self beyond understanding. I would never again be the same self that went to bed that night.

My parents' separation and divorce came at a time when divorce was relatively rare in our community. Although I believe that divorce is always damaging to children (see my book *Healing Adult Children of Divorce*[1]), the post-World War II era was a particularly vulnerable period for children. Fathers had gone to war. Some never came back. Many children had not seen their fathers for four or five years. When the war ended, a great emphasis was placed on rebuilding families. So the stigma of divorce was particularly devastating, not something you could ignore.

As the product of a "broken home," shame and fear dominated my feelings from then on. I became the focus of pity from adults and the target of ridicule from my peers. I knew several boys whose fathers had been killed during the war, but none who had been divorced. If my father had been killed, he would have been a hero. Divorce produced not pride but shame.

This all-pervasive shame deeply scarred my developing self. I felt angry, depressed, self-depreciating, and frightened for a long time. I felt robbed of my childhood and birthright—the right to grow up in a home with two parents. In self-defense, I became stoical, withdrawn, afraid of crying or showing any sign of weakness, and distrustful of anyone who said "I love you."

Thank God much of this damage has now been repaired, but not without a lot of grace, effort, and the loving patience of my wife. Not everyone is able to undo the devastating effects of divorce.

Significant damage to the self doesn't necessarily require a traumatic life experience like divorce or physical, sexual, or emotional abuse. We live in an imperfect world. Everyone is likely to be damaged in some deep way because of the presence of sin in all of us. As a consequence of the Fall, Christians believe that the self is flawed to begin with, but I will deal more with the topic of sin and the self in a later chapter. I want to focus here on the damage caused more by our environment and child-rearing practices.

The next chapter will cover the more serious "disorders" of the self. They represent the extreme consequences of dis-ordered child-rearing and unsatisfactory early childhood envi-ronments that severely distort the self and usually require pro-fessional help to correct. Damage doesn't always mean one is disordered. Unfortunately, the damage to the self I will cover in this chapter is common to all of us.

THE MAIN CULPRITS

Contrary to popular Christian opinion, not all psychologists see the self through rose-tinted glasses. We see more and more reality-based interpretations of the self beginning to replace humanistic pop-psychology. Many prestigious psychologists no longer paint the self as the embodiment of total goodness, just waiting to be released into its glorious personhood! The self is what we make of it. It embodies what a culture believes is a per-son's place in the cosmos—encompassing all of his or her limits, talents, expectations, and prohibitions.[2]

Psychology, particularly psychotherapy, has *failed the self.* By itself it has not helped us build a better world or a more perfect self. The self is being damaged, first by sin and then by a sinful environment. In this world in which the self must live, what are the *influences* that damage the self? And what are the *signs* of this damage?

Historical influences. We are all the product of history, the events which shape our world and largely determine where we live, how we live, whom we marry, whom we leave behind. Over the past two hundred years, several developments in Western culture have especially shaped the self as we find it today.

Industrialization and urbanization forced us into little boxes we call "homes." These individual units which usually house only the nuclear family rob us of a sense of community, especially that of the extended family—grandparents, uncles, aunts, and cousins. We find it more difficult to build personal relationships, maintain family units, or keep a marriage together for very long. The industrial revolution destroyed many of the rural, agrarian communities which promoted intimacy and a sense of belonging. Those people who shifted from the cooperative security of the family farm to the competitive work of business and industry—usually accompanied by the social isolation of apartments and single-family homes—lost the sense of "tribal living."

The sexual restrictions of the Victorian age gave rise to much of today's neurotic sexuality and preoccupation with orgasms and pornography. The sexual self of today is often obsessive and compulsive. Economic depressions and two world wars have further molded us into consuming selves. We are compelled to acquire material possessions to avoid the anxiety of insecurity. Secularism and media exposure has further fostered a lack of personal conviction and worth, a relative value system, and a predominant psychological philosophy that glorifies the self-contained individual. The ideal self of our day and age, therefore, is highly individualistic.

Societal influences. These same events have shaped the social influences that have warped the modern self. Huge city complexes are usually riddled with crime, gang-warfare, drug-trafficking, prostitution, and violence. To provide a safe environment, the affluent have escaped to the suburbs. This urban-flight further destroyed any larger sense of community by separating the "haves" from the "have-nots."

Culture is intended to explain and provide a context for the self. But modern-day social and economic separateness creates a sort of accidental apartheid. The self of today is being shaped by a one-sided, ethnocentric psychology, which is mainly Caucasian. I am appalled that very little of today's psychotherapy is relevant to those who live in the barrio or the ghetto. Humanism is a philosophy for the privileged. Selfism is a byproduct of affluence, not poverty. The one-on-one "talk therapy" of contemporary psychotherapy hardly makes any sense in the ghetto, just as it didn't make any sense to me when I grew up in South Africa and related to traditional African cultures.

Parental influences. Who you are as a parent has a major influence on the self of your child. The family is a complex interactional system that helps to define a young child's self. By actions more than by words, a person learns if he or she is worthwhile. The family shapes the conscience by its choice of punishment. It helps us to internalize pictures and attitudes that we will carry in our memory for the rest of our lives. If an adult cannot answer the question "Who am I?" satisfactorily, it will be because the parents have failed to teach the child who he or she is.

But parents are not totally to blame if they fail. Chances are they themselves came from families which distorted their own selves. The victims of "self-degeneration" are unprepared for the task of parenting. Extended family members were not there to compensate for their inexperience and to provide validation. Perhaps one parent grew up in a single-parent home where everything depended on Mom. No Dad consistently reassured the child, "you are a precious person who is deeply loved."

How do we arrest this vicious cycle that damages our selves? How do we stop the destruction that so impedes the work of God in repairing the self, or that prevents people from turning to God for spiritual healing in the first place? The answer begins with our own selves. We start where we have the greatest influence: within our own, deep, precious selves. And we begin *now.*

But I'm running ahead of myself. In order to diagnose our own condition—which is always the first and necessary step toward healing—we first need to decide how the modern self has been damaged. A clearer understanding of how the self is damage-prone will also help us as parents to be more effective in preparing our children to receive the work of God in their lives. At least we will be less likely to erect obstacles that prevent them from turning to God.

To illustrate the clearer reflection of the self that is currently emerging from psychology, I will limit myself to three recent "word pictures" that have been painted for us: the *empty self;* the *overinvolved self;* and the *overindulgent self.*

THE EMPTY SELF

The most obvious deficiency of the modern self is that of emptiness. Gavin is a classic example. He is in serious trouble at the age of twenty-one. Not legal trouble or emotional trouble *per se*. Rather, he feels lost and bewildered, adrift on the great ocean of life. His father died before Gavin reached adolescence and his mother continued to run the family business. While this young man has never wanted for anything material, he just hasn't found his niche in life. Something went wrong in his childhood to produce a feeling of estrangement from the world.

Up to the point when he left home to go to college, Gavin was outwardly a compliant, loving, responsive, and considerate son who had never given his mother any cause to worry. In fact she idealized him. Mom could rely on her son to come home when he said he would and to keep out of trouble. Their consistent church involvement had kept him exposed to reputable, loving young people. The fortunate teenager seemed destined to live a happy, fulfilled life.

Then Gavin went away to college. He felt drawn to the outcasts at his school and began to experiment with drugs. He got hooked because he felt lonely and needed peer support and friendship, because he wanted to know whether there was something in life that could fill or satisfy the inner vacuum that he felt. What had gone wrong? Why did Gavin feel so *empty* ? Had his family failed him in some way? His early environment had not led him astray. Gavin had apparently been double-crossed by life itself.

Dr. Philip Cushman, in an article published in the prestigious *American Psychologist*, labels this as the *empty self*.[3] A byproduct of contemporary life, it is a self with no substance, a vacuum. Because the self is empty, it must be "filled up" and soothed with food, electronics, music, celebrities—even drugs. Despite Gavin's healthy upbringing, his self had been damaged. But he has made an important discovery: the self is empty and restless until it finds its rest in the bosom of its Creator. He is fortunate. Many Gavins never discover the source of their emptiness. They become too preoccupied with numbing it by cramming junk down their throats.

The inner emptiness of the modern self can be described in several ways:

- An absence of a sense of personal worth: you don't just hate yourself, you don't even care.
- A lack of direction in life; a sense of aimless wandering.
- A lack of appreciation for what one can contribute to life.
- An absence of personal convictions: you don't believe in anything.
- A compulsion to fill the emptiness of life with food (which leads to eating disorders) or drugs (which leads to drug addictions).
- A compulsion to anesthetize the emptiness (other addictive disorders).
- A compulsive consummerism: filling the emptiness with gadgets, cars, and toys.
- A search for meaning in various New Age experiences, such as channeling or meditation.

All of these are negative results of the feeling of emptiness. On the positive side, this absence of personal meaning in life can produce a hunger for spiritual guidance and fulfillment, along with an openness to the gospel. Such a person is fortunate to experience his or her very real need for God.

What produces such profound emptiness? Spiritually, I believe it is a given, that the self is essentially empty as a byproduct of the Fall. We all experience some degree of emptiness, but some suffer from it more than others because of what has happened to them.

Psychologically, this inner vacuum is exacerbated by a strange cultural paradox: the self in our time is expected to function in a highly autonomous and isolated way. As the defined norms for health, we "individuate" and "differentiate" very early in life. Most of us are forced to separate from the family, to stand alone and "be ourselves" by being sent to school. We must become:

- *self-soothing:* learn to nurture yourself; you can't depend on others.
- *self-loving:* love yourself first; you won't always get it from others.

- *self-sufficient:* cut yourself off from the support of others.

Five or six is a very young age to be forced to learn such survival strategies. Where is the catch? These qualities are probably well suited to helping you adjust to an isolated life on an island—à la Robinson Crusoe. But these qualities run contrary to what it takes to be a loving parent.[4]

Good parents are self-sacrificing, willing to suffer personal discomfort in order to be nurturing. They often surrender a lot of their own desires in order to help their offspring get a good start in life. I could write a book about the number of times I have sacrificed my own desires, my own pleasure, my own dreams, just to make it easier for my own kids. But I certainly don't want my kids to feel guilty about this choice; I don't even want them to know I'm doing it. That's just the nature of love. I hope they'll do the same for their kids.

Even though sadly lacking in many qualities, the empty self is here to stay. The advertising media exploits this void to sell the products that supposedly can fill it. They create the desperate illusion that the empty self can be soothed with goods—cars, cans, or candy. But only God can fill this emptiness. A Christian psychology, rightly construed, should point us to this solution.

THE OVERINVOLVED SELF

The self can vary in the extent to which it gets involved in what is going on around it. I may, for instance, go to a political rally and hear a number of speakers hold forth on the economy, domestic policies, and world events. But the involvement of my self could be minimal. My own reputation is not at stake. If the issues seem to be remote and unconnected to my immediate life, I don't plug directly into the current.

But the modern self tends to be the opposite: it tends to be overly involved in most issues. Let's suppose I'm watching two prestigious colleges vying for the honor of having the best football team in the Rose Bowl. I really have no personal connection with either college, but perhaps a few days before the game I told my son-in-law who I thought would win the game. I'm competitive this way. He disagrees with me, but I'm determined to be right.

Now I'm watching the final quarter of the Rose Bowl. It's been a close game, but my adopted team is losing. They're fumbling a lot. I'm beginning to regret that I chose them. My self is very involved. My reputation is at stake with my son-in-law. I'm afraid that I'm about to be judged unintelligent. My self-esteem is on the line right along with the outcome of the game.

Self-involvement varies considerably from situation to situation. So what determines how much of my self gets hooked by a given issue or experience? Why does an exam capture more of my self than a tennis game I can easily win, or why does a political election in my own state captivate me more than the presidential election in a foreign country?

My involvement is largely determined by the *impact of the situation on my sense of personal esteem or value.* The greater the risk that my esteem will be damaged, the greater will be the involvement of my self in that situation. My senses will be more alert to what is going on and my emotions more affected by the outcome. Self-involvement serves to heighten my alertness. An opposite response of underinvolvement may serve as a protective mechanism to prevent the self from becoming damaged.

Sometimes the protective aspect of self-involvement goes wrong and the self creates other defensive behaviors to compensate for its deficiencies. For instance, if my self-esteem is fragile, the closing minutes of that Rose Bowl game may be too painful for my ego to observe. What will my son-in-law think of me? I've backed the losers. I'm not very smart. Perhaps this is one of a long string of stupid stands I have taken. He'll laugh in my face and gloat over his smart choice. (He's really not like that; I'm just speaking hypothetically.) At this point I would automatically try to find some defense for my self. I could say something like "I really egged you on, didn't I? I knew all along who would win." It wouldn't be true, but it might save me from humiliation.

What sort of defenses does the self bring into play as protection from such threats to its esteem? There are many, but let me mention two of the more important defenses: *repression* and *rationalization.*

Repression. Repression is a process by which we force or push down a memory so that it is pushed out of our consciousness. Psychologists believe the memory "goes underground" into the unconscious, where it continues to exert control over our feelings and behaviors without our awareness. One of the consequences of this process is that we forget painful events, and we remember only good things.

The more severe the emotional pain that produces the repression, the more likely it will be pushed into the remotest corners of our consciousness. In my Rose Bowl example, I could very well turn off the TV and totally forget that I rooted for any one team. My accusers might try in vain to convince me that I backed the loser. I would simply deny it, and even firmly believe my denial. But what if the experience was truly traumatic, as in the case of childhood abuse? I would be even more likely repress the memory. This kind of repression underlies a lot of our forgotten childhood pain.

Rationalization. Rationalization is what we do when we devise superficial explanations or excuses for our acts, beliefs, or desires. We convince ourselves by using some sort of logical reasoning—which is not always very logical—that we did or didn't mean what we said, or that we didn't do what others say we did. "I knew all along the other team would win. I just egged you on to make the game more exciting. Do you really think I care who wins? I knew all along who would really win—so there!"

This is rationalization, something we do all the time. Our selves are too fragile to admit defeat. In order to feel worthwhile, we must believe we are invincible, undefeatable, all-wise. We will go to any length to maintain self-protection and prevent discovery of our real imperfections, even if we superficially pronounce ourselves as unworthy.

Why do we develop such defenses? To a degree, these defenses can help us ward off dangerous threats to the self. In that sense, they can be a helpful coping mechanism. But these defenses often become so entrenched in us that they become unhealthy responses to reality, with tremendous power to distance the self and its ability to relate well to others. Parents sometimes foster unhealthy overinvolvement in their children without realizing it. When a child makes a mistake, they may make critical comments like "you're bad" or "you're stupid." Such negative generalizations breed unhealthy defenses. How is a child to develop a healthy self if it is bombarded with such criticisms?

The alternative is to offer suggestions for constructive change. Instead of "you're bad" or "you're stupid," a child should be told why something was the wrong thing to do and should be helped to solve the problem. "That's not the right way. Let me show you again how you should do it...."

Unhealthy and excessive self-involvement invariably leads to a heightened state of anxiety, which is one reason why such problems are so dominant in our age.

THE OVERINDULGENT SELF

Tom Wolfe, the journalist who promoted the protest writing of the sixties and seventies and who wrote the best-selling novel about flying-ace Chuck Yeager, satirized the seventies as the "me decade." Quite accurately, Wolfe perceived that period as heralding a time of self-centeredness and self-indulgence that we may only now be emerging from. During those years it became respectable to indulge your self, to talk about it, gratify it, and "let it do its own thing." Gone was any idea that you were responsible for anyone else. Banish the thought that you should feel guilty because your neighbor, or even your closest friend, was in need and you chose not to help. All that mattered was me.

This rampant self-preoccupation began in the early sixties with encounter groups. A whole generation joined these therapy groups. Getting violently angry at everyone and everything and swearing your head off became the mark of emotional maturity.

You could also be "born again" at Institutes of Rebirthing. All it took was meditation, fantasy, regression, and immersion in "self-awareness" therapy. Since this was the era in which I emerged as a clinical psychologist, I observed it all firsthand. Having begun my professional life as an engineer before turning to clinical psychology as a way of ministering to others, I was a bit late to the starting post.

I must confess that I was pretty confused myself. I lived in far off South Africa during the turbulent sixties, but moved to California early in the seventies. Therapeutic psychology was then dominated by "me" type therapies, such as assertiveness training, meditation, rolfing (a form of massage), and "body-work." Nudity gained a strong foothold when it was considered to be therapeutic to take off your clothes whenever you got a chance. Disrobing symbolized "breaking free" of society's restraints. It was a graphic way of discarding all your inhibitions and "accepting" the body you hated so much.

Was all this therapy any help? To be honest, much of it was revolting. At times I felt ashamed to be identified with a profession that merely used psychotherapy as a cover for carnality. Every professional convention I attended contained booths showing pornographic movies—under the guise of "sexual therapy." Many private gatherings of therapists reeked of marijuana's pungent odor.

Fortunately, this has all passed. Professional associations have clamped down. The women's movement helped to show how nude therapy and pornographic movies were a form of sexism and sexual abuse. Professional conventions banned the porno stalls. Ethics committees tightened up control, and anyone who engaged in sexual activity with a client was dealt with severely. For the most part, the mental health profession today is highly ethical and well-policed from within its own ranks.

One of the most damaging consequences of the "me generation" is a global rejection of the "self" by conservative Christians. The self-improvement movement of the sixties and seventies left a very bad taste in the mouths of Christians. This "new narcissism" was so revolting to the church that all references to the self were perceived as the equivalent of carnality. But we overreacted; we threw the baby out with the bath water.

The genuine value of this post-World War II era was that it introduced a new openness toward talking about the self. We could talk about our selves in a way that was healthier. Many people genuinely wanted to know their feelings better, to understand their deepest motives, and to have the freedom to be themselves more authentically. Godly people became open to "discovering" themselves and learning about what made them anxious, why they got tense, and what made them angry. But the Christian counter-reaction had begun, and is still with us today. The hedonism of this period has left the self with a very bad reputation.

On the one level, the "me generation" catered to a Dionysian feast that was wild, frenzied, and sensuous. But at a deeper level, some people were learning how to become more aware of themselves. Many ordinary folks were simply trying to rebuild their world, get over a devastating war, and find a place where they could genuinely live a more fulfilling life.

Simple self-discovery is not the same as self-indulgence. Self-gratification has to do with the Freudian id, that part of me that desires to please only itself and to indulge in every pleasurable activity. Scripture's term for the id is "the lower nature," a part of us which is driven by instinctive urges and desires to live according to the pleasure principle. True believers "put away" this lower nature and try to live according to "higher" principles.

But this is precisely where the confusion originates. The self is not identical with these instinctive urges for pleasure. The self is not the same as the id or the lower nature. It is not, in itself, narcissistic, proud, or vain. The self can be controlled by the id, but it is not the same as the id. The self is simply me desiring to live as me. It responds to "higher" desires and becomes focused or driven toward righteousness when it is centered on God.

A deep desire to understand your self through a process of discovery need not be equated with self-indulgence or self-centeredness. Self-discovery must not be confused with carnal self-release. Healthy self-awareness can help to render our world more manageable and to make us better people. When this self-discovery is guided by God's Spirit so that it is a *total* discovery—with full exposure of our real selves—it always brings healing and puts us in closer touch with our hunger for God. It helps us to became whole beings, with healthy bodies, wholesome minds, God-centered spirits, and emotions that heal rather than destroy. There is only one true "you" to be discovered. God can give you the courage to face your self as you are and as he intends you to be.

THE SHAMED SELF

Before the Fall of our first parents, the self felt no shame. What a blissful state, with no awareness of nakedness, no embarrassment. Just pure innocence and total transparency. The self could be itself in truth because it had nothing to hide.

After the fall, the self became riddled with shame. Now we have everything to hide, not just our bodies. We must hide our thoughts, because we fear we will be judged by them. We must hide our desires, because we know they will bring ridicule or rejection. We even hide our love for fear it will be rebuffed. The modern self is a self in hiding. And it hides mainly from itself.

Can I share with you a dream I often have? I have dreamed it many times, ever since I can remember. And I have often heard others tell of a similar dream. The setting is usually a public gathering. Sometimes it's a church service where I'm preaching, sometimes it's my office or a party. But always it is me discovering that I have no clothing on the bottom half of my body.

At first my nakedness seems quite normal. People are not shocked or running away from me, but then I always begin to feel deep *shame* as I desperately try to pull down a vest or shirt to cover my body. My embarrassment strikes at the very core of my self. I fear that I will never again be respected. And then I wake up. This dream never changes. I just lie there feeling so unworthy, so bad, so humiliated—like I've been robbed of my dignity and exposed as an evil person.

Where does this kind of dream originate? Perhaps as a very young child, I walked in on an adult gathering in our home with no pants on and people laughed. Perhaps I once saw a movie when someone was embarrassed by being caught without clothes. Perhaps my fear is imagined. Who knows! The point is that at a very deep, existential level, every self contends with shame. Our fear of nakedness reaches to the very core of our being. We can't escape it. We can try to push it away, keep it from our awareness, and even become ashamed of our shame, but these "psychological clothes" never cover the inadequacies of the self.

How are we to deal with our existential shame? Some people try to build self-respect by becoming a great athlete, a successful professional, or a "pretty good person." Some may even build what Nathaniel Branden calls "pseudo-self-esteem," a protective device that helps us to pretend that we are of value.[5] It doesn't help, but we keep on trying.

The only effective "cure" for this shame is God's grace—God stooping to our nakedness and covering us with his own garments. The fall of Adam and Eve rendered us such a brutal blow and developed such a one-sided sense of self-consciousness in us that only restoration to God's presence, through redemption, can help remove our shame of *being*.

THE BATTLE FOR THE SELF

I have discussed just a few of the ways the self can be damaged. but it is important to realize that a battle is raging over the self. While our adversary, Satan, seeks to destroy the self, God seeks to salvage and heal it. And in the midst of this battle, the problems of the self are changing.

The battle over the self is not simply an individual struggle. It is a war raged in the context of our society. Christopher Lasch, an ardent critic of our culture, has many stunning insights into how personality and its social context shape the self. In his book *The Culture of Narcissism*, he offers a penetrating look at the damaged self of our time: narcissistic, emotionally shallow, fearful of intimacy, and primed with pseudo self-insight. With a prevailing passion to live only for itself, the modern self tends to live simply for the moment.

Lasch traces the origin of this narcissism to the human potential movement of the sixties, when the therapies of Carl Rogers (Client-Centered Therapy) and Fritz Perls (Gestalt Therapy) emphasized such values as trust, openness, risk-taking, acceptance of self and others, capacity for joy (peak experiences), and empathy. He believes that this has resulted in an "isolation of the self."[6]

What has emerged are "neo-narcissists" who see the world as a mirror of themselves. Their interest in an external event extends only so far as it throws back a reflection of their own images.[7] The self has fallen in love with itself in a sick way, selling its future for whatever gratification it can get now. As a result, we have lost our capacity for love, we are fearful of intimacy, and we dread old age and death. Lasch depicts the modern self as chaotic and impulse ridden. What an accurate picture!

In his subsequent book, *The Minimal Self*, Lasch contends that people have not only lost confidence in the future but are now engaged solely in a battle for survival. Faced with long-term economic decline, environmental deterioration, crime, and terrorism, the modern self has retreated from committed relationships that once provided security and order—such as the family and church. The self has contracted to its defensive core and become a "minimal self."[8] Unlike in the recent past, the self can no longer afford to be grandiose, hedonistic, self-seeking, indifferent, narcissistic. Instead, the modern self hides in a shell like a hermit crab.

This is a significant shift. In these troubled times, everyday life has often deteriorated to a point of survival, not indulgence. Narcissistic self-preoccupation is a kind of luxury that many of us can no longer afford.

In fact, most people have developed a "minimal" self rather than an imperialistic one. It seems as if the pendulum has swung away from pleasure-centeredness to an urgent search for security and certainty. "Where can I get my next thrill?" has been replaced with "Where can I get my next job?" This root change in the nature of the game of life seriously alters the rules.

Human nature always remains the same, but how it plays out the game of life shifts through the ages. The achievement of an adequate sense of self has always been difficult in Western culture. The decline of the family as the primary haven in a heartless world, the growth of individualism, and the retreat from community loyalty and dependence have made it increasingly difficult for anyone to achieve an adequate sense of belonging in a hostile, fragmented world.

Christians have abhorred self-display and an over-emphasis on self-fulfillment. But now the battle for the self will be fought with the weapons of demoralization: a sense of inner emptiness, and the threat of the disintegration of the self. Christopher Lasch rightly indicates that our earlier culture of narcissism has now shifted to a culture of "survivalism."[9] People all over the world will have to learn strategies once common only in countries exposed to extreme adversity.

The *minimal self* is the self our children and grandchildren will have to contend with. It is not a self full of grand ideas or ego-fulfilling plans, nor is it a self that believes it has all the answers. It is an emptier self, searching for a more solid footing than mere success can provide and a deeper sense of destiny than a guaranteed three score and ten years can give.

The image of this minimal self is well portrayed in the modernist sculptures of the Swiss artist Alberto Giacometti (1901-1966). Razor-thin, hollow-eyed, and knobby, his emaciated figures seem to stare blankly into space as if the simple task of existence occupies all the energy they can muster. They are our modern icons of emptiness, nothingness—a minimal existence by a minimal self.

This battle for the self has also changed in another way. Under the guise of making us personally more productive, we're being surrounded by the emerging technologies of *self-consciousness*. Self-awareness no longer seems to be enough. We are being turned into self-conscious, navel-gazing morons. No matter which way we turn, some technology nags us to examine how we look, sound, express ourselves, and even think. It used to be just mirrors that reflected our images. Now the familiar whir of video camcorders serves as a technological mirror. Next we will be watching video telephones. The self enjoys new opportunities to see its reflection in a way previously unknown to humankind.

What is the effect of such technological advancement? It can only be a level of self-consciousness that will eventually damage the self. We are constantly viewing how we appear to others. Very soon, video recordings of virtually every business meeting will be commonplace. It's already a fact in Fortune 500 companies. Managers are constantly critiquing their performance "on camera." Did I say the right thing? Make the right gesture? Use the right posture?

We are becoming so self-conscious—so concerned about the "impression" we make and how to manage that impression—

that we will find it increasingly difficult to "just be ourselves." Gone are the days of simple self-awareness. Now full-blown self-consciousness is our constant companion.

Before voice recorders, I wasn't very conscious of how my voice sounded. It sounded okay when I heard it through my ears. Then tape recorders made me self-conscious. Before video recorders, I was oblivious to my hand gestures or head nods. Now I think about them every time I teach or preach. What will it be next? I can't even be private from myself. We are becoming neurotically preoccupied with impressions. A new vanity is on the rise from which there is no retreat.

What effect is this all going to have on the self? It is frightening to ponder. More and more of us will become dissatisfied with our looks, manners, spontaneity, warmth, style, and decorum. We will become a nation of actors and actresses, constantly performing on stage. Speech therapists, plastic surgeons, and tailors all have a rosy future. Who knows what miracles they will be called upon to perform? The self is in for some serious trouble ahead—and spell that with a capital "T." What are the Christian implications for this battle for the self? We may need to retool and refocus the gospel on more relevant themes. The "yuppie" phenomenon may be the tail-end of a narcissistic preoccupation. For instance, railing against self-interest, selfism, and self-fulfillment will soon fall on deaf ears. When people are just struggling to survive, or attempting to stay alive, being accused of too much narcissism becomes laughable.

On the other hand, self-consciousness is on the rise. We will find it increasingly difficult to just "make it" in our brave new world. I believe that psychology has already begun to deal with the realities of this "tough new world." Fortunately, the timeless good news of Jesus Christ will always be relevant—in the worst of times as it is in the best. The self faces rough seas ahead, but being centered on Christ offers us a sturdy keel.

The Disordered Self

M OST CLIENTS WHO SEEK HELP from mental health professionals or pastoral counselors these days suffer from *disorders of the self*.[1] But like so many who have been in practice for any length of time, I have seen a shift from more classical neuroses to the more diffuse, undefinable, vague complaints that seem to characterize the disorders of the modern self.

When I first began to see patients in the mid-sixties in South Africa, I frequently observed "classical conversion hysterias," such as the sudden onset of blindness, paralysis, or amnesia without any physical explanation. Such fascinating mysteries are the stuff of which novels and movies are made. I remember receiving a call early one Saturday morning from a missionary friend:

"Please, can you give me some advice? It's rather urgent. I'm calling from the home of an Indian couple who have recently converted to Christianity from Hinduism. Their seventeen-year-old daughter is due to get married this afternoon, but has suddenly gone paralyzed. She says she can't move her legs—they're lame. I'm convinced it has something to do with the impending marriage. Can you see her right away?"

Within the hour I was by her side. She lived with her parents

in a poor Indian sector of our city. Her grandparents had emi-
grated to South Africa after the First World War and now she
had been caught up in the struggle between tradition and her
new life. Her story is classic for transitional cultures. This young
woman was promised at birth to a marriage partner she had only
just met.

Six months before meeting her fiancé, she had fallen in love
with another young man—definitely a "no-no." In fact, it was this
young man who had evangelized her Hindu family and had
brought them to my friend's missionary church. All fairly new
Christians, they were very confused about what to do. Clearly the
apparent paralysis was connected to their conflict, a disorder
known as "conversion hysteria." In this disorder the anxiety
caused by overwhelming fear or conflict is "converted" into
some physical disorder as a way of resolving the conflict. Forms
of paralysis, blindness, and even amnesia can be created by the
mind as protection against intense emotional pain. There is no
physical cause in the conversion symptom.

As the young girl sobbed out her painful dilemma, my heart
really went out to her. Should she disobey her parents or be
joined in marriage to a pagan Hindu that very afternoon? In the
background stood the young Christian man whom she loved.
Her parents were also quite distraught. Should they honor a
commitment made seventeen years ago according to their cultural tradition? Feeling obligated as Christians to keep their
promises, what else could they do? What was the daughter to do?
The marriage feast had already been laid out. How humiliating
to call off the marriage just hours before it was to take place.

I sent my missionary friend to negotiate with the parents and
family of the groom, while I concentrated on trying to resolve
the girl's apparent "paralysis." I was convinced of the conversion
hysteria because I had seen it often under such circumstances, a
sudden paralysis with no history of injury. The pattern of paralysis makes no sense physiologically. It cuts across nervous system
boundaries.

I explained to the girl what was happening and reassured her
that something could be worked out. Hope was not yet lost. I
suggested that her strength was returning, prayed with her, and
asked God to give her courage and wisdom to know what she

should do. And slowly her legs began to move again. After a while she sat up. The hysteria had been resolved in a way that seemed miraculous, but the mind was only doing what it was designed to do in such conflicts. The paralysis was a defense mechanism triggered by the conflict to protect the young girl.

Just then my missionary friend returned with the message that all had been resolved. As it turned out, the young girl's intended wasn't that keen on the marriage either. He liked another girl and was very glad to be off the hook. The small feast that the parents had prepared would be used to celebrate some recent birthdays. Since they were poor anyway, little money was involved. The missionary would explain the change of plans to the group who were planning to celebrate the wedding, most of whom would be Christians anyway. Joyfully, they immediately began making plans for a new wedding.

I returned home exhausted—but deeply thankful for the special understanding God had given me for these types of problems. The mind is a wonderful organ, intelligently designed to protect us in the midst of severe conflict. We don't need esoteric or even supernatural explanations for such dramatic defenses. Cultures in transition often manifest these dramatic forms of psychological disorder, just as our own culture did during the first few decades of this century.

A CULTURAL SHIFT

When I first moved to the United States about twenty years ago, a few of my patients clearly had classic neurotic disorders, the sort that would have made Freud happy. Obsessions and compulsions that varied from excessive hand washing and continuous checking that windows were closed, to loss of voice and amnesia. One patient would always became paralyzed when sitting in the reclining chair I used for therapy.

But I have observed a gradual change over the years. Much of what we now see in clinical practice are not major aberrations of the mind, but rather *disorders of the self*—ranging from sexual identity problems, to feelings of being uncared for, or trying to escape one's existence through various addictions. Most modern people suffer from a profound erosion of self-worth, interpersonal stress, conflict, and identity problems. Depression with which the self cannot adequately cope often results from losses such as divorce, from diminished respect, absence of cohesion, loss of ambition, of hope, and of life-meaning.

Rachel is one example, a thirty-eight-year-old, middle-class, attractive but totally bored mother of two teenagers by a previous marriage. She married very young because she was pregnant by a young man who turned out to be irresponsible and lazy. Since her husband failed to earn enough money, Rachel went to work as a secretary for a real estate company. When her children were old enough to be placed in day-care, she moved into a sales position.

In the midst of a real estate boom, Rachel prospered. She divorced her no-good husband and began having affairs with married men—a help to her business, she said. Besides, what was a single woman to do? Then Rachel met a man who said he would divorce his wife to marry her. He was also in real estate. They soon settled down to build the "perfect" family. He wanted to have his own children, but Rachel adamantly refused to have any more kids. Their relationship grew increasingly tense and they gradually drifted apart. It was during this time that she suffered periodic depressions.

Then Rachel met another married man who "fell in love" with her. They both divorced and began living together. Her two children, now fourteen and fifteen, did not like this new arrangement. Fed up with Mom's lack of stability, they both began to act out. The boy, who was the oldest, started taking drugs and skipping school a lot. The girl became boy-crazy.

Meanwhile, business wasn't going too well for Rachel and her live-in lover. As the real estate market dove into the doldrums, Rachel began to feel the pinch financially. In desperation, she turned to gambling to make money. She bet on everything—legally and illegally—and also lost everything she bet. At the time I began seeing her, Rachel was borrowing and spending two to three thousand dollars a month on horses, the lottery, and an occasional poker game. Her companion knew little about this as she moved assets around to cover her losses, sold jewelry, and borrowed to the hilt.

Even as her financial mess escalated, it was Rachel's emotional pain that finally brought her in for help. She realized that she had become vulnerable to other men again, that her depressions were becoming more and more frequent, that her kids were out of control, and that her relationship was going nowhere. Her gambling addiction had provided an escape and promised to solve all her financial problems. Now it was also out of control.

When Rachel first sat down in my office, she literally collapsed in the chair and started sobbing. After she had described a long history of problems, she begged, "What's wrong with me? Am I a nut-case or what?"

I could offer no single diagnosis, as is more and more often the case. Many such clients end up being labeled "borderline," the current catch-all for vague and multiple problems.

When Rachel is depressed, she can be diagnosed. When she's pouring through the race listings, she can probably be called a "compulsive gambler." But when you gather up all her difficulties, what have you got? An ordinary person who has lost her way and doesn't know where to go. The only appropriate label is "disorder of the self."

Such disorders are the result of a failure to achieve a cohesive self, one with harmony, vigor, and a sense of directedness or purpose. Like a fish out of water, people with this disorder are at odds with their environment; they haven't quite figured out what life is all about. The resulting instability affects them in a variety of areas, including their ability to relate to others, and their problems with self-image.

A complete review and description of what can go wrong with the contemporary self would require a book in itself. To illustrate the range of possible disturbances, I will briefly describe some of the more common problems encountered by today's therapists.

While the self has always been prone to trouble, at no time in human history has it been as disordered and lacking in cohesion as it is now. Life is certainly more complex and pressured than it has ever been, but there is perhaps an even more telling reason for this disorder. At no other time has the self been so abandoned, so isolated, and so unsupported. The breakdown of the family, the prevalence of single-parent families, and the scarcity of an extended family is beginning to take its toll on all of us.

Unlike previous generations, our individualistic culture cuts the self off from natural human support. Many Rachels of this world have nowhere else to turn but to a psychotherapist, they have no "significant other" who can help them unravel the problems of the self. If we were living "in community" as God intended, professionals like myself would probably be out of business. Supported selves are quite capable of becoming healthy. It is the isolated self that inevitably suffers the most. Following are some examples of the disordered self so rampant in today's world.

TWISTED RELATIONSHIPS

Disordered relationships top my list simply because they both cause our problems as well as result from them. Every human being is created—some would even say "programmed" or "preadapted"—to actively interact with others. Babies focus primarily on their caretakers in their efforts to make sense of the world. Even a newborn somehow knows that the world revolves around *other people* rather than inanimate objects. Babies don't gurgle and smile at a pillow, but at a human face. They stretch their arms toward others, not toward the door. Being surrounded by a soft, down-filled mattress isn't enough. The baby wants to be cuddled by another warm body.

Within this context, the baby begins to become aware of its self. The initial lack of any sense of self is called a *virtual self,* one which has the potential to become a fully aware, self-conscious self. Selfhood typically emerges in the second year of life when the brain is sufficiently developed to distinguish between one's self and others. Prior to this time, the boundary is blurred. Now the child begins to realize: *"This* is me; *that* is you!" Psychology refers to *others* as *objects.* Such an impersonal term helps to clarify the distinction between the self and everything else that is not the self.

The healthy emergence and development of a sense of self requires a very important ingredient: the presence of others. Along with food and air, every human being requires appropriate interaction with people—from infancy to the end of life—in order to become mature and cohesive. Faulty experiences with others leads to *fragmentation* and *emptiness*. The self lacks any sense of fitting together. One feels like an uncoordinated conglomeration of body parts rather than an integrated whole. We all feel fragmented at various times in our lives, perhaps when we are fatigued or suffering some traumatic blow. Some people, in fact, feel that way all the time.

Faulty relationships can have a devastating effect on our development of self. Consider the young child who is physically or sexually abused by a family member who is supposed to be a protector and guardian. Such a self will be deeply damaged and will always feel vulnerable to abuse even in normal relationships. Injuries to the self can be devastating at any age, but those which occur during the formative years or at major developmental turning points can be disastrous. The child is extremely vulnerable to violations of trust and love. The abuse of this trust and love causes very deep trauma to the self.

Most adults who have problems with relationships have had unstable childhoods. They become exquisitely sensitive to rejection or shame, overly concerned about what others think of them, and devastated by the slightest hint of disapproval. They withdraw from intimacy, avoid taking risks with love, have few or perhaps no friends, and develop unstable relationships that vacillate from intense dependency to total abandonment. Recovery often involves a slow, painful process of rediscovering and repairing their fractured selves. The likelihood of total healing will improve if they can get out of any destructive relationships and find a relatively caring, unconditionally loving environment in which to rediscover themselves. Of course, no environment (or person) can provide unconditional love, but the more unconditional and accepting it is, the greater is the potential for healing.

AM I WHO I THINK I AM?

After disordered relationships, I would place *disorders of identity* as the next most significant disorder of the self. What characterizes a disorder of identity? Some people have described it as a preoccupation with the question: "Who am I?" I think this is too simplistic. An identity disorder is really characterized by the question, "Am I who I think I am?"

We all know enough about ourselves to be able to give some answers to the question, "Who am I?" Most of us can at least say, "I am a man" or "I am a woman." But what continues to puzzle those with identity problems is uncertainty about how they are to think about themselves. They receive such conflicting feedback that they don't trust their own self-evaluations. Their confusion further intensifies because their real self doesn't match their ideal self. "I know who I would like to be, but I don't know how to become this ideal person."

Throughout life we continue to be vulnerable to the absence, insufficiency, or inappropriateness of self/other experiences. One of their functions precisely entails helping the self develop a sense of *identity*. We come to know who we are through what others reflect back about us. Many critics say, "So what's the big deal about this identity stuff? Just *be* who you are and stop worrying about what you think you are or are not!"

But for many it's not so easy. They would gladly "be" who they are, if only they knew who they were or what it was they must be. Those who basically know who they are can't understand this dilemma. If you've never had a toothache, you can never really understand people who complain of toothache.

The concept of "identity" is not an easy one to grasp. The theorist, Erik Erikson, provides the richest and most insightful definition of identity: "The sense of ego identity... is the accrued confidence in one's ability to maintain inner sameness and continuity of one's meaning for others."[2] In simpler terms, identity means having a sense that I am who I think I am and who others think I am. I'm a unified whole. I can say to myself, "I'm always the same person."

We can distinguish several ingredients in this identity formula:

- Identity involves a feeling of *continuity* in one's sense of self. People change enormously over the course of a lifetime. Even as they grow bigger, older, and wiser, they continue to experience a sameness about who they are fundamentally, despite these changes. This feeling of sameness contributes to one's sense of identity.

- Identity also involves a sense of being *different* from others. If someone else is identical to you, you may have difficulty feeling you have your own identity. Identical twins, for instance, often struggle to define their separate identities. They are so much alike that they tend to think of themselves as a unit. In some disorders of the self, this struggle can occur even with total strangers.

- Indentity involves ongoing progress toward the *integration* of the self. A fragmented and disjointed self cannot develop a unifying identity because it lacks a cohesive foundation. Integration of the self involves bringing the various parts of your self into a harmonious whole. Your beliefs, attitudes, values, motives and everything else that makes up your identity are harmoniously integrated. You act as a whole. Your feelings are integrated into your actions and thoughts.

- Identity also involves a *connectedness* with a larger social group. No matter how individualistic any one of us feels we need to be, we cannot have a sense of personal identity unless we are connected to a reference group. If you were the only person in the world, you would have no personal identity. Personal identity does not come from isolation and separateness, but from belongingness and being a part of a community.

When the reference group you look to for your identity itself constitutes a social problem, then no matter how clear your sense of personal identity, you are a problem too. Such a dilemma is sadly the case with those who join the gangs that dominate our inner cities. Gangs are the only reference groups available to many young people, particularly those from impoverished neighborhoods. Gang activities act primarily as "identity factories." Unless and until we can find alternate reference groups for inner city kids, we will never eliminate gang warfare. These kids are only doing what their psyches were created to do—to find an identity. The problem is clearly a social one.

For all of us, though, a sense of identity must come from belongingness and connectedness to an acceptable community. For the Christian, the fellowship of believers should at least be one of these reference groups.

Many people face significant obstacles to developing an adequate identity. They feel fragmented, unacceptable, lost and bewildered by their many internal conflicts. Even being a believer does not automatically guarantee that you will not struggle with an identity problem. Fortunately, though, being grounded in Christ does provide invaluable resources for healing.

What are some of the causes of identity problems? The undeniable origins of identity problems are to be found in childhood and adolescence. While the questions of identity begin to emerge with the onset of adolescence, the foundation for these problems is laid earlier. How the child is treated, acknowledged, valued, disciplined, abused, and criticized will deeply affect how the sense of self develops, and whether this identity is unified, stable, and acceptable. When puberty brings rapid physical and emotional upheaval, the self is forced to reflect on the all-important identity question: "Who am I becoming?"

Internal conflict always arises at this point. On the one hand, the child has developed some idea of who he or she would like to be. But now the self is confronted with the *reality* of what is emerging. Just as turbulence is created wherever cold and warm oceans meet, so psychological turbulence occurs whenever warm ideals meet the cold waters of reality. An identity struggle inevitably ensues. Some settle it satisfactorily before they leave adolescence; some exist in a sort of cold war with themselves. Many never settle it at all, but continue to struggle with identity problems for years afterwards.

What are some of the symptoms of identity problems? Instead of one universal type of identity problem, we have many. And each has its own dominant set of symptoms. Here is a sample of the sorts of symptoms that can point to an identity problem:

- An inability to integrate aspects of your self into a cohesive and acceptable sense of self.
- Confusion about long-term goals or directions, or the choice of a career or marital partner.
- Significant vacillation about friendships, religion, group loyalties, or moral values.

- Frequent conflict regarding existing commitments, values, or religious identification.
- Certain behaviors, such as inappropriate sexual behavior or extra-marital affairs, which are inconsistent with one's outward or public image.
- Frequently feeling out of place or unwanted in both social and vocational settings.
- Failure to make progress toward developing a healthy acceptance of oneself; the tendency toward self-rejection.
- Frequently asking "Who am I?" and never being able to give a satisfactory answer.

A variety of secondary disturbances also tends to accompany identity problems:
- Mild anxiety and depressions, acute or chronic.
- An inner preoccupation with self or what is going on in one's life.
- Frequent conflicts with friends or spouse over irreconcilable differences in values.
- Self-doubt and a pervasive lack of confidence in one's own abilities.
- Difficulty making decisions and anxiety over decisions already made.

One of the main reasons for the preponderance of modern identity problems is the vast amount of change and flux in today's world. In the midst of such instability, people find it increasingly difficult to achieve a stable identity that remains intact throughout a lifetime.

I recently counseled a man in his late forties who had always felt secure in his work as an insurance broker and who felt a clear sense of identity as a believer. A good father and stable provider for his family, he suddenly lost his job for the first time in his life. The economy had forced his company to lay off hundreds of employees.

After six months of unsuccessfully searching for work, this man was understandably mired in a major depression. But the impact on his sense of identity was what really stood out. He simply disintegrated as a person. He could not relate to his family or continue to engage in normal church activities. Since he had built too much of his sense of self around his work, his identity collapsed along with his employment. The therapeutic task was to rebuild his identity outside of his vocation. He needed to have a feeling of worthwhileness that was independent of his performance.

These kinds of identity shifts and struggles are becoming commonplace. In fact, it may no longer be realistic to think that we can develop a single, stable identity early in life that will stand the test of time. Each significant change in our lives will force us to develop a "new" identity. Quickly disappearing is the traditional culture that maintained a stable environment. We can no longer count on relationships or institutions to remain intact. We ourselves may be here today, but gone tomorrow. For example, many women who have developed their identity around being a wife and mother have been forced to change because of divorce. Suddenly their world changes and they have to begin building a new identity around being single.

All of us must be prepared to face forced changes to our identity. We need to learn how to be more flexible and how to build support systems that can help us weather the inevitable transitions. Divorce, death, unemployment, catastrophic illness, or a host of other life-changing events can suddenly bear down on us. For some, these transitional stages may be frequent and demanding. Our identity must be flexible enough to undergo dramatic reevaluation at short notice.

THE SELF IN SHAMBLES

Borderline disorders have been the subject of controversy for over forty years.[3] The essential feature of such a disorder is that the self becomes *unstable*, which is reflected in large swings in mood and self-image. It also becomes *inconsistent* in commitments, attitudes, and behavior. A borderline disorder, then, is anything but predictable.

Now I must sound a word of caution here. The label "borderline" has become a wastebasket term into which we toss anyone who is not coping well with life. Many professionals use this catch-all category for anyone who is unhappy, angry, periodically depressed, or even antisocial. In fact, I have been appalled at the readiness with which psychologists and psychiatrists bandy this label about.

No constellation of symptoms can reliably characterize these disorders. The best we can do is to understand them as a disruption in the development of the self that shows up as "general chaos and enfeeblement." In other words, I'm not sure that it qualifies as a full-blown psychiatric disorder. But this disturbance of the self certainly warrants our attention. And our world seems to be turning out more and more people characterized by this generally chaotic approach to life.

Instability and *inconsistency* are its hallmarks, with *chaos* as its consequence. The individual with such a problem lacks genuineness. Outwardly, everything may seem intact, but inwardly bedlam reigns. On first encounter, they may seem perfectly normal. But after a while, you begin to ask yourself, "What's wrong with this person?"

This borderline state used to be considered a precursor to full-blown schizophrenia. Most professionals no longer make such a connection. Borderline states are now thought to be defensive maneuvers of the self, designed mainly to protect it against anxiety. Such people manifest a very low tolerance for anxiety, poor impulse control, and few healthy outlets for aggression. Some see it as a "disease of limits" in that the person with a borderline disorder cannot establish essential and reasonable limits.

A young man may borrow his girlfriend's car "just to go to the supermarket for a pack of cigarettes." Four hours later, he hasn't returned. She calls his home and asks his parents if they've seen him.

"Oh, Jim has been home for a couple of hours now," replies his mother.

"Can I talk to him?"

When she asks Jim about the car, he seems genuinely puzzled. "Well, you know I've got it. I'll bring it over in a while."

The young girl has every right to be upset. In fact, she should probably get out of the relationship. Borderlines don't make good husbands! They cannot set limits. They don't establish reasonable boundaries, and the self is without adequate borders. A normal young man would be able to predict his girlfriend's feelings about having her car "borrowed" indefinitely and would begin to feel guilty about presuming on her kindness. He would return it promptly, or at least ask her if he could borrow it for a longer time than he originally thought he needed it. The borderline lacks both sensitivity and the ability to set limits and can't understand why people get upset.

The development of a healthy self requires the awareness of reasonable limits—to oneself, to one's belongings, and to others. The "borderline" personality does not just show a lack of conscience, but a profound lack of awareness of where his or her self ends and other selves begin. Consequently, the boundaries are crossed freely and without any apparent discomfort.

Borderlines are also *unpredictable*. They spend excessively, gamble, take drugs, shoplift, overeat, and generally become self-destructive. They often use others for their own ends, either through subtle manipulation or through direct action. They lack self-control, become intensely and inappropriately angry, and experience long-standing uncertainties about gender identity, career choices, and relationships. Their mood changes often and quickly and they often feel empty and bored. Like a human tornado, they may leave a trail of chaos wherever they go.

We have a long way to go in understanding this disorder. While very clearly the problem is manifested as a *self in shambles*, we are not sure whether this is due entirely to psychological factors in childhood or whether there are genetic or biological factors (like brain malfunction) that may play a role. For now, the best we can offer is prolonged psychotherapy in which the victim learns to set limits to his or her self in the context of a supportive environment.

MULTIPLE PERSONALITY DISORDER

In 1817, S.L. Mitchell first reported a case of so-called "multiple personality disorder."[4] Any in-depth treatment of this topic would require a whole book in itself, but this disorder of the self warrants brief consideration here.

Mitchell's report concerned an American woman named Mary Reynolds who displayed two alternating personalities, each oblivious of the other, and each supposedly quite different. Mitchell's diagnosis of "duality of person in the same individual" created quite a stir. Public fascination with this phenomenon has been further spurred by such novels as Robert Louis Stevenson's *The Strange Case of Dr. Jekyll and Mr. Hyde*, published in 1877.

The story of "Sybil" is particularly fascinating because of so many different personalities being found in one person. From the age of three in 1926 until 1965, fifteen other personalities were "born" inside Sybil. As described by her psychiatrist, Dr. Wilbur, some were self-assured, sophisticated, and attractive. Others were fearful, angry, and extremely emotional. Two were males called Mike and Sid. One remained a perpetual baby called Ruthie; another a nameless teenager called "the blonde."

Supposedly true, stories like this strike a thinking person as incredible. Yet as a culture, we are very easily convinced by such accounts. We find it fascinating to contemplate so many personalities batting around inside one person's head. Perhaps the following explanation will help to dispel confusion about this disorder.

From the outset, professional circles wondered whether "multiple personality" was simply a clever deception rather than a legitimate form of psychopathology. Certainly, therapists sometimes help to create the illusion of multiple personality by unwittingly reinforcing the different so-called personalities. A clever therapist can easily convince a patient that there are many sides to his or her personality, and can even create the impression of different personalities. A lot depends, of course, on what you mean by the term "personality" in this context.

Whatever is meant by the term "multiple personality," it certainly does *not* mean that a given body has more than one person or self residing therein. I don't believe this is possible— psychologically, physiologically, or biblically. Many people have picked up this idea from the way multiple personality disorders have been described in the popular press. In fact, only one person or self can exist in one brain or body. If there are two brains, then that's another matter. Scripturally, God deals with only one self in each of us. Otherwise, who does God hold accountable? If we have multiple personalities, would we have multiple souls?

What then do we really mean by "multiple personalities"? Clearly a phenomenon of this sort does exist. Too often, however, psychotherapists rush to call anything that hints of ambivalence or that suggests feelings of disconnectedness as "multiple personality." It seems to be a current fad, even a status symbol to have several "multiples" under one's care. Having supervised many clinical psychologists in training, I have frequently had to dissuade some eager young therapist from believing he or she was dealing with multiple personality disorder.

Often the patient in question was clearly schizophrenic and evidencing dramatic changes in behavior from time to time. But schizophrenia is a *biochemical* disease, not a multiple personality disorder. At other times the patient was confused, muddled, and vacillating. Yet when the therapist did not reinforce that person's belief in multiple personalities lurking inside, the patient remained quite intact and in control. Diagnoses can become self-fulfilling prophecies.

While this particular diagnosis is faddish and over-identified in today's psychotherapeutic world, I recognize the existence of such a phenomenon. Multiple personality disorder has been identified by clinicians who have no bias and who could not explain the behavior of the patient any other way. But such persons are not "multiple" in their personhood; they just experience a great deal of internal disconnectedness. A far better label would be "fragmented personality" because this is more accurate than "multiple." Such fragmentation of their inner sense of self can be very serious and debilitating and give rise to the illusion that one has many personalities within.

This confusion surrounding multiple personality can be seen at the end of Flora Schreiber's account of Sybil. When Dr. Wilbur's patient was finally "cured," Schreiber says that "the selves as autonomous, independent entities were gone."[5] What does this mean? Where had they gone? Were they actually separate selves to begin with? Quite frankly, they never really existed as separate personalities. They were merely symptoms of a fragmented or "disconnected" personality, not multiple personalities.

The label "multiple" as applied in such a case is quite misleading. A personality can simply be so lacking in cohesion that it can disintegrate, through a process of unconscious fabrication, into displays of the many facets of its own personality as well as what it sees around itself. In Sybil's case, these so-called "different" personalities had finally been successfully "re-integrated" into her core personality. They were now contributing their uniqueness as various aspects of her rounded personality.

How does "multiple personality disorder" typically manifest itself? Let me now attempt to describe some of the *symptoms* of this fragmented disorder of the self.

- The person believes and behaves *as if* there were more than one personality present. (I say "as if" because there can be no proof that two or more actual personalities exist. The patient merely believes, or acts, as if there is.)
- The transition from one personality to the next is sudden but often associated with stress. Escaping to another personality is typically a way of avoiding stress.
- While in one personality state, the person is unaware of the other states. There may be a genuine "blocking" of memory or awareness of the other states.
- The original personality and all the sub-personalities are aware of lost periods of time.
- The different personalities are always discrepant and seem to be opposites, even of the opposite sex. This helps one to escape from the problems of the primary self.

Malingering can present a difficult diagnostic dilemma. Clearly, most so-called "multiples" derive some secondary benefit from claiming to have other personalities. Some may desire certain benefits that are associated with a certain personality—as, for instance, the benefits of being a child. They can claim to have a separate personality so that they can deny responsibility of certain behaviors. One recent well publicized case of murder is being defended on the grounds that the woman who did the murder claims that her "other" personality was responsible. Others can abandon themselves in permissive sexual behavior and not feel guilty. But setting aside the possibility of malingering, what do we know about the *causes* of this problem with the self?

- Childhood traumas, especially sexual abuse and incest, are very common in those with alleged multiple personalities. It seems that such traumas cause the severest fragmentations.
- Intense conflict with accompanying anxiety seems to always act as a trigger for this disorder. The damage is done in childhood, and then adult stress causes the mechanism to "kick in."

Since I don't believe it is possible to have more than one person in one body, what is really going on here? The self is so frightened, so traumatized, so torn by early conflict that it fails to learn how to act as an integrated whole. Drawing on its imagination and previous exposure to other people, the self "splits" up into different styles of being or into different compartments.

The human mind is a marvelous organ! Under severe stress, it can alter its identity, escape into one of the compartments, and sincerely believe it is someone else. It then behaves like this other person with all the gestures, accent, and temperament to match. The defense is complete. The sufferer can suspend the emotional pain for a period of time.

Multiple personality disorder is fundamentally a form of defense or denial. The escape helps to avoid the painful realities of the basic or "host" personality. The memory of the basic personality is blocked out so that when the self is playing the role of some other personality, it temporarily forgets the problems of the basic self.

That we, as a profession, have called this disorder a "multiple" personality is, in my opinion, unfortunate. As I mentioned, a better label would have been "fragmented personality disorder." We do not see multiple selves, but rather a fragmented self. Aspects of the self have been compartmentalized and consequently lack adequate cohesion or integration. A vivid imagination helps to reinforce belief in the phenomenon.

Not surprisingly, most so-called multiples claim to have only two personalities. This is all one needs to escape the painful reality of a conflicted existence. But anyone who lacks integration or cohesion of the self can be encouraged by others to invent additional "personalities." By escaping into these, the person can keep running away from the real self and avoid conflict and anxiety *ad infinitum.*

I realize I have only touched the surface of this controversial topic. I am not surprised that several Christian counselors have taken to dabbling in multiple personality disorders, even linking them to demon possession. The similarities are remarkable. But I don't think we need to go far afield to explain how the self naturally defends itself against childhood trauma by seeming to form multiple personalities. While not discounting how possession can manifest itself, I believe that most cases of multiple personality can be explained in these natural terms. Certainly, this is an area that desperately needs further research, along with a balanced theological and psychological interpretation and explanation.

MESMERIZED BY OUR OWN BEAUTY

Narcissistic disorders of the self are the final category I want to discuss here. These disorders are the ones we fear most as Christian believers because they have to do with the glorification of the self. In Greek mythology, Narcissus was an extraordinarily handsome young man, so attractive that all the girls who saw him longed to be possessed by him. But the heartbroken maidens failed to stir his heart. Even the fairest of all the nymphs, Echo, did not move him. Having been commanded never to speak to Narcissus, she would cast her longing gaze upon him at a distance. How could she make the beautiful youth pay attention to her when he never looked at any girl?

One day Echo got her chance. Narcissus was calling to his companions. "Is anyone here?" The nymph, hidden behind the trees, called back in rapture, "Here, here." He moved toward the voice but when he saw her, the scorner of love turned away in disgust, as he had done to so many other maidens as well.

One of these scorned maidens then prayed: "May he who loves not others love himself." The great goddess Nemesis—whose name means "righteous anger"—undertook to answer this prayer. One day, as Narcissus bent over a clear pool for a drink, he saw his own reflection for the first time and instantly fell in love with it. "Now I know," he cried, "what others have suffered from me, for I burn with love of my own self.... Only death can set me free." Narcissus pined for himself. One day, to get a better look at his beautiful reflection, he leaned too far over the pool, fell in, and drowned. What a fool!

Legend has it that the nymphs he scorned wanted to bury him, but couldn't find his body. It never rose to the surface but in the spot where it had fallen there bloomed a new and lovely flower which they called by his name, Narcissus. This flower still blooms in many ponds.

Today we use the term to describe those who love themselves too much. Actually, narcissism means several things: self-preoccupation, vanity, exhibitionism, even arrogant ingratitude. The fear of this grossly misunderstood term has caused many believers to become overly afraid of "self-love." We fear being narcissistic so we intentionally play down our feelings for ourselves. We don't want to be hedonistic, individualistic, or self-centered because we recognize such qualities as contrary to the Spirit of Christ. So we have perhaps pushed the pendulum too far in the direction of self-hate and self-rejection. Many Christians now feel that it is more spiritual to speak badly about themselves than to be honestly self-accepting.

I will devote a part of a future chapter to a more detailed discussion of the topic of healthy *self-esteem* and show how it is different from self-love. Here my focus is on disorders of the self. Whatever we mean by self-love, a narcissistic disorder has clearly gone too far.

As human beings, one of our primal needs is to gratify pleasure. Narcissism, then, has its roots in our very flesh and blood. But this legitimate need which has been programmed into us has been contaminated by the Fall. Our senses cry out for pleasure. Our instincts demand satisfaction. Infantile narcissism may start as an addiction to our mother's breast, but it soon encompasses addictions to other pleasures—from toys to trips to Disneyland.

This fundamental narcissistic urge, then, is the backdrop against which the self develops. It is easy to see, then, how vulnerable the self is to distortion. We start out being preoccupied with gratifying every need and desire the infantile mind can imagine. As we mature, this natural narcissism should become more balanced and begin to take into consideration the needs of others as well. Failure to achieve this balance creates a distorted self.

The term which in my mind accurately desribes this distortion is a *grandiose self*. It has three components: a pathological self-centeredness; a pattern of insecure relationships; and an insecure, fragile self-concept. Such a person has an exaggerated sense of self-importance, grandiose fantasies of unlimited success, and a tendency to devalue others in order to maintain his or her own sense of importance. When exposed for what it really is, the narcissistic self will retreat, temporarily, into a profound state of confusion and an exaggerated sense of unworthiness. The self, having become its own idol, is now fallen from its pedestal. It may even have been traumatized by the fall.

The narcissistic self constantly seeks admiration and attention. It is more concerned with appearances and with being seen with the "right" people. The language of such a person takes on a special flavor.

"How well am I doing?"

"What do others think of me?"

"But I'm entitled to special favors."

Always wanting the best for itself and desiring self-aggrandizement above everything, the narcissistic self often exploits others. It feels no hurt and may even be annoyed by the pain of others, especially if that pain gets in the way of satisfying its own pleasure needs. For instance, a young man may become furiously angry at his girlfriend for getting the flu because it means he must cancel the fun date they had planned. He has little, if any, empathy for her discomfort. He is unable to experience how she must feel and is concerned only with his own disappointment. Such a person also operates out of a sense of entitlement and expects special favors from others. When his girlfriend won't do what he wants, even due to serious illness, he is surprised and angered.

These are the hallmarks of a self distorted by narcissism of the worst kind. One can understand the normal response of disappointment when something you have looked forward to has to be canceled. But the narcissist is sick and cannot balance out this disappointment with understanding. This young girl would be wise to heed the warning signs and find herself another beau. Endearing herself to such a distorted self will only spell misery for the relationship. If she ever marries him, she will find herself in a living hell.

These then are some examples of how the self can be distorted. Some of these disorders can be corrected through psychotherapy, or in some cases they can improve simply by being in a loving, honest environment of caring friends. Others do not seem to respond well to any form of treatment. Short of a miracle from God, there is nothing we can do to change them. The self has been corrupted at such a foundational level that divine intervention is required to topple the old self, repair it, and then reconstruct it into an integrated whole.

Psychotherapy definitely has its limits. Fortunately, God is in the miracle business. No self is so damaged and distorted that God's Spirit cannot reach down and touch it at its core. This is what gives me confidence to do the sort of work I do. If not for God, the prognosis for the self would be a very poor one.

CHAPTER 7

Sin Leads to Dysfunction

But as for you, continue in what you have learned and have firmly believed, knowing from whom you learned it and how from childhood you have been acquainted with the sacred writings which are able to instruct you for salvation through faith in Jesus Christ. All scripture is inspired by God and profitable for teaching, for reproof, for correction, for training in righteousness. **2 Tm 3:14-16 RSV**

I FREQUENTLY ENCOUNTER PEOPLE who tell me they believe that the Bible is the only source of truth about ourselves. Of course, they insist that *their* interpretation of a particular Scripture is the only valid one. A tightness in my chest and a hollowness in my stomach warns me of danger—danger, that is, that I will offend these dear people. I don't mean to. After all, they mean well.

These Christians desire the same thing that I want—just to know the truth. But I sometimes suspect that they are more concerned about defending their own preconceived beliefs. I would encourage all of us to set aside preconceived ideas and to really try to discover what the Bible teaches us about ourselves, especially about the self.

Scripture is divine revelation. Those who wrote it were inspired of God. But the Bible is *not* intended to be a textbook of psychology, even though it has a lot to say about the self—just as it is not a textbook of astronomy, even though it describes the heavens, or of medicine, even though it has a lot to say about healing. The Bible is not a psychology text in the sense of describing how perceptions work, how we think, how we sense the world, how we learn, or how memories are processed or repressed. This may sound pretty basic, but I emphasize this point because I see so much anti-psychology sentiment fueled by the idea that Scripture is to be the *only* source of data about our psyches.

Scripture is much more than a textbook of psychology. It is a *textbook for life*. I see a huge difference. The Word of God gives us the grand plan for how God intended human existence. It also gives us the "bottom line" diagnosis for the human condition: alienation from God through sin. The essential healing prescribed for this condition is redemption through Christ, salvation by faith.

Scripture then proceeds to teach us doctrine and to point us toward correcting human behavior. It does all this out of the context of knowing the human condition better than any psychology will ever know it. But the Bible *does not* tell us everything. It doesn't describe how feelings are formed, what causes different types of depression, or how trauma can produce debilitating stress. This is not its purpose.

While Scripture is not a detailed textbook about the mind, it is the ultimate *standard* against which *all* truth must be judged. If some "psychological truth" is discovered which stands at variance with rightly interpreted biblical truth, a Christian would have to question the validity of that particular psychological discovery and repeat the experiment.

To date, *no such variance exists in my mind*. Either the "psychological truth" in question is merely the invention of someone's mind, or the particular interpretation of Scripture is someone's idiosyncratic view. There can be no conflict between the truth of Scripture and any scientific discovery. I hope to show in the next few chapters how essential biblical truths are in complete concord with our understanding of the self. I also want to show how they can help us deal with the human condition in the way God intended.

I certainly don't mean to imply that everything Christian psychologists say is true. They can be wrong too. Many well-meaning psychologists and psychiatrists who profess Christianity have merely uncritically borrowed the theories and techniques of secular psychology. Professing faith in Christ does not immunize us against distortions. Even those with the best of training sometimes rationalize differences with biblical standards and deny, or fail to understand, the work of the Holy Spirit in the heart.

Some even equate psychotherapy with surgery. "A Christian surgeon," they say, "just does surgery. He or she heals with the knife. There is nothing uniquely 'Christian' about this surgery. Any qualified person can do it." Similarly they say, "A Christian counselor or psychotherapist just does therapy. It is neutral activity, just like surgery."

I strongly disagree. Psychotherapy by a Christian professional may not be truly "Christian" at all, but this doesn't mean that no "Christian psychotherapy" exists where God is conjointly at work with what is being done in therapy. The job of a Christian psychotherapist is to *cooperate or collaborate with God* in the healing process. Neither does such a statement preclude Christian psychologists working with non-Christians. It just means they have access to different resources. Non-believers do not have the same resources for building a healthy self as believers do.

Scripture may not specify in detail how we can teach our children math, help teenagers discover their abilities, direct our grief over a loved one suddenly killed by a drunk driver, cope with the unfinished business of anger as an adult child of divorce, or manage stress. Nevertheless, God's written Word does lay down some fundamental principles about the human condition that must provide the foundation for our efforts to help one another to become whole persons.

THE MODERN TRAP

Our understanding of the self is fraught with difficulties. Various myths, world views, and theologies handed down through the ages have all influenced our modern understanding of the self. Unfortunately, Western Christendom has tended to produce a concept of the person that is strongly *individualistic* as well as *dualistic*.[1] Much of our modern interpretation of the self is colored by these two errors:

1. We see the self as primarily individualistic; in and of itself it is all that matters. Self-interest is the goal of all existence. This has fostered a "selfism" model in modern psychology.
2. We see the self as having two components: one is *natural,* tied to the flesh and nature; the other is *spiritual,* the object of divine grace. Even non-Christians believe in this "dual" nature. As a result, we have driven a wedge between the natural self and the spiritual self.

The first of these errors has mainly influenced the development of modern psychology. It has led us to remove the self from its context in community, thus downgrading the importance that others play in completing or fulfilling the self. The self has become "disconnected"—lonely, isolated, frightened, and lost.

The second of these errors has fostered a splitting off of the spiritual from the physical and psychological aspects of our being. It has especially influenced how we interpret Scripture and apply it to our understanding of the self. While we have a Spirit that transcends the body and continues to exist after we have physically died, I think we have gone too far in separating the Spirit from our natural self and elevating the spiritual side of human existence above the other components of the self.

This split is very misleading. In fact, it's a subtle form of an ancient heresy called Gnosticism. The Gnostics were a sect that taught a basic dualism between spirit and matter. They also taught the idea that salvation came by knowledge—especially self-knowledge—and fostered the idea that only what is spiritual is important. What you do in the flesh is unimportant.

We tiptoe around this same error when we espouse ideas such as: "Give priority to your spiritual development." "Don't be too concerned about your mind; just focus on your spiritual well-being." Or, "It doesn't matter if you are emotionally unhealthy, provided your soul is at peace with God." Separating the spiritual from the physical or psychological is a form of dualism. While we are in the body, we are *one* entity composed of body *and* spirit working together in harmony. Our job is to foster this harmony.

I work in a seminary setting where I observe firsthand the ways in which this dichotomy influences the development of emerging pastors. Many seminary students unconsciously come to believe that they can be "spiritual" yet neglect their bodies or personalities. They believe "praying people" need pay no attention to their tempers or how they treat their families. Such ideas border on heresy.

God has created us to be "whole" persons. Who I am in my spirit should not be divorced from my psychological make-up. To put it another way, my temperament and my worship are not in separate rooms of the house called self. In fact, this house contains no separate quarters at all—just one, big family living together in the one-roomed structure we call the self. My moral and religious values are not separate entities, but a unified "whole." My psychological self and my spiritual self are also not separate entities while I am in the flesh. My emotions cannot be divorced from my spiritual desires or practices.

Merely for the sake of understanding, we often speak of ourselves in compartmentalized fashion—as being made up of emotions, body, mind, spirit, and soul. But God always relates to us as a whole person, and holds us accountable for working with him to integrate the various aspects of our self. Scripture never gives us permission to pursue spiritual health while neglecting the well-being of our bodies or our minds. In fact, I find quite the reverse.

For instance, 1 Peter 1:13 tells us to "gird up the loins of your mind, be sober, and hope to the end." This admonition is not a reference to drunkenness. We are to be calm, collected, self-controlled, and even-tempered in mind and action. To "be sober" also means to be of a sound mind, reasonable and sensible, and to act prudently. Such advice stands as the antithesis of "to be beside oneself" (2 Cor 5:13).

In viewing us as *total* beings made up of spirit, mind, and body, Scripture calls us to be *totally healthy*. Our two-fold nature in no way implies that we live out a two-fold or "split" form of life. We are called to live an *integrated* life, where spirit and flesh together seek to glorify God as a unity.

SOUL AND SPIRIT

The relationship between the self and soul, and between the self and spirit is also a very confusing issue for many. I have used the word "soul" several times thus far, but what does it mean? I have labeled as "soul" that part of us that can be aware of God and open to his work of grace. But is the soul different from the self? And what about the spirit? How does it relate to the self?

Such questions open a theological Pandora's box. Since most Christians don't really understand the distinction between the soul and spirit, I want to take a moment to explain how they relate. In Jewish thought, the human being is presented as "clay" (or body) animated by "breath" or "spirit" (*ruah*). The nonphysical side of humanity is called "soul" (*nephesh*)—which means "the man himself" or the "individual," the person as a living being. To this conception is added "heart" (*leb*), which is the emotional/rational side of the person.

Two major theories explain how this all hangs together. First, the *dichotomous theory* holds that each person has a *two-fold nature* (like two floors in a house), material and non-material. According to this theory, we consist of body (the lower floor) and spirit (the upper floor). Scripture seems to support such a view. For instance, the Word of God "divides asunder" soul and spirit from joints and marrow (Heb 4:12). The interchangeable use of "soul" and "spirit" in Scriptures like Genesis 41:8, Psalm 42:6, John 12:27, and John 13:31 also seems to support the simple two-fold nature of persons.

The second theory, which seems to be more commonly held, is the *trichotomous theory*. According to this view, which actually has less biblical support, persons have a *three-fold nature* (like a three-storied house): body, soul, *and* spirit. Scripture does sometimes uses "soul" and "spirit" as contrasting rather than interchangeable terms, for instance: "and the very God of peace sanctify you wholly; and I pray God your whole spirit and soul and body be preserved blameless unto the coming of our Lord Jesus Christ" (1 Thes 5:23).

While some feel that the trichotomous view holds an element of truth it endangers our understanding of the unity of our higher nature by splitting and contrasting "soul" and "spirit."[2]

If taken literally, "spirit and soul and body" could imply a three-fold nature, but my theological colleagues tell me that this is not what is intended here. We are spirit. This is essential. We are not just mortal. But this spirit is embodied in the body or *soma.* So, then, what is soul? By the term "soul" we really mean the spirit plus the body—our total being. This would be consistent with the Old Testament's use of the term "soul." When we speak of "soul," therefore, we really speak of the *incarnate spirit,* a spirit which has a body. One way of understanding this is to see that a body with a spirit is a soul, but without a body it is just "spirit." Angels are pure spirits. Human beings are "souls." When Jesus in Matthew 10:28 says you can "kill the body, but are not able to kill the soul," he is referring to the spirit being separated from the body. Since soul is the spirit and body union, you cannot kill the soul, only the body.

But how does the "self" relate to the soul? One could think of the self as the human side of the soul. It is what we experience of ourselves while we are in the body. The self, then, does encompass the soul. Who I am in my self includes everything that I experience in my body as well as in my spirit.

Now I can almost hear the response. Wait a minute! Didn't Christ die to save my soul? Yes, he did. He died to save my whole self. Isn't my spirit the side of me that lasts forever? Yes, it is. And Christ came not only to save you for eternity but also that your self can become a whole and healthy self. So whatever way you want to divide yourself up, remember that redemption is for every part of you—body and soul, flesh and spirit. He came to save your *total being.* God wants to heal your self, the totality of who you are as a person.

DOMINATED BY DUALISMS

This now brings us to the essence of our problem with the self: many forms of dualism permeate modern Christian thinking. Many see humans as having two natures—the physical and the spiritual; or hold that people have two basic entities—such as mind and matter. Even the idea that we are soul and spirit holds great popular appeal simply because it seems so plausible. This kind of dualism pits mental health against physical disease, or spirituality against emotional health, and so on and so on. Dualistic thinking has become a serious obstacle to a healthy and integrated spirituality.

We naturally like to think in terms of opposites. It helps us to feel as though we understand things. But when we think like this we fail to do justice to the *unity* that must exist in all these apparent dualisms. Our mind cannot be separated from our brain and our body. The spiritual, physical, and psychological aspects of our being are integrated wholes. I am not advocating a "monistic" view. Monism is the doctrine that there is only one ultimate substance or principle. I am merely pleading for a greater understanding of the unity that should exist in our thinking between spiritual and physical or psychological aspects of our being as well as for our need to integrate the different sides of our being.

We might well ask whether or not this need for integration of the spiritual and mental or physical is scriptural? It certainly is. The biblical view of human nature points us away from a radical body/soul dualism and toward a *unity of the self.* The human person should be a coherent, consistent entity. While Scripture presents some polarity between the physical and spiritual (for example in Ezekiel 37 where "bones" and "flesh" come together, but live only when the spirit breathes life into them), Jewish thought strongly supported a unified self. Body, soul, and spirit were viewed as a whole entity, not as a dysfunctional family fighting it out in separate rooms of the house.

The New Testament points even more clearly toward the unity of the human being, even though its language and thought is more Greek than Hebrew. The Greek words are *soma* for body, *psyche* for soul, and *pneuma* for spirit. But in many instances, *psyche* is used to indicate "life" or the person or self, rather than "soul," as for instance in Matthew 6:25: "... Take no thought for your life, what ye shall eat, or what ye shall drink.... Is not the life more than meat, and the body than raiment?"

The New Testament clearly points toward unity of the person while in the flesh, not dualism. Redemption does not operate just on the spirit, as separated or abstracted from the body, but rather on the whole person, the self. Or, to put it another way: while our whole self may have its forms (body, mind, soul and spirit), they do not function separately. Like a well-rehearsed orchestra, the various parts harmonize beautifully.

I believe this emphasis on the unity of our being is extremely important for a Christian understanding of the self. Any attempt to compartmentalize our being, to separate the spiritual from the physical or emotional, will eventually lead us into error. Psychologists have been just as guilty of this error. In order to validate psychology as a separate discipline, mental health professionals unfortunately tend to separate the mind from the body and our feelings from our being. Recently, medicine has tried to reunite the human body with the mind in the concepts of "psychosomatic" illnesses or "holistic medicine." Even more recently, the field of psychoneuroimmunology (how the mind affects the tiniest parts of the body, our immune system) has helped to further integrate the mind and the body and to counteract the pervasive errors of dualism.

Sadly, psychology and theology are still very far apart for the same reason. The first is supposedly concerned with emotional health and the second with matters of the spirit. Modern Christian thought continues to keep them apart. This dualism is perhaps the most difficult of all to reconcile. But in order to present the full gospel to a broken world, it is absolutely essential that we understand the self as being both a spirit and a soul, both a spiritual and a psychological entity. The heart of the biblical view of the person is one of unity. Psychology needs to put the "soul" back into "psyche," and Christian teaching needs to put the "psyche" back into the soul.

THE SELF AS A MORAL BEING

The Old Testament Hebrew language had no single word denoting the concept of self or even personality. Various words have been translated as "person." The most frequent are *nephash*, becoming soul or person, and *ish*, meaning an individual person. The New Testament uses two Greek words, *proposon*, meaning face or person, and *hypostasis* meaning foundation or substance.

What then, constitutes a self or person in biblical thought? In summary, the Bible teaches us that the self is a living being which possesses intellect, will, emotion, self-consciousness, and self-determination. These qualities are not to be found in other forms of life to the same extent that they are found in humans. Some secular psychologists believe you can find at least some of the first four in animals, but they are scratching at thin air! The gap between what animals are capable of and what men and women are capable of is so great as to be of no comparison.

Even more than these qualities, the biblical view of the self is that it possesses a *moral* nature which clearly distinguishes it from all other forms of life. Because we are moral beings, God has placed in our hearts a standard, the work of the law (Rom 2:15). We have a personality. We are essentially spirit clothed with a material body and made in the image of God who is Spirit (Jn 4:25).

Interestingly, this moral aspect of the self causes us the greatest conflict with psychology, and is the most neglected in secular forms of psychotherapy.

THE QUESTION OF SIN

The central concern of nearly every critic of psychology is the matter of sin. Modern psychology, they say, makes no place for sin. And they are right. In the framework of secular psychology, psychopathology has replaced evil. These critics further argue that many Christian psychologists have also played down, or even ignored, the importance of sin in understanding the human condition. They tend to "pathologize" it. In other words, they see it as sickness, not a moral disease. I agree with this observation as well.

Sin is perhaps the single most divisive issue facing us as Christian psychologists. It separates us not only from our secular colleagues but also from one another. In other words, we too easily label as "sickness" or "disease" many disorders that should really be seen as manifestations of sin. But there are many conditions that don't need treatment so much as an old-fashioned call to repentance—perhaps more rightly the domain of the preacher than the therapist.

Calling someone a pedophile, nymphomaniac, alcoholic, or drug addict, such critics say, removes personal responsibility and thus reduces the possibility for improvement. I certainly don't disagree with their sentiment. Much that is passed off as Christian psychology lacks an adequate understanding of sin and how it contributes to pathology. Such a dearth of understanding has major implications for therapy.

No understanding of the self, therefore, would be complete without considering the sinful nature of the unregenerated self—how selfish, evil, degraded, and rebellious to God we are by nature.

My focus here is *not* on the problem of evil. Scott Peck tackled this issue quite admirably in his book *People of the Lie.*[3] Human evil is a reality. You don't have to look further than your local newspaper for evidence of this fact. Perhaps you only have to look at the folks in your neighborhood, or even inside your own heart. Human evil is all around us. But evil is not my concern here; sin is.

We need to ask: *why* does evil pervade the world? Simply, it is because *sin* poisons the human heart. While I agree with Peck that we need a "psychology of evil,"[4] I think we have an even more urgent need for a "psychology of sin." Sin precedes evil, and thus needs to be dealt with first. We cannot understand evil unless we first acknowledge the presence of sin.

Psychology has traditionally steered us *away* from sin's pivotal contribution to human suffering and psychopathology. For psychologists and counselors to neglect the role that sin plays in the development of dysfunctional patterns of behavior would be like physicians ignoring the connection between germs and disease. We can recognize the symptoms of emotional problems. We can even provide a significant degree of "symptomatic relief." But at the root level of cause, we will never "cure" emotional disease by ignoring the "germs" of sin.

The self itself is not *sinful*, but rather is *contaminated* by sin. Again and again, critics of the self make statements which confuse this crucial distinction. "For the Christian, the self is the problem," or "sin and the self" are viewed as one and the same. Such claims imply that everything sinful within the person can be subsumed under the label of "self." That's like saying, "the appendix *is* a disease," rather than "the appendix can *become* diseased."

What do we mean when we say, "love the sinner but hate the sin"? Precisely that the person is contaminated by sin, rather than that his or her essential personhood is sinful. While all humans are "fallen," not everything humans do is sinful. The self is not synonymous with sin. The self is contaminated by sin and capable of sin, but it is not sin itself.

Why is a doctrine of sin essential to a Christian psychology? Simply because it is essential to understanding the human condition and the work of God in our world.

What is sin? Is it really that difficult to define? Sin is the "lack of conformity to the moral law of God, either in act, disposition, or state."[5] Only a self is capable of sin. Animals without a self cannot sin. A part of the body cannot sin. An arm cannot sin, even while reaching out to steal food. A stomach busily digesting the stolen food is not sinning. The person who willfully steals food is the self that sins. It is the self that is *aware* of sin. Because we have this phenomenal ability to stand back and observe our inner selves, God holds us accountable for our actions. A comatose person is not capable of sinning.

But sin is not just a *state of action* against God's laws, it is also a *trait*. Outward thoughts, actions, and affections can certainly be recognized as wrongdoing. But Scripture also teaches that the very core of our being is sinful, the "heart" from which our actions spring (see Mt 5:19 and Heb 3:12). Sin is not only the *consequence* of wrongful acts but also the *cause* of my actions. As Romans 7:8 states, "Sin... wrought in me... all kinds of covetousness." According to Scripture, sin exists in the soul prior to our consciousness of it, even if we have never actually done anything wrong. God holds us accountable only when we reach an adequate awareness of our sin, but we are born sinners nevertheless.

Christian psychology tends to downplay the role of this sinful core by "excusing it." We blame it on a dysfunctional upbringing or some inherited trait. We excuse it by giving power to the human body or some inherent "weakness" that controls us. The scriptural view, however, is that sin is always the supreme choice of the self. Even if unfortunate life circumstances cause a woman to become a prostitute, and even if years of therapy are necessary to help such a woman restore her sense of self-worth, we must still reckon with the central role of sin and choice in her pathology.

We *excuse* sin when we reassure a delinquent teen, "you've just had a bad start in life," or a crack addict, "you're just trying to block out painful memories." While this may be true, it is not the whole story. We *excuse* sin when we fail to call people to account for their actions and confess them to God, or insist that they merely make the right choices. When we fail to emphasize the moral aspects of many actions, we fail to adequately address the person's estrangement from God.

We *excuse* sin when we blame parents for "wounding the inner child" of an adult handicapped by intense neurotic guilt and thus incapable of fun. Of course a child can be damaged by careless parenting, but mislabeled expressions of our sinful nature can easily distract us from the real issues at stake. Many "mental disorders" or "personal distresses" are in reality "disorders of volition." People are choosing to act in those ways. By making different choices or taking personal responsibility for their actions, they can alter the course and curse of their lives. This ability to choose and to take personal responsibility has the ability to bestow dignity on the self, but it can also bring great suffering.

But herein lies the rub. Sin not only *causes* many personal problems which ultimately end up in the psychotherapist's office. Sin also *robs* people of their ability to exercise responsible judgment and *handicaps* them mentally and emotionally so that they cannot exercise moral judgments. Unfortunately, many critics of psychology just don't understand this Catch-22.

Jane serves as a prime example. She was raised in an extremely dysfunctional family. Her father was a brute who lashed out at the slightest provocation. Her uncle had sexually abused her as a young child. While in his twenties, this younger brother of her father had lived with the family and was always willing to babysit Jane and her younger brother whenever her parents wanted to go out. But no sooner had her parents left the house than the uncle would put Jane on his lap, fondle her, and talk about sex. Jane's brother was too young to know what was going on and Jane herself was too afraid to resist her uncle or tell her parents. She cried a lot, but this didn't stop the uncle.

Jane came to dread those nights and still has nightmares even now, more than twenty years later. Clearly she has been severely traumatized, the victim of someone else's wrongdoing. But that's not all. Jane's grandfather was an alcoholic. Whenever he got drunk he would want to fight. The grandfather would often drop by to visit when he was in an intoxicated state, and the evening would invariably end with violent shouting that kept Jane awake for hours.

Every male in Jane's life—from her birth until she left home at seventeen—had been the source of intense pain. Being surrounded by unsatisfactory models, whose behaviors were of the most evil kind, had harmed her profoundly. This wasn't her sin, but the sin of others that was harming her.

But then Jane added her own. To escape her abusive situation and go to college, she left home to live with a slightly older man, someone she didn't really love. But this man also turned out to be demanding and abusive. Having jumped from the frying pan into the fire, Jane became deeply depressed. After trying to take her life by overdosing on sleeping pills, she came to see me. Even though she no longer trusted men, she felt helpless about leaving her abusive lover. She was even very suspicious of me.

So where does Jane's sin figure in? She is living with a man who is not her husband. She's allowing him to continue abusing her. Is her problem entirely her own doing? Why could she not just "choose" to leave her lover and start a new life all on her own?

Critics who know nothing of the incapacitating and debilitating consequences of sin—both personal sin and the sin of others—simply have no answers to these questions. They reply, "Just change your behavior," or, "Pray for strength to leave." They fail to understand how a self can be so abused and traumatized that healing requires *more* than merely changing direction.

Getting Jane to confess her sin, pack up, and get out of a sinful relationship is the easiest part of the intervention. But that is not all she needs. Her sinful behavior is only the tip of the iceberg. A tremendous weight of damage lies beneath the surface, yet to be healed. Is it enough just to pray for Jane? I'm afraid not. Of course we must pray for her; perhaps God will intervene and sovereignly heal the damage done to her self. I myself have witnessed such miraculous "cures." But I have seen many more who have not enjoyed such an instantaneous healing.

Jane may face a long, uphill battle in which she will need all the guidance and support she can get. Healing her broken spirit, disillusioned ideals, distorted perceptions of men, depressed mood, and demoralization requires expert care. Her own moral choices need to be bolstered until she can live responsibly on her own. Christian psychology can help to facilitate this work of God. Sin detours us from the road of healthy living, but then also prevents us from finding our way back. This is the "double jeopardy" of being a fallen self.

What is it about personal sin that causes us damage? I believe we are harmed because sin is essentially a *selfish state.* I don't mean just an exaggerated self-love, but rather our tendency to put our selfish needs *at the center of the self.* Sin breeds self-centeredness. The self is not born self-centered; it learns to be self-centered. The Fall has corrupted the core of the self with sin, and as the rest of the self (our personality, beliefs, values, etc.) develop, they too become corrupted to varying degrees. Sin elevates self-gratification above all the other needs of the self. The self prefers to cater to itself, thus maintaining a state of animosity toward God. Only the re-creation of a new core of the self (known as "regeneration") can save us from this pathway to self-destruction.

THE SELF AND THE "FLESH"

Many equate the self with the "flesh" or with the "lower nature." What does Scripture mean by these terms and how do they relate to the self? Paul discusses the "flesh" in Romans: "For I know that in me (that is, in my flesh,) dwelleth no good thing.... So then with the mind I myself serve the law of God; but with the flesh the law of sin" (Rom 7:18, 25). "So then they that are in the flesh cannot please God.... For if ye live after the flesh, ye shall die" (Rom 8:8, 13).

The Greek word translated as the "flesh" is *sanx*. It occurs one hundred and forty-three times in the New Testament, but with several different meanings:

1. The soft substance of all animals and humans (muscles, blood, tissue etc.), as in Luke 24:39.
2. The body; the whole material part of the living being, as in Hebrews 2:14.
3. Our offspring, as in Romans 4:1.
4. The weak, creative side of the self, as in Romans 6:19.
5. Sometimes the carnal side of the self, but not always, as in Galatians 5:17: "the desires of the flesh are against the Spirit, and the desires of the Spirit are against the flesh; for these are opposed to each other, to prevent you from doing what you would." Verse 19 continues to detail the works of the flesh.

This last reference to the "flesh" is actually the most important for us in our discussion of the self. Here our natural inclinations are seen as pitted against our spiritual side. Yet notice how carefully Paul distinguishes between "me" and "flesh" in Romans 7:18. A *part* of the self is the "flesh," but *not the whole*. When the self surrenders to the sinful side of itself, we say that it is "in the flesh." What is quite clear in these references is that the "flesh" does not signify our body, but our whole being when destitute of the Spirit of God.[6]

Scripture sees the seat of sin as being the soul itself rather than our physical form or body. The *body* is just a machine which does what it is programmed to do; the *self* controls the program.

Just as with computers, it is a matter of "garbage in, garbage out." If the self can surrender to sin, it can also surrender to the Spirit (see Rom 8:4-13; Gal 5:24-25).

So don't blame your body when you sin. It's neutral in this state of warfare between your flesh and God's Spirit. Flesh means more than the body. It is your self left to itself, standing by itself, without God—precisely why the flesh, incapable of pleasing God, is doomed to die (see Rom 8:8, 13).

But what about the "lower nature" or "carnal mind" as mentioned in Romans 8:7 or Ephesians 4:17? The mind of the self can be given over to carnality (just another word for sin), pleasure, and sensuality. While not synonymous with it, the flesh is prone to carnality, drawn to sin just as a fly is attracted to rotting food. It is the flesh that gives in to sin; the flesh is not sin in and of itself, just as the self is not sin.

As Dallas Willard writes, "It is the carnal mind—not the flesh—that is at enmity with God...."[7] He argues strongly that the flesh is not the "fallen" aspect of the self. The flesh is capable of lust; it is not lust itself (1 Jn 2:16). Scripture tells us that God would pour out his Spirit on all "flesh" (Acts 2:17), that indeed the flesh cries out for God (Ps 84:2). Even Christ had "flesh" (Acts 2:31).

Willard goes on to further define the relationship of the self and the flesh. As we seek to discipline ourselves and be transformed by God, the flesh is one of the two components of the self with which we have to contend. Our practical, everyday walk with God depends on disciplining the self and its "flesh." The other component of the self is the spirit. But layer upon layer of our life experience—including all its distortions and damage—have shaped the "flesh" component such that it does not immediately harmonize with the regenerated spirit of the believer. So the flesh continues to exert its distorted tendencies, even after conversion.

This is why Scripture warns us that the flesh and Spirit are opposed to each other (see Gal 5:17)—meaning the Holy Spirit, not our spirit. But because God assumes control of the human spirit after regeneration, it is also in conflict with the old ways of the flesh. Herein lies much of the struggle that Christians face.

How crucial that we uncover the damage that the "flesh" part of the self has suffered at the hands of an abusive world. It is also crucial to foster prayer, simplicity, sacrificial living, meditation on God's Word, and Christian service. These personal disciplines provide food and nurturing for the spiritual side of the self.

SPIRITUALLY BANKRUPT

Secular psychology is spiritually bankrupt. It does not fathom, nor can it ever understand, this second dimension of the self. The nature of this warfare between the spirit and the flesh within the self is foreign apart from revelation. But as we thoughtfully apply this concept of the "flesh" to our understanding of how the self can be damaged in other ways, we will become better helpers to those who are troubled.

At bottom, the real issue is whether or not secular psychology is the *only* solution to the dilemma of human existence. Clearly it is not. Psychology may be able to help us *diagnose* the pain and problems of the human condition, but it can never explain the root problem nor provide anything close to complete healing.

The most powerful support for this understanding of secular psychology's limits does not come from a Christian. The social anthropologist Ernest Becker (1924-1974) may not have been a believer, but he was about as honest a human as I have ever encountered. He died shortly after completing his Pulitzer prize-winning book *Denial of Death.*"[8] After many years of careful research, Becker concluded with several classic statements about the limits of psychotherapy. Psychologists, both secular and Christian, need to heed his comments.

At best, Becker says, psychotherapy can only confront us with the terror of real existence. He suggests that all therapists should put up a small sign over their office door that reads, "Danger: Real probability of the awakening of terror and dread, from which there is no turning back."[9] He believes such an honest statement would relieve us of some of the guilt we feel when we experience the occasional suicide of a patient.

Becker further suggests that at worst psychotherapy encourages the myth of "paradise through self-knowledge" or a "constant joy." Not that psychotherapy cannot bequeath tremendous gifts to tortured people or add dignity to anyone who can utilize self-knowledge. Therapy can certainly help people deal with neurotic guilt (as distinct from true guilt), become less fragmented, and find release from self-defeating habits and wrongful choices. Becker concludes: "Yes, psychotherapy can do all these things, but there are many things it cannot do and they have not been aired widely enough.... Not everyone was as honest as Freud was when he said that he cured the miseries of the neurotic only to open him up to the normal misery of life."[10]

What keen insight! What refreshing honesty! The best we humans can do is to whitewash the barn we call the self. We can make it look neat and feel clean and smell clean, but underneath, the wooden foundation will still be rotten and decaying. Sooner or later the whitewash will fall off and the ugliness of the core will show through again—unless that core has been redeemed and renewed by God.

The redeemed believer stands in a different place at precisely this juncture. And this is where Christian psychotherapy ought to differ as well. God works to renew the core of the self. His surgery is right at the "heart" of the self. Scripture talks of a "new" heart and a "renewed" spirit (Ps 51:10). As we shall see, Christian counselors or psychologists certainly have a role to play. We can help believers to "work out" their salvation so that it permeates every aspect of their beings and their selves (1 Thes 4:3).

Before I discuss this healing of the self, we should examine one very important biblical perspective. What does it mean for my self to be created "in the image of God?"

8 | Made in the Image of God

And God said, "Let us make man in our image, after our likeness." ... So God created man in his own image, in the image of God created he him, male and female created he them. **Gn 1:26-27 KJV**

THE FIRST VERSES OF the Scriptures paint this beautiful picture of men and women created in God's image. As the summit of all God's work, having been made in the "image" of the ruler of all creation, humanity stands in a unique relationship to God. The *imago Dei* holds special significance for our understanding of the human self.

But what does it mean to be created in God's image? What are the implications of this likeness? Can we continue to be the same, whether we know this likeness exists or not? Most important of all, what is it about us that represents this likeness? It can't be our bodies. They are but atoms (or the biblical equivalent of atoms, namely "dust"). They age, decay, and finally die. It can't be our personalities. They are too different from one another, and unfortunately, too different from God to represent this likeness.

Could this unique likeness be reflected in the fact that we have a self? An intriguing question. Let's examine this question from a biblical and theological perspective. The meaning of the "image of God" is expanded in the New Testament to include the idea of a "mold" or "pattern" after which something is to be formed. For instance, "For whom he did foreknow, he also did predestinate to be conformed to the image of his Son, that he might be the firstborn among many brethren" (Rom 8:29). God then empowers us to become like this image ourselves, as he forms us through Christ.

We can discover yet more about the doctrine of the *imago Dei*. Far from an accidental quality, the image of God is *essential* to the make-up of the self. It is what gives it autonomy, a separate existence. Martin Luther believed that being made in the image of God meant having the "freedom to choose obedience" to the will of God. But humanity has misused this freedom. Thus sin and the Fall entered into the picture.

Did the Fall remove the image of God from us? Martin Luther believed it did, but others do not. As I will discuss in the next chapter, I think sin has concealed or "covered" this image. No matter how sullied because of sin, we have not lost this image. Our regeneration or new birth restores that image to its rightful place at the core of the self. It may be a matter of semantics, but this picture gives me a clearer understanding of the *imago Dei* than the idea that fallen selves are devoid of this image.

Another meaning of God's image is that it distinguishes human beings from animals. Common sense dictates that animals are different from us. They don't have a "self" in the sense that I have been describing it: one that can be held accountable for its actions because it can know itself and foresee consequences. If animals possess any such qualities, they are too rudimentary to count.

Some psychologists have demonstrated that chimpanzees can devise a rudimentary system of language, or figure out how to pile boxes on one another in order to reach a banana suspended from the ceiling on a piece of string. I don't believe such facts disprove the uniqueness of our creation in the image of

God. All this tells me is how far I am above the beloved and cute chimpanzee. I can have faith in a living and loving God. All the chimp desires is to eat a banana. Big deal!

Following the teaching of Aristotle, some theologians identify our capacity to think and reason as the essential reflection of God's image. I see this as just a variation of what I have already said about the autonomous self.

Liberal theologians stress that being made in the image of God means that human life is sacred, that we can do what needs to be done on earth and to the earth. They think of it as a "relational" concept. In other words, because I have the capacity to love you, I must have the "image of God" in me. While this is all very true, I find such reasoning lacking in substance. Surely this *imago Dei* represents more than just whether or not I like you enough!

I suppose I would agree most with Paul Tillich on this matter, though not on all matters. Tillich (1886-1965) opposes the understanding of the image of God only in relational terms. Believing that the image of God involves *more* than our ability to love and forgive, he is convinced that it is rooted in our "being," at the very core of the self. Tillich doesn't just mean the possibility of being, but the *fact* of being. Our very make-up—what I am calling the self—*includes* the image of God. *Imago Dei* is precisely what makes us capable of becoming what God has created us to be.

Perhaps we can think of this image in the person who has not yet come to faith in Christ as lying dormant, waiting for heavenly sunshine and rain to bring it to life. It is like the dried seed buried in the desert. When the rain of redemption comes to that seed, it will discover, and others will behold, the germination of a glorious "re-image" of the Creator.

TOUCHING GOD

Whatever we believe about the *imago Dei*, it must at least mean that just as God is Spirit, so also are we spirit. It is this spiritual dimension which defines us uniquely as being created in the image of God. Something in us resonates with God and responds to his promptings. Even while we are still in the flesh, some part of us is capable of transcending our creatureliness and touching God. "God is a Spirit: and they that worship him must worship him in spirit and in truth" (Jn 4:24).

Being made in the image of God also means we are free to act according to our own choices, either responsibly or irresponsibly. A part of us can bring peace to the warring members of our bodies and minds, and restore us to a harmonious relationship with our Creator. We have this unique capacity to take control of our inner selves.

Our spirit, then, is an important part of our self. This nonbodily power of the self is that part of us that can "connect" with God and draw strength from God. Without this spiritual dimension, we would be mere animals wandering aimlessly through life with absolutely no purpose to our existence. Without spirit, we would be left to our own devices—and consequently stunted, mutilated, deformed, weakened, and in various stages of disintegration. What point is life without spirit?

But the self must be grounded in its Creator. It must be "hooked" or connected to the Spirit of God in order to be complete.

The doctrine of the *imago Dei* includes this truth that no self is complete on its own. The spirit of the unconnected self is lost and wanders aimlessly. According to Scripture, it is in fact doomed (Jude 15). We can only achieve full "selfhood" by reconnecting the self with the divine image after which it was created.

Once we have been "reconnected" to God, we can expect the image of God to influence us in three specific ways:

1. The image of God ought to "empower" the self.
2. The image of God ought to "mold" the self.
3. The image of God ought to be a "motive" for the self's existence.

EMPOWERED BY THE IMAGE OF GOD

The spiritual aspects of the self need to be restored in their rightful connection to the Spirit of God. As an important resource for the rest of the self, the spirit holds the "connection" to God's Spirit, just as the plug holds the connection for an electrical cord. It is the seat of faith, hope, and love. I don't love with my hands, glands, or brain. I love with my spirit.

Anything I do that transcends my humanness is done in my spirit. My brain is too mechanical, too earthbound. It can't soar with joy or love with depth. My mind is just electrical impulses batting around as in a large computer, causing minute chemical explosions, connections, and reconnections. Certainly my spirit needs these impulses to give expression to what it experiences, but my spirit transcends all this. It sees the "whole" picture and knows what is going on.

Sometimes the spirit is embroiled in a bloody battle with the mind (Gal 5:17). But when it is fully grounded and "correctly integrated into and dominated by God's spiritual kingdom," the spirit has the power to win the battle within and without.[1]

The spirit, then, is another reality in my self that enables me to tap into the "power" that God provides through his Spirit. Just like the electric cart that I see gadding about on a nearby golf course, the spirit must "recharge" periodically. Without this recharging resource, the self can never be whole. The self can never cope with the ultimate issues of life because it was never designed to "go it alone."

Our task, then, is to discover how we can harmonize our total being with the God who has created us in his image. Our task as counselors is to help others reconnect as well. No psychology of the self is complete without understanding the vital role God's Spirit plays in empowering our spirit and in building a healthy self. To rightfully focus on the spirit means that we also nurture that aspect of the self as a part of the healing process. Contemporary psychology especially fails us here. All it can do is nurture the non-spirit side of the self.

But the winds of change are blowing—although mostly in the wrong direction. One of my students randomly surveyed one thousand psychotherapists belonging to the American Psychological Association to find out how their religious or non-religious beliefs influenced how they dealt with suicides. We were amazed to discover forty percent said they were "very" religious," and seventy-three percent said they were "very" or "somewhat" religious.

Many referred to themselves as believing Christians, but quite a number labeled themselves as "religious" because they were dabbling in "spiritual" matters.[2] Many were also involved in channeling or New Age practices, but what especially interested me was the apparent shift away from hard-nosed, reductionistic, I-only-believe-what-I-can-see type of thinking. Psychologists are genuinely beginning to acknowledge the "spiritual" dimensions of human existence. If only they can discover the *real* source for this hunger—namely that it is God calling us back to himself.

Nurturing the spirit is not just the task of overworked pastors. Christian counselors can make an important contribution to this endeavor as well. They can encourage believers in their spiritual disciplines and show how they can be better integrated into the total life of the self. Almost any emotional problem can benefit from spiritually nurturing the self. Many psychological ailments such as depression, anxiety, guilt, anger, and resentment have spiritual dimensions as well.[3]

Dallas Willard cites particular activities that are helpful for nurturing the self.[4] One category includes *disciplines of abstinence*, such as solitude, silence, fasting, chastity, and sacrifice. Abstaining from normal needs such as food, sex, convenience, and comfort is not intended to be a form of self-punishment, but rather a way of focusing on the essential needs of the self.

Having authored a book on the topic of "hidden addictions,"[5] I am very aware of how easily food and certain behaviors can become anesthetics for the self. They numb our real feelings and force a false escape from reality. Disciplines that help to break these addictions of the self—especially the addiction to stimulation and excitement—can powerfully reconnect us with our spirit, and through our spirit to God's Spirit. If we can get over our "withdrawal" symptoms before we end our period of abstinence, such spiritual disciplines can help us to break these addictions.

Willard also lists *disciplines of engagement*, including study, meditation on Scripture, worship, prayer, confession, and submission. Such disciplines serve to "till the soil" of the spirit so that new seeds can be planted and a rich harvest reaped. We reap what we sow, physically as well as psychologically. Try eating too much food and see what you reap in a stomachache. Or try being angry all day and see how this anger pervades your personality and invites outbursts from others.

This same principle especially holds true spiritually. Not only does sin have its own wages, but if you starve the spirit, it stagnates and remains stunted. If you feed and foster the spirit, it matures and strengthens the rest of the self.

Tricia struck me from the start as being someone who had conscientiously nurtured her spirit ever since becoming a Christian in her teens. Now at age thirty-five she faced a frightening prospect: her husband of four years had taken up with another woman and was threatening to walk out. Tricia was confused, scared, angry, and depressed. But I recognized an inner strength that would see her through. Unlike so many believers I have counseled, she was intimately in touch with her spirit. Having nurtured and fed it over many years, her spirit helped Tricia to be strong. She sensed God's reality, knew how to pray, paid attention to the inner promptings of God's Spirit, and understood with a high degree of sophistication how God works to mold and refine his children.

So why was Tricia seeking help? I can just hear many of you asking this question! Can't this believer just rely on her spiritual maturity to see her through, or just pray and let God take care of her husband? She could. She did pray. But Tricia was also mature enough to understand the value of sharing her problems with another.

One aspect of maturity that is so often overlooked is not trying to do everything by ourselves. Spiritually mature people understand the importance of not always trusting their own judgments or isolating themselves when they are in emotional pain. Maturity involves a willingness to depend on others and to value the importance of "burden bearing" (see Gal 6:2; Col 3:12). Pastors are vulnerable to emotional breakdowns partly because they are forced to depend only on themselves. They find it difficult to "let down" and be on the receiving end of ministry. But that's true for doctors and nurses as well. We all feel that we should be self-sufficient. Spiritual maturity opens us up to "other-dependence" and helps hold us accountable. It fosters encouragement and helps us to keep a proper perspective. So Tricia wisely sought help.

I did not have to give Tricia a lot of advice on how to manage her life through this period of turmoil. She didn't need advice so much, just someone to support her. I provided her a listening ear, which is perhaps eighty percent of what good counseling is about anyway. Tricia was able to do the rest and maintain her composure. Rather than overreact out of anger, she adopted a Christian spirit of love toward her wayward husband. And he responded by dropping the affair and finally reconciling with his wife. It was not that she was permissive, just that she didn't give full vent to rejection and anger. Her husband was able to face up to himself, and to change.

The value of listening cannot be underestimated. Those who attack counseling often unwittingly foster a tight-lipped attitude in other believers. Often those same critics need help the most. They tend to keep all their hurts to themselves—and consequently hurt all the more. Listening helps troubled people to "externalize" their thinking and feelings. Once pain is on the "outside," it becomes a lot easier to understand and to apply spiritual principles of healing.

MOLDED BY THE IMAGE OF GOD

Augustine (354-430) emphasized the distinction between being created in God's *image, tselem* in Hebrew, and in his *likeness,* or *demuth.* Genesis 1:26 actually implies both.[6] Debate later raged about whether the image was lost in the Fall. Luther argued that it was destroyed for all practical purposes. John Calvin felt that "reason," which comes from the image of God, is defaced but not totally destroyed. Even sinners could have notions of justice, integrity, and honesty. But Calvin sounded an important warning: the higher reason aspires, the more it errs.[7] In other words, the more the self tries to be a true self, *by itself,* the further it gets away from God. How true!

More recently, theological consensus about the *imago Dei* has not fostered a dualistic view which distinguishes the image of God from the likeness of God. Both are used to reinforce a single idea: we are created in his *image, and* we take on his *likeness* as the human self is regenerated and renewed by his spirit. Without getting caught up in a theological controversy, I think it is safe for us to assume that the human spirit—once reconnected and restored to God—can begin to take on a "likeness" to God. His image or likeness is to be emulated. It is a "mold" to which we must conform. Since Christ also manifests this image, he is held up as a model for us to emulate.

I don't see how we can believe that we were merely created *in* the image of God, and then deny, as some theologians do, the importance of becoming the image and likeness of God. Surely the one follows from the other!

The New Testament is full of references to this "molding" or shaping aspect of God's image:

> Learn of me. Mt 11:29
>
> For I have given you an example, that you should do as I have done to you. Jn 13:15
>
> Now the God of patience and consolation grant you to be like-minded one toward another. Rom 15:5
>
> Let this mind be in you, which was also in Christ Jesus. Phil 2:5
>
> Forgiving one another... even as Christ forgave you, so also do ye. Col 3:13

God's image becomes a call to model ourselves after. His image is not only a picture we adore, it is a blueprint for growth. This aspect of the image of God as a "mold" or "pattern" for my life is beautifully illustrated in the passages about refining and about the potter's wheel. "For thou, O God, hast proved us: Thou hast tried us as silver is tried" (Ps 66:10). "Behold as the clay is in the potter's hand, so are ye in mine hand..." (Jer 18:6).

One of my own hobbies is making jewelry. I absolutely love to craft beautiful adornments out of gold and silver. Perhaps I should have been a goldsmith! My family has to hide rings, pendants, or any other precious metals from me, because I love to recycle the stuff into something new. I can't stand to see a ring remain the same, year after year; I yearn to make it more lovely.

The jewelry-maker uses a wax master that is shaped according to a specific design. This wax master is then made into a mold by pouring a special casting powder over it. When the master is heated at high temperature, the powder turns hard but the wax melts, vaporizes, and vanishes, leaving the shape of the wax inside the mold ready to receive the molten precious metal. It's called the "lost-wax" process. You sacrifice the wax in order to make something more precious.

But how the artist handles the metal makes or breaks the beauty of the final object. Getting a good likeness in the mold is easy. Cleaning the gold is very difficult. You can never get dirty gold to polish properly. While it may look shiny and smooth, the precious metal can be contaminated by very tiny flecks of foreign substances that scar the jewelry and keep it from being as beautiful as it could be.

How do you clean the gold? Just as God purifies our spirit: lots of heat and additives that congeal the dross and force it to the surface where it can be removed. Then the gold is ready to be poured into the mold and finally polished. The cleaner the gold, the more brilliant the shine.

This is a beautiful analogy for the molding of the self. Having been contaminated at many points, the modern self needs cleaning. The "heat" of life—its failure, disappointment, or suffering—often cleans more effectively than success and easy living. Self-actualization can be an erroneous quest when it tries to substitute "actualization" for refinement, when it seeks acquisition, accomplishment, ascendance, and prosperity instead of a purer spirit. Even such positive qualities can become the "dirt" that contaminates the self-gold. Rather than adding brilliance, they dull and tarnish. Proper self-actualization can help to make the self truly beautiful, as we will see. But it is *an actualization of what God seeks for the self, not what the self seeks for itself.*

I constantly have to remind myself: *God is not in the success business; he's in the refining business.* Success is merely a bonus, not the primary goal that God has for the self. We build much more character through trials and suffering than we do by achievement and success. We will look at this more closely when we examine the self's need for esteem. Those who have scrambled to the top of the heap do not feel any better about themselves than the drop-outs of society. This is the great paradox of self-esteem!

This "refining" motif runs throughout Scripture. Peter chides, "Beloved, think it not strange concerning the fiery trial which is to try you, as though some strange thing happened unto you" (1 Pt 4:12). After all, "the trial of your faith, being much more precious than of gold that perisheth, though it be tried with fire, might be found unto praise and honour and glory at the appearing of Jesus Christ" (1 Pt 1:7).

There is no escape from the refiner's fire. If you have surrendered your life to God, you have also consented to be changed into his likeness. Being conformed to God's likeness means change and change proceeds from the "fires" of life. The self that surrenders to this refining process is the self that is free to rise above everything and conquer life.

"The self is the one and only thing we own," writes E. Stanley Jones.[8] It is the only thing we brought into the world and it is the one and only thing we will take out of the world. Day by day, hour by hour, minute by minute, we live intimately with ourselves. The kind of self we are determines the kind of life we live. God has a plan for us to become a fully functioning or "actualized" self, but his plan will not be fulfilled by traveling down the road of success, self-centeredness, or self-investment. I'll have more to say about this in the final chapter.

MOTIVATED BY THE IMAGE OF GOD

Whatever happened to the *imago Dei* at the Fall, regeneration enables it to become a vital component in shaping and forming the spiritual self. The renewing grace of God is essential to our full restoration to God. There is no other way. The hub around which the Christian self revolves, the image of God, becomes our motive for living and loving, doing and dying.

We could probably have many disagreements over what it means to be "created" in God's image. With so few biblical texts to clarify what it really means, this doctrine has come to mean different things to different people. But surely we can agree that it means we are *personal* beings, as God is personal. We are mirrors of what God is and we are called to become like him. At our core we are spiritual beings. We "image" God in living out the gospel message in our lives, through suffering as well as through triumph.

The classic Reformed teaching is that humans image God through *rationality* and *morality*. Being created in God's image means this and probably much more, all of which holds tremendous significance for our understanding of the human self. The *imago Dei* provides for a rich, multi-faceted existence, one that comprises actions, feelings, emotions, capacities, virtues, and relations. No aspect of the self is left untouched. Any conception of the "fulfilled" self that does not include the touch of God's image and the call to become like that image is bankrupt. It has nothing to offer. Secular psychology is but an empty shell waiting to be filled by this image.

The image of God, therefore, is the sole motive for "becoming a self." If we are already a self, what does "becoming a self" mean? Because of its brokenness, the self is incomplete, empty. It has been damaged by sin and distorted by evil. When God's Spirit is released in the empty or damaged self, healing and repair inevitably ensue. The scriptural word for this is "sanctification," a process of being purified and made free from the domination of sin. God's Spirit now turns his image into a reality.

Understanding the *imago Dei* sheds light on the limitations of so many popular psychological phrases which can be quite misleading and even erroneous. Let us examine a few of them.

Become yourself. Becoming yourself is not the same as "becoming a self." Here the phrase implies that if you just let yourself be yourself, you automatically "become" yourself. Assuming that the self is good enough for itself, this approach is an encouragement to be more authentic. Just let it "become." Dr. Carl Rogers fostered this idea. Just help people become more self-directing and self-confident, and they will "become themselves" more.

Such a direction is not determined by God's image. Rather, it moves away from it. By itself, the self is bankrupt. If it becomes more like itself, it will only become more bankrupt. If it fulfills more of itself, it only creates more of a problematic self.

Know yourself. Socrates advised "Know thyself." He meant that we should make our own decisions about the conduct of our lives, and not simply go by the rules of others, however they are derived. Today his dictum has taken on an entirely different meaning, something like, "all the truth you need to know lies within yourself, so just know yourself better." This approach fails to recognize that God's image is shut off from the unregenerated self. The unbeliever doesn't have direct access to a "pure" model for the self from within. Sin has blanketed this image with distortion and deception.

I am not saying that we should not "understand" ourselves. Every sinner must know he or she is a sinner in order to come to repentance. Also, I don't mean to say that we should not "know" our feelings, thoughts, and desires. The more we know our true selves, the better. But just *knowing* these things is not enough to bring wholeness. God's image must be freed to become our ideal and to renew us.

Actualize yourself. Humans exhibit an innate drive to grow, develop, mature, and thus actualize themselves by becoming fully functioning. We cannot take issue with the general idea of self-actualization—provided the self is properly understood as the regenerated self, and that the power and purpose of actualization is God-prescribed. Actualizing a sin-filled self only produces a more sinful self, rather than the idealized, spontaneous, flexible, confident, creative, and open self. God certainly desires such ideals for us, but the self must first be recreated and the damaged core repaired before it can be fully "actualized."

To put it another way, there is a sense in which self-actualization should apply only to our spiritual walk. Who doesn't want to be the complete Christian—loving, obedient, and sensitive to the Spirit? But the self first needs to be liberated by Christ and empowered by the Holy Spirit. Then, and only then, can it be spiritually actualized and freed to manifest the talents and gifts that honor God. I will devote the final chapter to a more complete discussion of this important topic.

Affirm yourself. Advocates of a certain model of self-esteem believe that if you say only positive things to yourself, you will feel better about yourself. I believe self-affirmation should be more of a result than a cause. If your self is in tune with God and your spirit in touch with God's Spirit, affirming your self can be a meaningful and necessary spiritual discipline. God wants us to tell the truth about the self.

The Apostle Paul was always ready to call church leaders to account for their weaknesses, but he quickly affirmed their commitment. To Philemon he writes, "I thank my God—hearing of your love and faith..." (Phlm 4-5). To affirm is simply to declare that something is true. The Christian especially needs to affirm the work of the Spirit in the self and the actions of faith by the acting self. But affirming a self that is without God is of no spiritual value.

However, humans need affirmation very deeply. While we should not affirm the self in its lostness, we should still affirm the self as a self. For instance, every child needs to be affirmed by his or her mother and father. Every wife needs to be affirmed by her husband. We can always affirm persons for being persons, whether they are Christians or not. This is just an expression of our love. Ours is not to judge or reject, only to love. We don't love selectively; we love all who God puts in our way.

Sadly, many Christian parents are so afraid of affirmation that they deliberately play down their affirmation of a teenager who is acting out his or her rebellion. They fear that unless they are constantly critical, their children will interpret their lack of criticism as an affirmation of their bad behavior. Not affirming our children, just for who they are, is a major cause of rebelliousness and delinquency, especially in our Christian subculture.

Self-determination. This popular psychological phrase really has two meanings: first, the self is determined *to be a self;* and second, the self is *determined* that by any means, it will become a self. Both ideals are admirable. The important question is: what sort of self are you determined to be? Is the self you want to become one in which the spirit has been set free, or is it a self that is determined to become more self-centered? The very phrase "self-determination" implies that we want to act according to our own mind or will, without outside influence. This literally excludes God's Spirit from the process.

These misleading statements about the self arise primarily from humanistic psychology. My contention is that they fail to take into account the true nature of the self, devoid of its fullness when separated from the image of God. None of the humanistic notions about the self apply without qualification to the unregenerated self. Carl Rogers, Abraham Maslow, and others who have developed a humanistic psychology of the self often see it as gloriously positive and inherently magnificent. Scripture and the doctrine of sin paint a very different picture.

Even so, their portrait of the self may be more accurate than we realize in terms of the ideal that God himself holds out for the regenerated self. I believe humanistic psychology is really describing the ideal self that God wants us to become after we are saved. The mistake of humanistic psychologists is that they believe the self can reach this pinnacle apart from the grace of God. This puts humanistic psychology in a whole new light. Everything these popular statements hold out for the ideal self is exactly what God wants it to become. The difference is that he's the only one who can provide the means for this becoming.

Since regeneration is so crucial to understanding the process by which the self is transformed, the next chapter will offer a more detailed treatment of this topic. For me, it is the crux of the matter of the self. Everything revolves around what God does through forgiveness and salvation. The essence of the gospel surrounds God's renewing work in the heart of the self and the full restoration of his image in every believer. We call this regeneration.

PART THREE

Healing the Self

9 | Grace Heals the Evil within

Jesus answered him, "Truly, truly I say to you, unless one is born anew, he cannot see the kingdom of God." **Jn 3:3 RSV**

He saved us, not because of deeds done by us in righteousness but in virtue of his own mercy, by the washing of regeneration and renewal in the Holy Spirit.... **Ti 3:5 RSV**

WITH A GROWING NUMBER OF CHRISTIAN believers seeking help from professional counselors, I am surprised there hasn't been more attention given to two extremely important questions: *What does God do for us, and what must we do for ourselves?* For me, the whole debate over the role of psychology boils down to this: *How does the work of God through his Holy Spirit relate to the work we do in counseling?*

All across our country, thousands of Christian psychotherapists lay claim to helping people deal with emotional problems, dysfunctional families, addictions, and neuroses of all kinds. But few have a very clear idea of how their professional efforts interact with the work of God through the Holy Spirit. What is the relationship between God's healing and the healing that can come from Christian psychotherapy?

Some merely see themselves as Christians "doing" psychotherapy. Their approach is often very traditional, with perhaps a little modification to make it Christian. They may pray at the end, but what they do is very much the same as what a secular therapist does. Some believe strongly that psychotherapy is a "natural" discipline, like medicine or dentistry, and should be kept separate from spiritual matters. "Go to a spiritual advisor" if you want spiritual help.

To help their clients grasp the "true meaning of life," some might avoid "mechanistic" therapies like behaviorism or cognitive behaviorism and follow existentialism or other such therapies to try to get at the "deeper" issues of existence. While acknowledging that the self is also spirit, prone to anxiety and guilt, they then try to solve these problems purely from a psychological point of view.

Still others render their therapy "Christian" by quoting Scripture and using "Bible talk," hoping to baptize what they do with the Holy Ghost. Occasionally they may tackle some troublesome spiritual problem like helping an obsessional personality understand what the Bible really says about the "unforgivable sin." Or they may quote various theologians to support their perspective. But mostly, Christian psychotherapy has remained very much apart from the spiritual disciplines. We have suffered from the lack of a clear model of how our professional efforts relate to the work of God.

Up to this point, I have attempted to show how the modern self is an empty self, easily troubled and fragmented. It is a highly conscious self, extremely aware of how it looks, feels, sounds, thinks, and expresses itself. But it is also naturally sinful, devoid of any real substance apart from God. The more the self tries to "become itself," the further away it moves from the true source of healing and nurturance.

Many understand the reality of a "false" self that is not centered on Christ. It cannot be anything but "false" in the sense that it is grounded on nothing substantial. A "real" or true self is built on the solid foundation of Christ. But what is the role of the Christian counselor or psychotherapist in helping someone to be a true self in Christ? What does God do, and what do we do? Do we do anything? Or is it all God's work? Are we not a means of grace as therapists, just as preachers are a means of grace?

I have lost the reference, but I recall reading an article in a Christian magazine in which a pastor claimed that counseling was a waste of time: "There is a place for the pastoral call in times of sickness and death, crisis and uncertainty. But there is room to debate where there is a place for hours upon hours of the traditional pastoral counseling which yields such little fruit."

How sad! What a pessimist! I'd hate to be a member of his congregation and fall into serious trouble. Perhaps he simply does not understand how counseling fits into the work of grace that God does in the heart. I know many pastors who are "burned out" on counseling. They hate it because it is so slow to bring change. But this doesn't mean it is of no value to the one who is troubled.

For many years I have taught a course on the "Emotional Hazards of the Ministry." One of the topics I address is how the work of God relates to the work we try to do in the hearts of people. This model, which has served to clarify my own role as a Christian psychotherapist, holds crucial significance for our understanding of how the self is healed.

GOD MAKES US NEW

What constitutes a healthy self? What is self-esteem all about? To answer such questions, we must first consider the work that God does through spiritual regeneration. Psychotherapy must place this divine healing at the center of all we do. The model I propose takes into account the following essential points:

1. God is actively involved in the healing of the total person, including emotional and behavioral problems.
2. Sin is a reality that contaminates our psyches and shapes many of our emotional problems.

3. The core of the self, biblically referred to as the "heart," is sinful but this does not mean that the total personality is depraved.
4. Many nonbelievers can still be altruistic and upright people, even more moral than believers, but still have sinful cores.
5. The Holy Spirit is vitally and necessarily involved in the healing of the total person and in the maturing of the self.
6. The work of Christian counseling and psychotherapy, when properly conducted, facilitates the work of the Holy Spirit, not usurping it but collaborating with it.
7. The spiritual disciplines are necessary and extremely helpful in facilitating emotional healing and in producing a healthy self.

Every evangelical Christian ought to hold dear the doctrine of regeneration, which simply means "rebirth." It is our attempt to understand how God acts to redeem and reform the soul and transform the will. How God regenerates the human self should be central to any "integration" of psychology and Christian faith. Any Christian psychology that fails to reckon with this rebirth is bound to be inadequate. It is the essence of what Christ came to do on the cross.

More than three hundred years ago, Philip Jacob Spencer stated in a series of scriptural expositions: "If one doctrine of our Christian faith is essential, then it is certainly that of regeneration. This is the spring from which everything which is good in our life must flow forth."[1] Why, then, don't we hear more about it? The word "regeneration" has virtually vanished from our Christian vocabulary. Instead we use its parallel term, "being born again." But that phrase doesn't quite convey the depth of meaning that regeneration does. The latter signifies a more profound and permanent work of grace in the heart.

Is it just too antiquated a word? Has liberal theology obliterated it? Do we fear becoming pharisaical if we teach that God actually causes us to be "made anew" and restored? Perhaps the real reason for our reluctance to talk about regeneration is that our age has become too "therapeutic." We even psychologize our Christian experience. We sometimes reduce conversion to merely a "peak experience," but see no ongoing work of God. Thus we water down the real significance of our spiritual encounter with God.

Carl Henry, the well-known theologian, made this statement: "Supernatural regeneration is *the* solution to the human condition. It is the hope of a new world. Without it all human endeavor to improve the quality of life, mental or physical, is limited." If this is true, and I believe it is, we need to seriously reconsider what it is we are doing in both our preaching and our psychotherapy. No wonder so many people are suspicious of all therapy. As commonly practiced, it often lacks any recognition of the divine work of grace in the heart, or any recognition of how this work can be fostered and developed.

Let me address one puzzle before I proceed. If there is such a profound work of renewal in our hearts, then why do so many people continue to exhibit the same nasty, unlikable, and even immoral behaviors after conversion? I don't mean to be a pessimist—quite the opposite. I'm trying to be a realist. Many people do manifest dramatic turn-arounds. They may quite miraculously give up drugs, alcohol, or crime, and make other dramatic life changes. But we all know people who claim to be "born again" yet don't seem to be all that different from those who are atheists, or from what they were before they were converted.

The changes in many ordinary people who confess Christ may be a "flash in the pan." We may see a dramatic drop in temper or a period of ecstatic joy for a while, but sooner or later these people revert to the old patterns. Continuing in the faith soon becomes hard work. Does this mean that regeneration is merely a good idea without substance? Does it mean that it is perhaps just a psychological "peak experience" that is only temporary? Absolutely not.

Assuming that a person has undergone genuine conversion, regeneration is *real* and *profound.* Being born anew is a vital and necessary experience, but it is only the *beginning* work of grace. Its focus is on healing the *core* of our being, not our whole being in one fell swoop. Our personality may be altered only slightly, except for the immediate thrill or joy. Many appetites will still stay the same. Old habits may quickly return. God first renews our hearts, and then begins the slow and often painful change in our personality, habits, attitudes, beliefs, and actions. We call this continuing process "sanctification."

Regeneration is more than making a "fresh start," more than beginning a new relationship with God. It applies the gospel to our hearts and ushers in a profound healing that literally gives us "new" hearts. Let us now examine how this renewal at the core of the self actually begins the healing of the whole self.

THE FORTRESS OF THE SELF

Keep in mind that I am presenting merely a "model" which must not be taken too literally. It is merely a representation that helps us to understand concepts which are otherwise very difficult to grasp. First of all we need a model for the structure of the self. The one I have found most helpful was first outlined by two psychologists, Lawrence Brammer and Everett Shostrum, in their book *Therapeutic Psychology*.[2] Their "multidimensional" approach is essential, given the many opposing theories that we have in psychology today.

Basically, Brammer and Shostrum propose that we conceptualize the individual—which I will call the "self"—as a series of ever-widening rings, such as we would see if we cut down an old tree. The young baby begins with just one ring, but as the child grows and "differentiates," it develops successive rings that constitute his or her personality. By adulthood, most people display a high degree of differentiation.

We can simplify these multiple "rings" of the adult personality to basically five components, as shown in Figure One.

Covering the outside is a protective "bark" or outer ring, designed to protect the more vulnerable inner parts of the self. The bark may be "tough" or impenetrable, as in someone who is tough, unmoved by pain, and difficult to get to know. Or it can be "soft" and spongy, offering little protection to someone who is sensitive and easily hurt.

Many have called this outer bark or outer defense system a "facade." Carl Jung called it a "persona." It is the "face" we put on for the world, the role-playing shell of the personality. We

THE STRUCTURE OF THE SELF

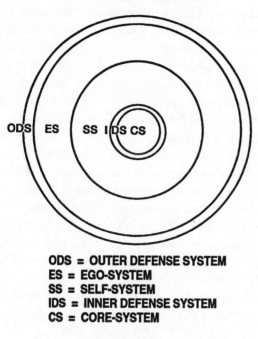

ODS = OUTER DEFENSE SYSTEM
ES = EGO-SYSTEM
SS = SELF-SYSTEM
IDS = INNER DEFENSE SYSTEM
CS = CORE-SYSTEM

Figure 1

often hide behind this mask so that no one will really know what we're feeling. This outer layer functions like the walls of a fort to defend our "self"—that private, inner part of us—from attack or over-exposure. We can erect a smoke-screen to hide our motives and escape embarrassment. We can clam up when we are hurt. But then, we can also open up to receive someone we trust.

One way of understanding psychosis is to see it as an absent outer defense system. The person is sick precisely because he or she cannot defend the inside of the self. The neurotic, on the other hand, has an extremely rigid defense system. Being overly concerned about exposure, this person has a greater need to hide from peering eyes or probing questions.

We all have such an outer defense system, learned from babyhood. But it can be either a healthy or unhealthy defense. What makes the difference? The ideal persona or defense system is one with the right *balance* between being open and being closed. If it is too open to everyone, we lack protection. If it is too closed, we become too private. Our outer walls should be *perme-*

able, able to close down or open up according to the situation.

Many psychological problems concern this outer bark. These are spiritual problems only secondarily. For instance, problems of intimacy often mean a person's outer walls are too rigid without enough gates. Nothing is allowed in and nothing is allowed out. One remains too private. The outer defense system is so rigid that it restricts the personality within. Expressing love or being open to receiving love is very difficult if not impossible.

What causes this kind of rigidity? Usually being hurt or abandoned as a child restricts a person's capacity for intimacy. Children begin life *without* any outer defense system. They gradually discover shame and embarrassment when they allow their inner selves to be too exposed. So they learn to close up. "Nothing's ever going to hurt me." "You won't catch me being vulnerable." "No way will you ever see me crying." Such thoughts flood those with too rigid an outer defense system. They learned this protective stance in childhood.

One of the functions of psychotherapy is to help such a person "loosen up" this defense and make it more appropriately open. In the confidentiality and safety of therapy, one re-learns how to be vulnerable. One experiments with being more transparent and risks exposing inner thoughts and feelings, only to find they are not as frightening as once thought.

How can such growth not be helpful? How can it be "anti-Christian" or interfere with God's Holy Spirit? If anything, increasing our capacity for intimacy helps us to open up to God as much as it helps to open us up to others or ourselves. Sadly, a rigid defense system is also rigid toward God. Problems with intimacy prevent us from becoming intimate with God as well.

THE FILTRATION SYSTEM

As we move past the defense system, we encounter two "inner" parts: first, the *ego*-system; and second, the *self*-system. The distinction is somewhat arbitrary, because the line separating them is not a distinct boundary but more like a region. These two systems are descriptive of the two major components of our inner self: the *conscious* and the *unconscious*. (I am using these phrases in a non-technical sense, not to be confused with Freud's more limited use of the term unconscious.)

Assuming we can pass through the outer bark, we first encounter that part of the self that is consciously aware of itself. We call this the *ego-system.* It knows *what* it is doing and *why* it is doing it. This conscious self doesn't feel too threatened at the outer edges, but quickly feels more vulnerable as one goes deeper. Even if I have a rigid outer bark, I could see my favorite football team losing a big game and say, "Yeah, I'm real mad. They were just stupid to blow the game the way they did." But I'm just tapping into factual stuff which is not personally threatening or very embarrassing. It is the "I," "me," "myself" part. The ego-system contains my intellect, habits, traits, behaviors, and feelings that help me "fit" my self into the larger world.

The conscious part of this ego-system is not very thick. Close to the outer edge is a dividing line separating the more confusing and threatening area of the self. This third ring or "self-system" starts out semi-conscious, but then becomes more and more unconscious as we move toward the center. Now we're in the region of the "real me" or the "real self." We don't know this landscape too well; it's too threatening.

Let's notice these two gradients as we go from outside to inside. The first involves going from what we know about ourselves (the conscious) to what we are totally unaware about ourselves (the unconscious). We also go from low vulnerability (just inside the bark) to extremely high vulnerability deep inside. As we will see, we are all frightened by what is deep within ourselves. It doesn't always feel "nice" to discover your real self.

This ego-system not only helps us interface with the world outside but also serves to filter what gets through to our deepest core. This filtration system selects what we attend to and rejects what is unacceptable. So within the ego, a whole system of defense can also develop that filters our experiences. If anything barges through our barriers, we can experience a serious crisis deep within. Defenses like *denial, rationalization,* and *intellectualization* serve to stop the flow of information in and out of the ego-system. They protect us from the severe anxiety that sudden exposure of our unconscious self-system can create.

This self-system contains all the deep motives, values, hopes, and dreams that we are not always aware of. If you ask me why I'm angry about a personal remark someone made at dinner, I may not be able to give you an honest answer. My response may be more subtle, but most likely the reason is itself too threatening for me to bring to consciousness. How many of us own up to our need for power or our craving for possessions? How many of us are honest even with ourselves about our sexual feelings or disappointments with love? How many of us are aware of our feelings of disappointment about our children or bitterness toward our parents? Not many. These very personal or unacceptable feelings are often repressed.

Psychotherapy attempts to make us more aware of these deeper, unacceptable thoughts, feelings, attitudes, beliefs, and actions of the self-system. As we uncover more and more of the self-system, the dividing line between the ego- and self-systems is moved further inside. More about us becomes obvious—"in the light" of the ego—and less is left hiding in the recesses of the self where it often eats away like a cancer at our happiness and fulfillment.

By definition, the immature self is one with too much "hidden away" in the self-system. The values you live by are not obvious, so you make wrong choices. Your hopes are driven by unrealistic expectations, so you never really feel as if you can succeed. Too much unconscious material in the self-system can easily set you up for a "mid-life" crisis. You can suddenly find yourself attracted to someone else or confronted by "hidden" motives or unfulfilled dreams. So you rush out to try and replace them as quickly as possible.

THE PRISON WALL

We now come to the crux of this model. The first three components of the self are relatively easy to grasp. We can all recognize our "bark," our "conscious," and our "hidden" selves. But as we dive deeper within the self, we encounter a *second* major defense system. This fourth ring protects the very *core of the self,* what Scripture refers to as the "heart." In contrast to the exterior fortress walls, Brammer and Shostrum describe this *inner defense system* as a "prison wall," whose principle function is to keep the deepest parts of our being totally concealed.[3]

This core contains the fundamental needs and drives that describe human beings, such as sexuality, aggressiveness, acquisitiveness, and dominating forces. This common denominator of all humans includes everything that makes us selfish, but it is totally hidden from us.

Now the big question is: How much of this core is good? Some say it is all good. Others say it is all bad. Freud called it the "id" and saw it as "bad." Carl Jung saw it as the "shadow," which held a dark side. "Depth" psychologists don't want to label this core as either positive or negative. A few would say that it contains both the lowest and the highest, the worst and the best of our humanness.

If we place the *imago Dei* at the center of this core, then we could say that it holds the potential for good if the divine image were allowed to reign supreme. But I believe Scripture reveals that this core is so contaminated that the impact of the image of God, even though it might be at the center of the core, is temporarily suspended. To put it in a nutshell, *the core is the sinful part of our nature.* Understanding how this sinfulness at the core of the self suppresses the image of God in us is the key to developing a Christian approach to psychotherapy.

THE HEART

The inner core of our being is the equivalent to what Scripture sometimes calls the "heart." I am again reminded of Ernest Becker's suggested warning to be posted on every psychotherapist's door: "Danger: Real probability of the awakening of terror and dread, from which there is no turning back."[4]

What is he alluding to? Since his book is entitled *The Denial of Death,* is it just the terror that accompanies the knowledge that one is going to die one day? Becker does make much of this "final terror of self-consciousness." He builds on Kierkegaard's idea that human existence exacts one great penalty: a certain anxiety about not living.[5] We don't find this dread in animals, only in humans.

But this is not the terror alluded to in Becker's warning. Rather it is the dread that comes from the heart or the "core" of the self when it is fully unmasked. Before it has been redeemed and renewed, our fallen core hides all that is dark and dirty about the self, all that is selfish and so self-centered that it could be labeled as "evil" through and through.

Scott Peck's book, *People of the Lie,* paints a vivid portrait of how pervasive and diverse human evil can be.[6] It is not enough, however, to accept that humanity is locked in a titanic struggle between the forces of good and evil, as Peck suggests.[7] We must also reckon with the evil created by the sinful core of the human self. With virtually no help from the outside, our fallen nature can singlehandedly work such evil havoc as to defy description.

I think we make a great mistake to always "externalize" evil, seeing it as satanic in origin. A natural evil springs from the human heart. It is our discovery of this deep sinfulness that strikes terror and dread in the self. Yet we must come to see the true nature of our inner core. It may not be a pretty sight, but it is the first step toward God's healing of the self.

The dark nature of the core has led many psychotherapists to believe that it is really unknowable. Many wounded people erect such massive defenses to contain the darkness that it becomes virtually impenetrable. Outwardly, we can behave as upright and honest citizens only because we maintain such tight control of our inner core. Perhaps most of us fall into this category. We're not Jeffrey Dahmer or Adolf Hitler. We are ordinary, run-of-the-mill sinners. But who knows what would emerge if we hadn't learned to control our sinful cores?

How does this view fit with Scripture? The metaphorical label of the "heart"—used one hundred and forty-eight times in the New Testament—denotes this core of emotions and personality. In Hebrew thought, it refers to our thinking and remembering, as well as to the seat of our morality. When God speaks to us he addresses the "heart" as the source of sin and evil. Mark 7:21 makes this clear: "For from within, out of the heart of men, proceed evil thoughts, adulteries, fornications, murders...." Jeremiah 17:9 makes the same point: "The heart is deceitful above all things, and desperately wicked: who can know it?"

Scripture considers the heart to be the seat of sin. And as Scott Peck points out, it is not "sins" that characterize evil people, but rather the persistence and consistency of their wickedness.[8] It is the core that is the root problem, even though its outward expression can certainly wreak havoc.

The belief that the heart is basically sinful is what separates us from secular humanists. They believe that there is nothing at the core of the self that is intrinsically evil. Many Christian humanists have adopted this position as well, but mainly because they believe we have taken the idea of the Fall too far. Fearing we have too earnestly pressed this notion of our basic sinfulness, they point to abuses in history where Christians even encouraged forms of child abuse to "break" this inherent sinfulness.

IS THE WHOLE SELF EVIL?

Perhaps our point of confusion centers on the question of whether it is just the core or heart that is sinful, or whether the whole self is evil. Not believing that all of the self is evil, I would propose that what happens to the rest of the self follows the model depicted in Figure 2.

HOW SIN CONTAMINATES THE SELF

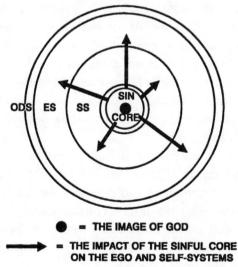

● = THE IMAGE OF GOD

➤ = THE IMPACT OF THE SINFUL CORE ON THE EGO AND SELF-SYSTEMS

Figure 2

This presents basically the same structure as Figure 1, except that I have now added a small inner circle at the center of the core labeled the "image of God." I believe that at the very center of the heart of all of us is God's image, the very image that characterizes us as spiritual beings.

Every human being, even Adolf Hitler, has been born with this divine image, which was disastrously contaminated by the Fall. The "core" or heart of the self—originally created to be the mantle that could be brilliantly lit to show forth this image—was extinguished. The fallen core of the self now surrounds this image of God, like Dracula's black cloak. Yet even in our fallen state, we still retain this *imago Dei* as a part of the self.

As the rest of the self begins to differentiate and develop, this sinful core has not yet erected an inner defense system. The fallen nature, therefore, begins to contaminate the emerging self, both its ego- and self-systems, to varying degrees. I believe the spreading contamination is only partial. While the ego can become self-centered *to some extent*, the spoilage is not total. Even though we are significantly shaped by heredity, most of the ego-system and self-system is *learned*. Our personality *per se* is not sinful, only the behavior we learn.

As we begin to relate to the outside world, we shape the form of our emotions, attitudes, and beliefs—while the sinful core is always exerting its influence. At the same time, we learn how to control and imprison this core by building a huge prison wall of defense to contain it. The sinful core, then, is the most unconscious part of the whole self. Most of us, if not all of us, haven't the slightest inkling of what lurks deep inside—until God's Holy Spirit convicts us of sin, forcing us to look behind the prison gates at who we really are.

The natural state of the self that emerges is depicted in Figure 3. God's image is encapsulated by a fallen sinful core that becomes surrounded by stiff defenses. But before it can be adequately contained, sin will have contaminated the rest of the self, both ego- and self-system, leaving us tainted by evil, replete with many bad habits and tendencies. This is shown by the wavy line running in and out of the self.

THE CONSEQUENCES OF A SINFUL CORE

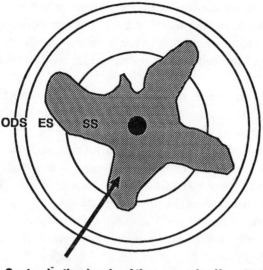

Contamination by sin of the ego and self-systems

Figure 3

This model clarifies several important points:

1. It helps to explain why many unbelievers are basically moral people. The whole personality is not sinful. Some people outwardly seem to be less sinful than others. They may be more altruistic, socially just, and honest. Their "contamination" is less because their core has been more contained. They have built better defenses against the influence of their sinful cores. Perhaps parenting and environment influence the spread of this contamination. Personality and other aspects of the self always fare better when given a healthier environment. Nevertheless, all men and women have this sinful core and suffer from some degree of contamination.

2. It explains why some people seem to be more evil than others. The degree of contamination varies from person to person. How do we explain someone like Hitler? That Satan controls him more? Perhaps. But even if this were the case, it happens because a person's inner defenses against his or her sinful

core are less effective. Sin, and hence evil, overruns one's self-
and ego-systems, contaminating them to such an extent that
Satan can easily control behavior. Whole selves are distorted
to such an extent that murder, even mass annihilation of others, comes to be seen as a virtue or social good. Such severe
distortion of the self can be produced by an unrestrained sinful core.

3. It explains why we all experience some degree of contamination. I don't mean that we all have a sinful core; that is a given.
I mean that *all* of us exhibit the influence of our sinful core in
our personality, our behavior, our attitudes, and our beliefs—
in fact, in every part of the self. None of us totally escapes.
Every one of us will at some time or another sin. This act of
evil betrays the trait of sin still within us.

4. It also warns us that unless the core of the self is dealt with and
the inherently sinful nature of the core removed, *any* human
being is capable of the most vile evil imaginable. The inner
defense system or prison wall is normally impenetrable, but
Satan can tempt us to remove it or circumstances can con-
spire to erode and weaken it. This explains why decent, honest people can become evil and destructive if their defenses
are destroyed. This may sound frightening, but I believe it to
be true. Regrettably, a severe psychosis can break down someone's inner defense system and release uncontrollable evil,
just as an underground aquifer poisoned with pollutants can
eventually contaminate a whole neighborhood. Such persons
become a danger to themselves and others precisely because
they are unable to maintain their defense system due to psychotic illness.

GOD'S REMEDY

The healing of this core of the self is what regeneration is all
about. If the heart is a core that is deceitful and desperately
wicked (Jer 17:9), then the only true remedy is that also presented by Scripture: the heart must be "made anew" or "reborn."

The unbeliever can be likened to an apple infected by an

insect. The outside may be pretty and most of the inside healthy and edible, but the core is rotten. The seeds of corruption have been planted within the core of the self by the insect of sin. This corruption has slowly spread to contaminate other parts of the apple. If left untreated, worms begin to multiply and burrow into the healthy flesh of the apple, slowly turning it brown and useless. These worms are like the acts of sin. The core is damaged by the sinful nature. The emerging worms are the evil behavior that continue to eat away at the self, completing the process of destruction.

Regeneration is how God acts to make the core whole and holy again. His grace does not normally remove all the worms in the apple immediately, but it does restore the core to wholeness. And because at the very center is God's image, the regenerated core of the self is now free to take on the image of God it previously suppressed. The self is slowly transformed according to this image, just as a piece of film can be imprinted by rays of light when left exposed. Thus, a long process of "sanctification" begins to remake us. The flesh—the rest of the self, both ego- and self-system—becomes conformed to the likeness of the Creator.

God creates a new heart within the human self. His work of regeneration provides a new source for righteous living, new aspirations, and a new power for service. As God promised through Ezekiel: "A new heart also will I give you, and a new spirit will I put within you: and I will take away the stony heart out of your flesh, and I will give you a heart of flesh. And I will put my spirit within you and cause you to walk in my statutes..." (Ez 36:26-27).

This beautiful description fits so perfectly the model I am presenting here. Jesus completes the picture when he tells Nicodemus: "Except a man be born again, he cannot see the kingdom of God" (Jn 3:3). Regeneration, then, means a whole new heart, a new life, a new hunger for righteousness, a new power. Paul sums up this divine transformation: "Therefore if any man be in Christ, he is a new creature: old things are passed away; behold all things are become new" (2 Cor 5:17).

How do we receive this renewal of the self? God responds to

our repentance and acceptance of Christ as our Savior. His divine power alone can work the change in our hearts. The Holy Spirit renews our core and plants a new spirit within us. The regenerated self then takes on the form depicted in Figure 4.

THE REGENERATED SELF

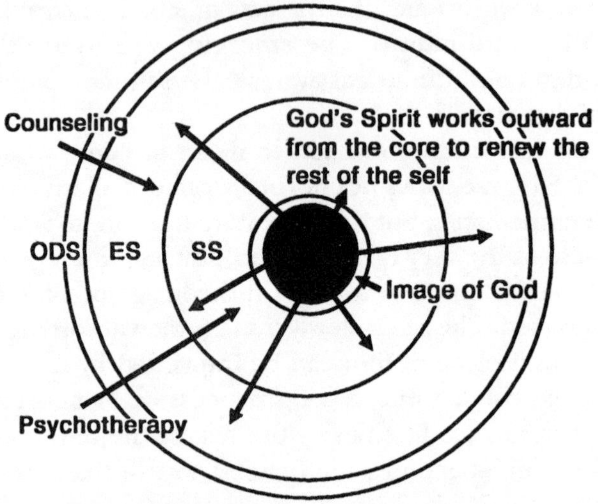

Christian counseling and psychotherapy work from the outside inward to facilitate the work of God's Spirit

Figure 4

God understands the hopelessness of the human condition. His solution was not to merely remove the worms, but to first renew the rotten core. Without this renewal, all other attempts at self-improvement fall miserably short. But this new birth offers even more than a change in our relationship to God. The other part of the miracle is the newness of our spiritual lives. The renewed core becomes able to attain all those ideals for the self held out by humanists.

Some puzzling issues become clearer in light of this model which I have presented. While God restores his image in our core, it must still become a reality in the rest of the self. How much our personality and behavior changes depends on many other factors. We will often retain far more of our old selves than we would like. But at least the heart has been renewed, which is the essence of salvation. Some people experience a dramatic release from incapacitating habits and gross immorality. Some have more worms left crawling around inside than others. In our own critical eyes, others may appear to be little changed by God's work of regeneration. But only God can see the heart.

God's transformation of the core is normally compressed into a short span of time, but it may take on the appearance of a process. Coming to a place of surrender may take a while. Did you ever learn to dive as a kid? You stand on the edge of the pool for a long time, thinking about taking the plunge, but afraid of getting hurt. You walk away; you come back. Then one day, you finally take the plunge. That's sometimes how it is with letting God have his way with us.

Even though we are all affected differently by the renewal of our hearts, a number of similar characteristics can often give evidence of this change. The heart moves from a state of carelessness about God or distorted fear of him, to one of passion and longing to know him better. Fear and hate turn to admiration. We experience greater receptivity to the promptings of the Holy Spirit. It is as if a receiver has been implanted at the core of the self, and it begins to feel urges corresponding to God's leadings. We desire less and less to gratify our "lower" instincts or to pursue sinful behavior. We become more aware of displeasing God; we grieve sin more.

Our attitude toward others changes as well. Feelings of hate and a desire for revenge begin to moderate. We treat others more carefully and lovingly. We become more concerned about the spiritual and eternal aspects of life, more aware of the true meaning of our existence. Scripture becomes our "survival" food, the milk that nourishes the renewed heart. We begin to resonate with God's truth in a way we never have before.

THE WELL SPRING

Finally, let's return to our original question. How does Christian counseling and psychotherapy relate to God's work of grace in the heart? Are our efforts and God's independent of one another? I would say that regeneration of the human heart is the wellspring from which all change must flow.

Therapy works from the *outside* in. First, the outer bark or defense system must be penetrated. The therapist builds rapport in order to overcome any natural resistance on the part of the client. Then ego-system issues are explored. Together, therapist and client seek to understand obvious and conscious aspects of the self such as habits, traits, and personality. How do they contribute to the problem that brought this particular client in for therapy? Resistance may periodically increase with the discovery of deeper feelings. Sensitively pacing this process helps it to continue.

The next stage of psychotherapy involves working with the deeper self, exploring the less conscious feelings, values, and motives. Here the client often becomes highly defensive because the self feels strangely vulnerable. It is easily damaged by ruthless exposure. Pulling the curtain back gradually allows what is discovered to be accepted and assimilated. Changes can be implemented to produce a healthier self.

The final stage of therapy is exploring the core, which requires penetrating the inner defense system. Here again we need to exercise great caution. The fallen core in an unregenerated self holds potential for great harm if its poisons are released into the larger self-system. Humanists think otherwise. They believe all we need do is break down a person's inner defense system to release a glorious core of goodness, and then nurture the self to maturity. Most depth psychologists warn that improperly exposing this core can actually drive someone crazy.

If the core of the self has been born anew, then a deep healing has already taken place. God's own image is then released into the whole core as therapy continues to break down the inner prison walls. While the therapy works from the *outside in,* God's Spirit works from the *inside out,* sanctifying and reconstructing the ego and self-systems, working to eradicate the worms of sin left over from the old core.

Even if the core has been renewed and God's image released for inner healing, many have been so traumatized that God's Spirit is not free to work as he desires. Our free will must still *choose* to cooperate with God's work of sanctification. Therapists can especially help damaged selves to identify the obstacles in their lives that block God's work of grace. Some biological conditions can hamper full emotional and mental health. Chronic depression, psychosis, and organic brain disorders can sometimes keep believers from acting responsibly. Treatment with medication may be necessary to remove such barriers.

Pastoral counselors, marriage and family counselors, psychologists and social workers—anyone who does "talk" therapy—is merely a handmaiden to the Holy Spirit, helping to facilitate full surrender to the healing work of God. Christian psychotherapy in particular can help to identify those blockages and weaknesses which would sabotage the self's journey toward full health. It can increase the self's understanding of its own evil tendencies and clarify the self's deep need for God's love and mercy. It can help believers to overcome the resistance to grace that is sometimes caused by trauma and abuse.

Christian psychotherapy is never capable of reconstructing the core of the self. That is God's prerogative alone. Grace as applied through the Holy Spirit changes the core. Therapists must collaborate with God in this process of sanctification by recognizing the presence, power, and work of the Holy Spirit. They need to be open to discernment or the leading of the Spirit in focusing on important issues within the self or on a particular obstacle that may be thwarting the grace of God.

A Christian therapist always points the client back to spiritual realities, such as the importance of confession and repentance in cleansing the self of contaminants. Whenever possible, unbelievers need to be pointed back to their need for renewal. No psychotherapy is fully viable without God's healing at the core of the self. Apart from its Creator, the heart is doomed to wander on a stormy sea of anger and depression. The heart that comes home to God, like the prodigal son, will know true peace. With this model in place, we can begin to explore what it means to be a "healthy" self.

10 | The Healthy Self

And the peace of God, which passeth all understanding, shall keep your hearts and minds through Christ Jesus." **Phil 4:7 KJV**

I FIND IT MUCH EASIER TO DEFINE a damaged or disordered self than to describe a healthy self. Controversy rages even between the major psychological theorists about what constitutes "healthy." Further disagreement surfaces between psychology and Christian belief systems.

Linda is characteristic of the many who are searching for their "ideal" self. She naturally wants to be healthy, happy, and fulfilled. But she's having trouble achieving it. I have never met this young woman personally. I know her only through her mother's eyes, but I have no reason to doubt her mother's story.

Linda went away to college at nineteen, and then on to medical school. After working as a physician for a while, she is now in her early thirties and training to be a psychiatrist. As part of her residency requirements and also to deal with some personal issues in her life, Linda is herself undergoing psychoanalysis.

In a "classical" approach, Linda lies on a couch five days a week exploring early sexual "forces" that have shaped her self. Her analyst sits behind her, out of sight, and asks Linda to "free associate" as much as possible. As his client minimizes conscious control and tells everything that comes to her mind, the analyst expects that more and more of her "unconscious" mind will emerge.

During Linda's therapy, a "transference" relationship with the analyst will develop. Strong feelings will emerge, both positive and negative, and the analyst will then use these feelings to uncover and understand Linda's deepest needs. Also, her dreams will be carefully dissected to help flesh out Linda's current and longstanding conflicts.

But in Linda's case the therapy apparently went wrong at one major point. Instead of "reconstructing" her basic personality—the ultimate goal of psychoanalysis—Linda became bogged down in a quagmire of anger. Somewhere she lost control in her quest for self-understanding. At any provocation Linda became full of rage. And her mother was most often the focus of her rage.

Linda's mother was totally bewildered and took it all very personally. She sobbed as she recounted her daughter's vicious verbal attacks. Linda blamed her mother for all her troubles. Her father had died when she was only ten years old, for which she also blamed her mother. Linda had felt much closer to him and resented the twist of fate that had taken her father instead of her mother away from her. Now all of her resentment was coming out. But the therapist was not helping Linda examine the legitimacy of her anger. He just let her go on believing that it was her mother's fault that her father had died.

This analyst even encouraged Linda's rage—not in so many words, but by allowing her to continue to vent it in therapy. She later acknowledged that her imagination allowed her to "invent" childhood traumas involving her mother, just to feed her rage. The therapist seemed to be less interested in discovering the truth than in fueling Linda's angry fire. As a result, Linda did not become healthier. She became increasingly distraught, distrustful, and disturbed.

The mother also became extremely agitated, not so much about being rejected by her daughter. "If she wants to go her own way and never see me again, I'll be hurt, but I'll get over it," she would say. "But I can't take this constant bombardment of letters and telephone calls in which she attacks me constantly, blaming me for every little thing I did wrong, and for a whole lot of things that I know never even happened. The real issue is that she hasn't gotten over her father's death, and her analyst doesn't seem to care about what the real issues are. He just wants her to keep being upset at me so she can keep coming to therapy. He says that now she is becoming healthy... she's letting out all her feelings. She's not getting better, she's getting worse. What sort of a psychiatrist is she going to be if she can't get her own life under control?"

I must confess I had a lot of sympathy for the mother. Too many therapists believe that the rest of the world owes it to their patient to be a "chopping block." You can go and beat up on anyone else you please, they believe, without regard to how they feel or will be damaged. What matters most is that you get better. If "they" don't like it, that's their tough luck!

Isn't such an attitude basically selfishness in the service of the self? I would ask these therapists: What gives anyone the right to hurt others so that they can feel better? What makes us believe that if we can find someone else to blame for our troubles, these troubles will get better or go away?

But what struck me forcibly about the mother's statement about her daughter's therapy was the phrase, "He says that now she's becoming healthy." Many therapists have been prone to label uncontrollable anger as a "healthy" emotion. An entire "anger industry" thrives on the promotion of uncontrollable anger. Unless you throw a tantrum at least once a day, you are not being "true" to yourself. Unless your marriage has a mammoth Vesuvius-type explosion weekly, you're not "clearing the air" in your marriage. Such ideas show no regard for the feelings or rights of those on the receiving end of that anger. Uncontrolled rage is selfish and, more importantly, sick. It doesn't lead to health, only selfish and self-serving behaviors.

There was nothing I could do to help Linda. She wasn't asking for my help. But I could help her mother. I showed her how to establish some boundaries with Linda and taught her a few assertiveness skills about how to handle Linda's anger. Surprisingly, when Mom began to stand up to her daughter and refuse to accept responsibility for her imagined grievances, Linda began to improve. She started to question the validity of her memories. She began to realize how she was inappropriately blaming her mother. Then the analyst began to get mad! He wanted Linda to stay rageful—at least for a couple more years—but Linda realized she needed to move on.

I've picked up many "Lindas" in therapy over the years—people who have traveled the wrong road to health. Not every model of therapy views emotional health in quite the same way. I am appalled to discover how easily some people are misled, how often so-called "memories" of childhood trauma are fabricated or blamed on the wrong person, and how unhealthy patterns of behavior can be encouraged under the guise of "psychological health."

If you don't understand what "healthy" means, you can easily take the wrong direction and end up more troubled than when you began your quest for healing.

WHAT DOES PSYCHOLOGY SAY?

A quick review of how a few of the major psychologies define the healthy self will help to set the stage for what I would propose as a Christian psychology's definition.

Psychoanalysis. Contrary to Linda's experience, psychoanalysis does have as one of its ultimate goals the development of greater conscious awareness of basic issues.[1] Perhaps we could give her analyst the benefit of the doubt and say that Linda was only "in process" about her feelings toward her mother. As the patient works through earlier painful and traumatic experiences so that they are no longer denied or distorted, they are able to maintain greater self-control. The healthy person has good ego-strength, meaning the self is able to make responsible decisions and regulate its life.

Two problems arise with Freud's psychoanalytic approach.

First, it is *deterministic;* what happens to you is really beyond your control. It blames sex for a lot of human problems. Second, it is *mechanistic;* you are just a machine, made up of parts that may or may not work together. Classical psychoanalysis views the self as being irrationally driven by biological, primitive drives—leaving no room for spirit. Such an inadequate model of health needs a lot of adjusting to fit human beings made in God's image.

Psychodynamic theories. There are a number of theories that spring from psychoanalysis which claim to focus on understanding the deeper and richer aspects of the self. While these theories also see "hidden" forces and unconscious factors as very important, they de-emphasize the role of sex as a determinant of behavior. A healthy self is viewed as one that has *individuated* and *separated,* i.e., one that is capable of autonomous living and relating. It perceives the world and other people with less distortion, and is thus able to trust others more freely. This definition is broader than that given by psychoanalysis. The approach called "object-relations theory" is perhaps the best known here. Objects are persons we view with strong emotion. They become symbols that influence how the self develops.

Existential psychotherapy. This approach focuses on concerns rooted in the individual's existence. Its strong respect for people's unique experiences works against forcing everyone into the same mold. The central health theme is that of *becoming*—the process of trying to discover your true self and make sense of your existence.

Existentialists ask admirable questions, especially in the context of encouraging us all to find meaning in our existence. Who am I? Who have I been? Who am I becoming? A central idea in this approach is reconnecting the self to the spirit. Existential anxiety helps us to make authentic choices. A healthy person is defined as "being a self in truth."

Jungian therapy. Following the theories of Carl Jung (1875-1961), some therapists see the self as a sort of archetype or pattern of inborn images that shape our existence. They believe that all of life is a *movement toward selfhood,* often a painful and difficult process. *Self-realization* is a lifelong process of becoming an individual. It is more an ideal we work toward than an actuality that can be achieved in the course of a lifetime. Health is viewed as coming only from becoming an *authentic self.*

Although Jung clearly gives a lot of credence to "spiritual" issues, Jungians trust the psyche or inner self to guide itself, rather than relying on any external spirit. They don't really see the need for the self to be "saved." Christians often use a well-known test of temperament, called the "Myers-Briggs Type Indicator" (MBTI) which builds on Jung's ideas.

The MBTI uses the "introversion/extroversion" categories of personality and expands the personality type indicator into several categories. A person is identified as expressing some combination of sensing, thinking, feeling, or intuitive processes. Unfortunately this test has been overutilized in popular circles and, in the opinion of many, has lost its professional credibility.[2] Lay people, however, often find the labels a convenient way of describing themselves.

Cognitive/behavioral therapy. Another group of therapists focus on how thinking and behavior patterns both cause and result from emotional problems. Their emphasis is on changing these patterns as a way of healing the self. Health is seen in terms of *self influence*—such as having rational and healthy thinking patterns —and on having *right beliefs* that can shape one's life. It stresses that thoughts and behavior are *controllable* and have significant consequences for one's life. Many Christian therapists find this approach quite compatible with their faith.

Client-centered therapy. One of the "person-centered" therapies was developed by Dr. Carl Rogers. Also known as "nondirective" therapy, it emphasizes that the client "directs" the therapy. More focused on health than pathology, it has been a primary source for the humanistic approaches so heavily criticized by Christians.

In client-centered therapy, health is defined as the harmonious meshing of what one wants to become with what one perceives one's self to be. The healthy self is fully *aware, honest, personally satisfied,* and *spontaneous.* Increased trust of self and openness to experiencing life *in the present* is supposed to lead to a new kind of freedom. Healthy people choose to direct their lives from within rather than to be controlled by the external world. This approach strongly emphasizes personal growth, self-acceptance, and being "in touch" with your feelings.

Maslow's ideas. We could continue to examine many other methods of psychotherapy, but Abraham Maslow's ideas perhaps summarize what many of them have to say. He believes that all humans have basic *needs,* governed by a hierarchy which determines which needs must be met and in what order. The ultimate need is to be a *self-actualized* person with the following characteristics:

- You accept yourself and others.
- You are spontaneous.
- You are an autonomous self.
- You have creativity.
- You are open to "peak" experiences.
- You have a humanitarian character.

As you can see, these are variations of the themes I have already described. Pooling all the theories together doesn't actually yield much variation in what constitutes a healthy self. Disagreement arises more on the methods of these therapies, *how to achieve* these goals of health. Yet because we realize that they are only tools, the methods are often the least bothersome to Christian psychologists. Rather, *who* uses the tools and for *what purpose*—these are the crucial issues.

We can sum up the totality of psychology's model of human wholeness then as as follows. A healthy self is:

- *Cohesive:* it sticks together and functions as a whole.
- *Vigorous:* it is strong, robust, energetic.
- *Balanced:* it has equilibrium, stability.
- *Open to feelings:* it can quickly identify and accept feelings and incorporate them into present experience.

- *Honest:* does not try to deny fears or anxieties or to defend against unpleasant feelings.
- *Controlled:* able to exercise self-control and make healthy choices.
- *Individuated:* it is its own self, not subject to undue control by others, able to resist manipulation.
- *Growing:* it is "becoming" a true self, and finds meaning in human existence.
- *Actualizing:* it finds appropriate outlets for self-expression and fulfillment in achieving something meaningful.
- *Spontaneous:* it is aware of the present and able to fully express itself in the present without fear of rejection or humiliation.
- *Congruent:* it is authentically the same on the inside as it is on the outside, fully harmonious, free of hypocrisy.
- *Trusting:* it knows when to trust and when to be cautious and is able to abandon itself in love or protect itself from abuse.
- *Self-accepting:* it is free of self-hate or self-rejection or any need to be self-punishing or to rob the self of any ability to enjoy pleasure.
- *Abiding dignity:* it fosters respect for itself and for others and honestly accepts strengths and weaknesses in the self.
- *Equanimity:* it is emotionally flexible and adaptable, relatively content with both the joys and sufferings that life inevitably brings, and able to live fully in the present, yet have long-term goals.
- *Transparent:* it is appropriately open to the outside world, free of facades or masks, and not preoccupied with social roles or "what others think."
- *Self-sufficient:* it takes responsibility for itself but not for anyone else, is not overly dependent on outside sources of affirmation or approval, and able to be self-nurturing and self-affirming.
- *Game-free:* the self is free of "games," maladaptive transactions, people-pleasing, and a need to manipulate others.
- *Unafraid:* it is not afraid to face itself, to face the good facts about itself as well as the bad.

This long list is far from comprehensive in detailing the models of health espoused by most theories of psychotherapy. Even with the most critical eye, one cannot help but affirm practically every one of these characteristics as ideal for the human self. Psychology has actually done a pretty good job of defining what constitutes a perfectly healthy self.

So what is the problem? First, I protest not so much about *what is* included, but rather *what is not*. Second, I seriously question many of the *means* for achieving these ideals. The underlying assumptions of many of these theorists is that humans are fundamentally good and healthy and only need an "opportunity to blossom." This assumption needs to be seriously critiqued from a Christian biblical perspective. The self first needs to be redeemed and regenerated before it can achieve these ideals. The highest aspirations of the self come out of its hunger for God.

WHAT IS MISSING?

While we can paint a beautiful picture of the ideal or healthy self, the self cannot achieve this ideal on its own. Scripture portrays our core as essentially sinful. While many human beings are beautifully whole, highly functional, altruistic, and loving, the ego- and self-systems that constitute the rest of their personality and self are still tainted and in need of renewal. The self, outside of Christ's renewal, poses more of a problem than a promise of self-actualization. Trying to fulfill a self that has not been regenerated inevitably turns out to be an empty and inadequate endeavor.

So what is missing? The regenerating work of God. A self can never be totally healthy until it is reconciled to God. I find that many of psychology's goals remain very appropriate for the born-again believer, even though self-fulfillment, self-actualization, self-direction, self-acceptance, self-esteem, self-responsibility, self-realization, and all the other self-what-nots seem to be so abhorrent to many Christians.

I believe this promised new self is a reflection of God's image, with the freedom to become all these things in a healthy way. Being a *real self,* a *whole self,* and an *honest self* can be both Christ-centered and Christ-directed. The healthy self yearns to be the best it can be in order to reflect the purity of God. Such an aim is not selfish, selfist, or self-focused.

Every one of these ingredients for a healthy self takes on new meaning for the regenerated believer. The Living Bible contains a beautiful rendering of Romans 5:1-2 that portrays this new self's quest: "So now, since we have been made right in God's sight by faith in his promises, we can have real peace with him because of what Jesus Christ our Lord has done for us. For because of our faith, he has brought us into this place of highest privilege where we now stand, and we confidently and joyfully look forward *to actually becoming all that God has in mind for us to be*" (emphasis is mine).

Christians can strive for each of the characteristics that define a healthy self. We can rely on God to provide us with the means for achieving these ideals. And we can thank him for the grace and power that make it possible.

Who wouldn't want to be a fully actualized Christian self, dedicated to becoming the best we can be for Christ? What's the alternative? Remaining unfulfilled and self-rejecting? This is not what God wants for us. A healthy self is never the enemy of contrition, penitence, humility, obedience, or faith. Quite the opposite. A healthy self helps us to achieve a more complete spirituality.

The self needs the process of sanctification as much as it needs regeneration. It needs to learn how to align its will with that of God, how to surrender its "rights" to others, and how to bring justice to a broken and unjust world.

But how can we encourage people to passionately pursue spiritual excellence, while at the same time telling them that they should not allow the "self" to get in the way? The regenerated self has *got to be in the way.* We won't get off first base without it. The self is at the center of the divine drama, the target of all God's wooing, the focus of the change that God wants to work. It should respond with great enthusiasm to God's call for righteous living, balanced values, and sacrificial love.

"But won't the self become too self-centered even in its pursuit of spirituality?" question the critics of Christian psychology. I don't hear this fear voiced so much by liberal Christians who don't always take the claims of Christ seriously, but more from those who have a great investment in a biblical view of life. Indeed, protecting the centrality of the gospel is a proper concern.

But we also need to be concerned about the confusing messages we send to Christian believers. Those who remain centered on Christ will find many guides to protect them from self-centeredness in their walk with God. Yes, some do become narcissistic in their spirituality. Their worship and walk with Christ is very self-serving, self-pleasing, and self-glorifying. But I don't believe the majority of believers fall victim to this problem. The healthier they become in themselves, the healthier will be their spiritual life and their walk with God.

PUTTING CHRIST AT THE CENTER

We often contrast "putting Christ at the center" of our lives with having the self at the center. I do not find this an accurate way of portraying "Christ-centeredness" in living. When a person's heart is made new, *Christ is automatically at the center of the self.* He may not be in control of the ego- or self-system, but Christ is always at the center of our core—the heart.

Sanctification is not a matter of *displacing* the self. Where else on earth is it supposed to go? Allowing God to completely occupy the rest of the self is a more accurate way to think about how God becomes central to our being. When we talk about "putting Christ at the center," what we really mean is letting Christ control the whole self. If he already dominates our core-self, we allow the Holy Spirit to do the work of sanctification by our cooperation. It is through the process of sanctification that we achieve the ultimate "integration" of the self.

Besides the direct work of the Holy Spirit in response to our pleas and dedication, what else helps us to achieve a healthy "integration" of the self?

Hearing the Word of God. I am often amazed at how hearing the Word of God preached, in and of itself, provides a means of grace. I have seen good preaching achieve profound (and often inexplicable) spiritual changes in a person's life. But we often overlook another important dimension of proclaiming the gospel: preaching itself is a form of psychotherapy!

Preachers can not only teach God's word but provide practical help from the pulpit on how to apply the spiritual disciplines to the daily issues of life. Sound, common-sense psychological advice can sometimes help people understand their ego- and self-systems even more effectively than therapy.

The preacher is certainly not *merely* a therapist. In fact, the Holy Spirit is the most effective psychotherapist of all. Proclaiming God's Word helps people receive God's work. Through its ministry of preaching and fellowship, the Christian church has been practicing spiritual psychotherapy for twenty centuries—long before psychology ever invented it. Biblical sermons help hurting people deal with guilt, anger, loneliness, and depression. Whenever we proclaim the good news, the Holy Spirit helps us to apply that word to the healing of the ego- and self-systems.

Effective preaching accomplishes four ends:

1. It helps people discover what God wants them to do—not just in their living but in their very selves.
2. It helps people discover the truth of their selves, both their unworthiness and their true value to God.
3. It helps illuminate the blockages, obstacles, and hindrances that prevent the self from becoming an authentic, Christ-like, and healthy self.
4. It points people to the resources of God that can be applied to the healing of the self, especially Scripture, prayer, and other spiritual disciplines.

Biblical preaching addresses itself to the immediate, practical concerns of the hearer. Jesus always spoke to the total human condition and we should do the same. The preacher enters the pulpit for the express purpose of showing how God can help people achieve a more fulfilling and effective life. Hearing the good news brings healing to the self at a very deep level. Frankly, preaching often makes the slow, limping ways of psychotherapy look like a tortoise!

Psychotherapy. Psychotherapy can be an important means to achieving health, especially one that is based on a Christian value system. Not every therapy used by Christian psychologists is necessarily Christian. Some see themselves merely as Christians who practice therapy. Of course, God uses the mind of even non-Christian counselors or psychotherapists to bring healing. God cannot be limited in how he works. But a Christian psychotherapy holds to a different set of values and beliefs about how God works through his Holy Spirit.

Why do we need the help of psychotherapy? Not everything we do nor every problem we confront is necessarily directly tied to spiritual issues. Many emotionally troubled people, including Christians, suffer from problems of overactive endocrine glands, disturbed body chemistry, or physical damage to the brain that can cause bizarre behavior or incapacitating depression. Stress disorders can cause headaches as well as emotional problems. Dysfunctional family patterns can disrupt the normal development of children, causing them to be distrustful and unable to engage in intimacy in later life.

While these are not specifically spiritual difficulties, many of them become obstacles to God's work in the self. Many sufferers find it seemingly impossible to live a Christ-centered life or to experience God at a deep emotional level. The severity of their problems prevents them from reaching out and receiving God's help, yet they are often told to rely *only* on God's help. I see people struck in this kind of dilemma all the time. What are they supposed to do if the help psychotherapy can offer is denied them? Sheer frustration often forces them to seek out a therapist anyway, but they may feel terribly guilty about not being able to solve their problems through prayer alone. Such people need encouragement, not criticism, for trying to get help from pastors and Christian leaders.

Connectedness. In addition to hearing the good news and receiving psychotherapy, supportive relationships can go a long way toward helping us become healthier selves. Scripture urges us to "Share each other's troubles and problems, and so obey our Lord's command. If anyone thinks he is too great to stoop to this, he is fooling himself" (Gal 6:2-3, LB).

American culture especially cultivates independence and self-reliance. And these values can be healthy, to a point. But how far should we go in this direction? Can a self really be happy and live a fulfilling life when isolated from others? I doubt it. A distorted drive for independence and self-reliance can easily foster a "disconnected" self, a phenomenon nowhere more prolific than in the modern family.

Connectedness is essential to a healthy self. We must be connected to Christ, connected to absolute values like honesty and goodness, connected within ourselves, and connected to others. The family, church, social networks and friendships are all aspects of community that help us to become healthy selves. Selfism encourages isolation, rather than fostering this connectedness.

Many believe this isolation is exacerbated by an overemphasis on *individual* psychotherapy. Even when a problem involves more than one family member, usually only one person "gets help." Most therapy excludes offspring—unless the child *is* the problem—as it does parents of older teenagers or adults. One valuable corrective to this overly individualistic emphasis and understanding of the self that we see in modern psychotherapy has been the increasingly popular "family systems" approach. Since we do not live in a vacuum, difficulties are seen to be "problems in living," not just problems within the self. This type of therapy focuses on the *whole troubled system*, rather than just on one troubled individual. The systems approach especially values the interpersonal *relationships* in everyone's life, and examines how the family system functions to foster health or dysfunction.

An awareness of rural and tribal life in Southern Africa increased my understanding of how other cultures differ from our Western independence. An injured or diseased villager would often walk many miles to reach the nearest missionary clinic. But not only the patient came. *Every member of the family* would come to the clinic whenever anyone was sick. For every patient, six to ten other adults and children would also arrive on their doorstep. Why? Because they believed that *all sickness* was a family matter. Everyone contributes to and suffers from the sickness of one member of a family. We have slowly lost this community concept as a result of our individualistic way of thinking.

This principle holds true even more for emotional or other psychological problems than for physical illness. The pain of an appendicitis is focused in the patient, but the problems of a drug-addicted teenager in trouble with the law take their toll on the total family system. Indeed, the larger system *is* the problem, at least to some extent, and needs help *just as much as* the troubled teenager.

Today's overemphasis on individual pathology and treatment carries in its wake a strong anti-family slant. Therapists sometimes purposely turn family members against each other as a way of supposedly helping people achieve independence. Early in Freud's practice, he always believed his patients' descriptions of childhood sexual abuse and supported their estrangement from their families. Only later did he learn through outside information that the reports were frequently fabricated as a part of the therapy process.

Many are currently repeating the same mistake as therapists zealously hunt for evidence of sexual abuse. Just as in Freud's day, scores and scores of relatives are being accused of the most atrocious crimes. Cases of abuse are abundant, but many actually turn out to be false. In a study conducted by the American Academy of Child Psychiatry examining child custody battles involving sexual abuse, as many as thirty-six percent of allegations provided to be untrue.[3] Misleading questioning by adults and the power of suggestion of therapists can lead children to make statements that can send a parent to jail and destroy families. Behind the scenes may be a therapist who "discovers" this information, yet doesn't take the trouble to talk to the whole family. The focus is only on the individual.

In order to support the family in its rightful role as the shaper of the healthy self, these potential dangers of an overly individualistic approach need to be recognized and avoided. Unhealthy families certainly harm the child. Breaking the cycle of dysfunction passed from generation to generation often requires outside intervention.

A healthy family helps the development of a healthy self in several ways. Here are a few of the primary ones:

1. By helping us to face up to the reality of our world and teaching us to respond positively to its challenges and crises.
2. By providing encouragement, support, and an "honest mirror" so we can see how we are responding and make changes.
3. By teaching us how to cope, communicate and care about one another. The self develops a less selfish and more rounded personality by being "in community."
4. By teaching us how to express love and appreciation for one another, it serves as the primary source of self-esteem for the growing self.

In order to be healthy, the family and the self must also be connected to a meaningful community. The church, the fellowship of believers, is our "second" family, which provides vital support, as do friendships and other social involvements.

Other cultures often highlight the deficiencies of Western individualism in creating the right environment for self-growth. Our sense of self tends to have sharp boundaries that stop at one's skin, clearly demarcating your self from your non-self. Asian cultures, for instance, view kinship and even the neighborhood as *extensions* of the self, rather than discrete entities. Cultures that value community over the individual create a more permeable sense of self, where the *me* merges with the *we* more easily.

The selfist, individualistic ideas of our Western world are really in conflict with what Scripture teaches. The Word of God as inspired by the Holy Spirit presents human existence as part of an extended community. A worldview which emphasizes the *I* can create immense conflict and shape our personality in an undesirable direction.

We Westerners tend to be more selfish and angry, and consequently more anxious and depressed when things don't go our way. God's Spirit faces a greater battle within us because we tend to think more of *me* and less of *us*. Our expectations tend to be oriented around ourselves, rather than the larger community to which we belong. We thereby create a self that is embattled, easily demoralized, and beaten down.

Because individualism and selfism are woven so finely into the social fabric of our culture, we cannot easily separate ourselves from it. One of the few "havens" or safe places is the Christian church, a crucial counterbalance to the influence of our "me" culture.

GOD'S LOVE BREAKS DOWN THE BARRIERS

Some sort of sickness in the self seems essential to prepare us to receive God's love. If we were perfect, we wouldn't need God! As a consequence of the Fall, no ego- or self-system escapes the contamination of the sinful core—no matter how "good" it may look on the outside. The emerging self is then thrust into a world dominated by other sinful cores, causing pain and distress. Some extremely isolated and rejected people live on the verge of suicide every day. "If one more thing happens to me," one lady told me recently, "I'm just going to end it all. I can't take any more pain."

This kind of pain may be the gateway to God's healing. Our *extremity* is often God's *opportunity*. We know that each human being faces a limit to the physical pain he or she can endure. Have you ever watched someone in the terminal stages of cancer? The agony can seem unbearable. But the deeper pain in the heart and mind often defies description.

One of our friends recently faced a crisis with her husband. "I've had enough," he said. "I want a new life. I've found someone else," he said. With no warning whatsoever, he left her. Having deeply loved her husband, she was utterly devastated. Grieving the death of a spouse can be a lot easier than living with this sort of personal rejection. Death is usually unavoidable; the breakup of this marriage could have been avoided.

Even watching her grief was itself quite painful for us. Is her grief unhealthy? Not really. Often the healthier self feels this sort of pain even more deeply. Callousness is not one of the attributes of emotional health. But what can such a hurting self do to continue on?

Often at such a crucial juncture, God's love reaches out irresistibly to the hurting self. If that person finds one who *really forgives*, he or she can find a strength that enables them not to become embittered or estranged because of the offense. Furthermore, if the self finds one who bears the injury of personal sin and yet still loves unconditionally, that self can be healed as surely as day follows night. The power of divine forgiveness that loves even the vilest of sinners holds tremendous appeal for each of us. God has specifically shaped us to respond to his divine forgiveness. The self is irresistibly drawn to it.

Our friend found herself drawn to this forgiving love of God. Before her husband's rejection, she was only a nominal Christian. The pain which quickly thrust her into the arms of God didn't disappear, but it did become bearable.

The self hungers for this unconditional love above everything else. It will devote all its energies to serving this love. In the firm grip of God, the self enjoys being occupied with the larger purpose in life inspired by his love. The self that finds its way back to this love is a healthy self. Success or failure in the eyes of the world makes no difference. The self is content to just "be" in the presence of a God who loves this way.

A pastor who recently took one of my doctoral classes wrote to me: "I've been trying to identify what it is you did for me in this course. Now I have a notion. You were being used by God to unleash the presence of Christ within my heart in that area of my being called the *self* so that, by Christ's presence, I could begin to exercise self-control." His sentiments just about sum up what I believe to be a "healthy" self.

SPIRITUAL RESOURCES FOR BUILDING A HEALTHY SELF

I do not want to give the impression that the only effective resources for building a healthy self come from the domain of psychology. While I try to resist making distinctions between psychological and spiritual factors in health, since we are made to function as integrated, whole persons, nevertheless some resources clearly have more of a "spiritual" focus. They are equally, or even more, important as tools for building a healthy self. Allow me to mention a few of them:

Obedience to God. I think it goes without saying that a healthy self is an obedient self. What is important, of course, is to whom you are obedient. Since God knows what is best for you, why wouldn't you want to be obedient to the max? The more you obey, the closer you come to God's ideal plan for your life. But obedience is also important because it teaches us a lot about ourselves. The points we resist can serve as mirrors to help us see ourselves honestly. Obedience also releases God's power in our lives. When we do something out of obedience, God helps us to accomplish it.

Repentance and confession. Repentance and confession are not only necessary to salvation, they continue to be the essence of the life of faith. God's forgiveness can only be claimed in response to confession (1 Jn 1:9). Furthermore, "He that covereth his sins shall not prosper" (Prv 28:13). In a very real sense, the self that does not address sin directly and remove its ongoing power cannot become healthy. Such a self refuses to participate in the process of sanctification and must thus become stifled and stagnant in its growth.

Love of God. It is the love of God that draws us to salvation, and it is the love of God that continues our sanctification. We desire to be possessed by and to possess God's love. A healthy self is able to both love God and be loved by God. Through prayer, the self becomes more and more inspired by and humbled by this love.

Love of others. The hallmark of a healthy self is its capacity to both give and receive love. We have yet to discover in psychology just how crucial this is and how easily family and other relational dysfunctions can damage this capacity for love. A self that desires wholeness, therefore, must be given to developing this capacity for love—a capacity that God makes possible if he is allowed to indwell us. How can we learn to be more loving? Ask God for the power to love—and then just keep doing it. It becomes easier as you practice it!

Self-disciplines. There are a number of self-disciplines that help to build a healthy self. I don't just mean learning self-control over habits that would otherwise destroy us, but also the disciplines of humility, self-sacrifice, and thanksgiving. The more God is allowed to control our total selves, the more we are able to achieve a healthy self. It's as simple, yet as challenging, as this. And the more we achieve progress in the disciplines of faith the more we are able to respond in ways that further develop the healthy self. This is the synergism of spiritual and psychological health. They work together to produce a complete whole—and this is the total wholeness that should characterize every believer.

11 | The Gospel of Self-Esteem

B EN HATES HIMSELF. He says so quite openly, almost as if he is proud of it. He dislikes everything about himself—his physical appearance, his intellect, his personality. In short, he would rather be someone else. Even though Ben can't abide thinking about himself, he actually thinks about himself a lot. He avoids large groups and displays obvious signs of discomfort when he is the center of attention. Although now in his mid-thirties, this guy feels so inferior that he has never made an attempt to court a girl, although deep down nothing would please him more than getting married.

Perhaps Ben is an extreme example, but he suffers from a very common problem: a primary defect of the self which can render it incapable of thinking well of itself. Ben needs a large dose of *self-esteem*, what *Newsweek* calls the "latest national elixir," which is really nothing new.[1] This special tonic promises to cure everything from poor grades to bad teeth. It preaches the message that there are no bad people, only people who think badly of themselves.

Many skeptics, however, fear that self-esteem has become the mantra of social science, psychology, psychotherapy, education, and even religion. And I agree. I think we've created a monster just by naming it. But what else can we call it? Insisting that our esteem should come solely from Christ, many critics of psychology abhor the idea of *self*-esteem.

No matter how much we may object to the term "self-esteem," the existence of such a phenomenon is undeniable. The self is sufficiently self-aware to form an "image" or global picture of itself. Once having gone that far, who among us fails to adopt a value judgment about that image? Whether we accept or reject the name we have assigned it, we cannot escape the fact that *the self has an attitude toward itself.* This crucial concept often determines the difference between a self that functions smoothly and one that just muddles along. We must look this issue squarely in the eye and try to avoid the pitfalls as we try to understand self-esteem from a Christian point of view.

We all stare dumbfounded when Muhammad Ali quips: "When you're as great as I am, it's hard to be humble." We hope he boasts with tongue in cheek. On the other hand, Mark Twain says, "Deep down in his heart no man much respects himself." We cringe, fearing someone's been peeking into our souls again. Somewhere in the middle of these extremes, can we find a safe road to travel on our journey toward a balanced understanding of self-esteem?

NAVEL-GAZING: A NATIONAL PASTIME

Self-esteem has been a hot topic ever since it was first labeled. People continue to squabble about its meaning. "High self-esteem" is interpreted as anything from feeling good about ourselves to having a sense that we could master whatever comes our way. "Low self-esteem" is interpreted as inner feelings of incompleteness, emptiness, self-doubt, and self-hatred.

Almost every disorder is blamed on low self-esteem. Too little holds a person back in life, results in teenage pregnancy, sets someone up for addictions, or triggers eating disorders like anorexia nervosa or bulimia. While it has become a paradigm for analyzing almost every problem in the American culture, many see low self-esteem as a byproduct of our relentless search for a deeper understanding of human existence.[2]

Low self-esteem has become a sort of "meta-addiction" that afflicts everyone. This "national elixir" has infiltrated the church right along with the secular world. Christian leaders spanning the theological spectrum espouse its importance, or perhaps more importantly, its appeal to ordinary folk. From Robert Schuller to Oral Roberts, achieving self-esteem seems to have become as important a message as getting saved.

But self-esteem has its enemies. Many critics of psychology call it the cardinal symptom of selfism. In sweeping and over-generalized statements, they proclaim that encouraging humans to build a sense of self-worth is "exalting humankind." They equate it with a "what's-in-it-for-me" approach to the gospel.[3] Those in this camp suspiciously eye self-esteem as a state of self-deception. Believers should take no thought for themselves, but only for pleasing and glorifying their Redeemer. If we were to take such admonishment literally, we would never exercise, eat out, or even comb our hair—all ways of "having thoughts for ourselves."

But critics are not attacking such reasonable efforts to care for our well-being. Beneath their over-reactive and generalized rhetoric lies a genuine concern. Granted, we human beings should feel enough self-worth to care for our legitimate personal needs. Without it, we wouldn't even want to exist, let alone turn to God for salvation. *But how much self-concern is normal and how much becomes narcissistic and self-serving? And from what source should this esteem come?*

These statements put the problem in a nutshell. We need to introduce *balance* into our notions of self-esteem. Yes, the "gospel of self-worth" has gone too far. But the remedy is hardly to replace it with a "gospel of self-hate." I believe that the self saturated with Christ can achieve the right balance. I find it very unrealistic to tell people that they should never think about how they feel toward themselves.

A troublesome imbalance is brewing around this whole issue as the secular world increasingly looks to self-esteem in a rather unrealistic way to fix many of its problems. The concept of self-esteem has established itself in almost every area of society. At least ten national and regional conferences in 1991 focused on self-esteem problems.[4] The State of California has appointed a state commission to promote self-esteem. In Minnesota, a program called the "Very Important Kid" encourages positive self-regard in children ages three to six.

In fact, nowhere has this concept taken root as firmly as in education. From toddlers to high-schoolers, "Project Self-Esteem" workshops or programs are starting in many cities. Because repeated failure is so destructive to a child's ability to self-esteem, the San Diego school system tried to abolish failing grades in all its schools. An outraged public rescued the "F" grade before the plan could take effect.

Is our confidence in self-esteem justified? If we could cure all self-esteem problems, would we solve all our social ills and salvage our youth from self-destruction? Like so many complex questions, the answer is not simply yes or no. Clearly we must attend to how our young people are feeling about themselves. However, the solution cannot come entirely from within the self.

But those who ardently reject self-esteem as a humanistic invention refuse to see the whole picture. Even the wealthiest of countries faces mammoth social dilemmas. Certain groups are increasingly being disenfranchised, resulting in rampant self-esteem problems. Extreme competitiveness takes its toll on many youngsters. They easily become confused about their identity or develop a pervasive sense of self-rejection, even self-hatred. Only a few ever experience enough success to avoid damage to their self-image. The rest lose confidence in themselves and become self-rejecting.

While we may have become overly preoccupied with the idea or carried it too far, the problems associated with self-esteem offer great cause for concern. Growing numbers of people are turning to drugs or alcohol to dull the pain. Teenage girls in search of love and approval give in to sex and get pregnant. Criminologists tell us that delinquency is often caused by kids trying to show off. To help them feel better about themselves, they "perform to an audience" to earn external respect.

The phenomenon of self-esteem exists because the self exists. But serious flaws haunt the solutions being offered. Becoming a nation of flatterers, ignoring all wrong behavior, and only praising right behavior will not correct the self-esteem problem.

Abolishing all criticism and failing grades will not strengthen the human character. Such a quick-fix may only make it more vulnerable.

Trees able to withstand hurricanes are the ones which have always battled strong winds. They put down the strongest and deepest roots so that nothing can shake them. Saying *only* nice things to children doesn't necessarily make them stronger, more secure, and full of esteem. It more often turns them into shallow and ineffective adults who will be blown away by the first storm of real trouble.

Children certainly need encouragement. Lots of it. But they also need honest feedback about their faults and weaknesses. How else will they change? They also need a realistic view of a world filled with prejudice and intolerance. Sooner or later, they will be forced to take responsibility for their own shortcomings. The sooner they become aware of them, the better.

Honest feedback of both *strengths* and *weaknesses*—offered in the context of love and acceptance—helps to fill this need. Flattery does not build character, nor is it selfish or boastful to celebrate one's real strengths. Children need to learn how to be aware of their deficiencies as well as rejoice over their gifts and talents.

While our attitude toward our selves is a serious issue, I believe it an exaggeration to blame every social ill on low self-esteem. Tremendous efforts are being expended to fix this deficiency so common among our youth. Five states are following California's lead in establishing self-esteem task forces. Others are urging national legislation to address the problem. The field of education is flooded with reformers.

But do we really believe low self-esteem is the *root cause* for our social woes? Doesn't sin figure in here somewhere? Can children as well as adults really feel good about themselves when they remain broken and alienated from God? If we abolish the word "bad" and give some kind of award to children every year, will they instantly guzzle that potent elixir called "high self-esteem"? I doubt it. On the other hand, a child who is yelled at all the time, rejected, or told "you're stupid" will almost certainly develop self-hatred.

PARADOX OF PARADOXES

Evidently, whatever it is we call self-esteem is a lot easier to *destroy* than it is to *create.* What makes this so? When we examine the phenomenon of self-esteem more closely, we come up against some surprising paradoxes. Because confusion about this issue swirls even in the world of psychology, the American Psychological Association recently published its own book on the topic. In it we encounter the following insightful comment: "From a common sense point of view, trying to understand the origins of self-esteem involves several paradoxes and contradictions. One of the most intriguing is *why so many successful, competent people seem to be plagued with problems of chronic low self-esteem.*"[5]

This book then describes the reflections of one seventy-year-old man: "My whole life has been a succession of disappointments. I can scarcely recollect a single instance of success in anything that I ever undertook." Who was this man? An alcoholic who had thrown away home and family for a bottle of booze? A down-and-outer living on the street? Willie Loman, the defeated character in *Death of a Salesman?* The writer who expressed these sentiments was none other than John Quincy Adams—a man who served with distinction as the sixth president of the United States, a senator, a congressman, and a vital participant in many of the early events influencing the nation. His life had clearly not been dominated by failure, nor was he an object of scorn. Yet he apparently suffered from what we would call low self-esteem. More recently a famous feminist, Gloria Steinem, admitted that she herself has had to battle inner feelings of incompetence, emptiness, self-doubt, and self-hatred.[6]

Doesn't this capture the common plight of humankind? Most people who try to achieve self-satisfaction through their personal accomplishments are plagued with disappointment and are dissatisfied with themselves. Even the most successful people do not develop an enduring immunity to their own imperfections. Yet most of us continue to believe that if we could only achieve something great or be successful in a particular endeavor, we would feel great about ourselves. What a myth!

Why does human achievement not guarantee high self-esteem? The American Psychological Association's guidebook to self-esteem interestingly points us to some conclusions:

1. Preoccupation with external success ignores the role that internal factors play in forming the self-attitude.
2. Regardless of degree of success, affection from "significant others" is a greater determiner of esteem than great achievements or acclaim from non-significant others.
3. Unless a person learns how to receive regular *negative* feedback—such as criticism or failure—self-esteem is damaged no matter how much success is achieved.
4. Unless a person can receive and enjoy favorable feedback, he or she doesn't form a favorable self-esteem. In other words, most people tend *not* to believe the good things they are told about themselves, for reasons that are yet not clear.[7]

The bottom line seems to be that we tend to look for self-esteem in the wrong places. Clearly, we need to develop a more biblical understanding of the phenomenon we call "self-esteem."

WHAT'S IN A LABEL?

Labels often help to determine the character of the things they represent. Self-esteem carries an unchristian connotation to those who equate it with "self-love"—not the healthy kind, but the self-worshiping and self-preoccupied form. Even if we merely mean it as "treating ourselves with respect" and not being self-hating or self-rejecting, some Christians still have a problem with that particular term.

What if we substituted alternative terms like "self-valuing" or "self-dignity"? How about "self-efficacy," meaning a sense of confidence in undertaking tasks? We would still fall short of capturing the reality in question. Several separate concepts often get mixed up with esteem, like "self-love," "self-awareness," "self-image," and "self-evaluation." Clarifying how they relate with self-esteem may be helpful.

Self-love. I won't say a lot about self-love since we've already discussed it in earlier chapters. But all too often, self-love implies self-adoration or self-worship.

While it might be appropriate to talk of loving some particular aspect of myself, I doubt if I could "love" *every* part of me. Certain things about me should not be loved. In fact, they shouldn't even be tolerated. I don't love my bad temper. I don't love my selfishness. So the self that is to be loved can only be a *part* of the whole.

Then how am I supposed to love the good parts? Should I set them down in front of me and admire them? Must I bask in a warm, fuzzy feeling about my goodness? Is it the kind of passionate and possessive love I feel for my wife? The protective and affectionate love I have for my children or grandchildren? The addictive love I have for ice cream or chocolate? None of these types of love strikes exactly the right chord.

So what do we mean by loving ourselves? In the healthiest sense of the term, we simply mean to "stop hating ourselves." We stop rejecting ourselves or being so negative about our abilities. We try to be more honest and accepting about who we really are. Self-love is more the *absence of self-hate* than the presence of warm feelings.

Self-awareness. I see this second concept as the place to rightly begin our understanding of self-esteem. As the pinnacle of God's creation, human beings have been given minds capable of reflecting upon themselves. We know about ourselves; we know that we know. We are capable of standing apart from ourselves and reflecting on what we feel, do, and say.

Without adequate self-awareness, we can do a lot of damage without even realizing it. Healthy self-awareness can make us more conscious of our bad behavior or our feelings so that we can repair them and take greater responsibility for our sin. But self-awareness can be carried to an extreme. We can become so obsessed with our failings that we never accomplish anything, or we can be constantly worried about what people think of us.

Self-awareness, then, is most helpful when it is objective or neutral, when it does not fuel self-rejection but helps us to simply accept the fact of our existence. It is a necessary *prerequisite* to self-esteem, but it is not synonymous with it. Out of self-awareness come the ingredients for how we feel about ourselves.

Self-image. Out of our self-awareness, we begin to build "pictures" of who we are. Out of the abundance of approvals, rejections, successes, and failures, we begin to form a mental image of ourselves. Others reflect back what they see and how they feel about us. We view ourselves not just in mirrors, but through the eyes of others. The global picture we form constitutes our "self-image" —sometimes called the "self-concept." Notice, it is *not* the same as self-esteem, which comes *after* the image is formed. Many people confuse these two concepts.

One valuable exercise involves "capturing" this image on paper. I wish we had psychic cameras which could photograph our inner pictures, but since we don't, we have to rely on word pictures. You can either verbally tell stories about yourself, or you can write a list of characteristics that you think describe you.

a. Begin by listing your *physical* characteristics. How tall are you? What sort of build? How do you stand, walk, talk, gesture, grimace, or gesticulate? One of the values of this exercise is to check out how accurately you see yourself, which gets harder the deeper you look. Ask a friend. Are your ideas either exaggerated or underemphasized?

b. Now move to your *psychological* self-image. How do you see your personality? Are you always honest? What are you afraid of? What do you like or dislike about yourself? What motivates you? What do you want out of life? Where do you think you fail as a person? As you answer these kinds of questions, you will begin to develop a clearer understanding of your psychological self-image.

c. How about your *spiritual* self-image? How do you feel toward God? How do you react to God's call for obedience? Are you a prayerful person? Do you even really feel like a Christian?

Other aspects of your self-image could be explored as well, but these few serve to illustrate how you can work toward developing an accurate self-portrait. Remember to keep your personal *evaluation* of these characteristics—either positive or negative—out of the picture as much as possible. This comes into play in the next step. At this stage, the self-image part of self-esteem ideally has no value attached to it.

Self-evaluation. This fourth step moves into the area of *feelings.* Whenever human beings are faced with personal information—whether true or false—we immediately want to attach meaning or value to it. We automatically appraise the trait as good or bad.

For example, if a high school student sees himself as incompetent at sports, he probably hates his lack of coordination and fears none of the girls will pay any attention to such a klutz. If his sister is overweight, she definitely won't be happy about it. If his father receives praise as a good tennis player, this will definitely please the old guy. If his mother has just received a promotion at work, she will proudly boast about it. Basically, we value success and we hate failure—at least as defined in the eyes of our culture.

Self-esteem. As we begin to add up these positive and negative values about our self-image, an overall sense of value gradually comes into focus. We have given the label of "self-esteem" to this particular phenomenon of attaching a *global value* to our generalized self-image. Perhaps we could have come up with a better name with more careful thought, but now this particular label seems to have stuck.

Let me summarize how these individual ingredients combine to make up what we call self-esteem. *Self-awareness* leads to the formation of *self-image*, which automatically provokes *self-evaluation*, which creates a global sense of self-value, which we call *self-esteem.*

Even though we may take issue with the label, *we cannot deny our tendency to value ourselves.* We would have to blot out the brain's ability to store self-images in files labeled good and bad. What we *can* do, however, is try to develop a healthier picture of ourselves. We need to try to understand what we mean by self-esteem, not just criticize it as a faulty term. Then we need help not to inappropriately attach positive or negative values on this self-image.

The Apostle Paul gives us as clear a prescription for self-esteem as you will find anywhere. He first calls us to dedicate our lives to God and to be transformed by the "renewing" of our minds. Then Paul goes on to say, "By authority of the grace God has given me, I say to everyone among you: Do not think too highly of yourself, but form a sober estimate based on the measure of faith that God has dealt to each of you" (Rom 12:3).

"Sober estimate" here means "honest and truthful." While Paul is especially concerned about the danger of inappropriate pride or conceit, his admonition applies equally to the opposite extreme of self-hate or self-rejection. We are to form an honest and truthful estimate of ourselves, based on the measure of faith that God gives us. This biblical prescription provides a perfect remedy for our problems with self-esteem.

The final outcome of self-esteem, then, is our "judgment" or evaluation of the facts that make up our self-image. By understanding these four components as separate entities in a total process, we can more clearly see to individually influence each step. Such an analysis helps us to build or heal self-esteem problems. We can address both the *formation of the self-image* ("form a sober estimate") and the *judgment* we place upon it ("do not think too highly of yourself"), in order to effect a more balanced final outcome: healthy self-esteem.

MENTAL GYMNASTICS

With this background in mind, I would now like to present a more biblical understanding of self-esteem. Figure 5 represents this model. (See figure 5 on the following page.)

Follow this diagram as I describe the process by which self-esteem develops. Starting at the top, we see the self's ability to reflect upon itself and form a "self-image." This is nothing more than an internal "self-picture." In addition to our own mental snapshots, other people usually play a major role in helping us form this self-image. We receive reflections of our-

THE STRUCTURE OF SELF-ESTEEM

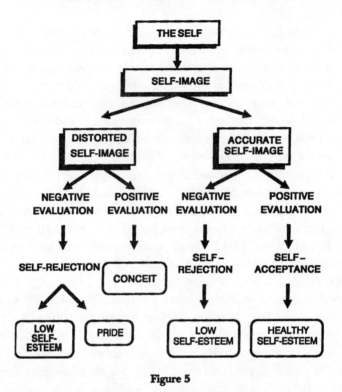

Figure 5

selves from parents, relatives, siblings, and friends.

In an endless feedback-loop, the way we behave also influences the reflections of others. A crying baby may elicit a sympathetic hug or a disapproving frown. The toddler who throws food on the floor will likely be reprimanded by the parents and simultaneously giggled at by the siblings. The young winner of a race garners rave reviews from relatives, but perhaps angry glares from defeated foes. Especially over the formative years of early childhood, these reflections gradually accumulate to form a general self-portrait. This self-image will be primarily either *accurate* or *distorted.* It will most likely be distorted since it forms at such an immature and highly impressionable age. We cannot always accurately perceive the reflections of others because the mind is not always rational or objective. Instead, it is highly selective. The mind cannot possibly process all of our available sense perceptions.

Absolute self-honesty is virtually impossible for even normal people in our culture, let alone young children. This universal distortion of the self-image is the beginning of our trouble with self-esteem. If not for this natural propensity, we would probably not be so preoccupied with such problems.

Marianne typifies so many of today's young adults. When I first met this young woman in her mid-twenties, she seemed to have a lot going for her. Quite attractive, intelligent, friendly, and talented, Marianne had even been voted the most popular girl of her senior class in high school (an unofficial poll of course). One couldn't help but like her. She seemed so open, accepting, and uncomplicated.

Marianne was just beginning to build a very successful career for herself in advertising. So why in the world did she seek out the help of a therapist? At first, Marianne had difficulty identifying and verbalizing what was bothering her. She began talking about a recent disappointment in love, a young man who had taken a serious interest in her a year earlier.

Marianne described her teen years to me. She had a few boyfriends, but had deliberately delayed any serious dating in order to concentrate on finishing her studies and starting a career. Her decision to put "first things first" received the full support of her parents. But as we talked, she began to question whether this was her real reason for not dating more seriously.

This young man she had been seeing at first appeared to be a fine person—considerate, polite, and faithful. But after a while, Marianne began to notice that he had a bad temper and would "sulk" for days at a time if he didn't get his way. The closer they became, the less he could control his temper and the longer he took to get over his sulks. Marianne became increasingly uncomfortable in the relationship. This clearly wasn't the sort of person she wanted to marry, so she finally ended the relationship.

This disappointment in love started her thinking. Why had she waited so long to date? And then when she did, why did she immediately take up with a real loser? Slowly Marianne began to get in touch with her feelings about herself. What emerged was the awareness that she did not like herself. She had never confronted these feelings before. Now they were screaming at her!

For a long time, this young woman had unconsciously fantasized that she was someone else, someone quite different. Her dreams often played out such fantasies. When I pushed Marianne to describe this "someone else," one theme began to clearly emerge. This other person was tall and slender. Marianne perceived herself as short, frumpy, and plump.

As long as she could remember, Marianne had idealized "tallness" and "slenderness." She would spend hours pouring over fashion magazines and admiring the thin, elongated shapes of the typical models displayed on glossy pages. Models never looked short. I pointed out that you cannot actually be sure of someone's height purely from a photograph of one person alone, but I was wasting my breath. This wasn't about *facts*. It was about *feelings*.

What made matters worse was that her older sister looked just like these models. Intellectually, Marianne knew she was well-proportioned. In fact, she looked fine even in a bathing suit. But still Marianne felt disatisfied with her appearance.

The more we explored this issue, the more Marianne realized that these feelings about herself had been around a long time. Could it be, she wondered, that these feelings had unconsciously prevented her from dating before? And then when she could no longer come up with a plausible reason not to date, was it possible that she took up with a flake because she didn't feel she deserved anything better? All very possible. But we can never really be sure about such things. We can only speculate.

What was clear to me, however, was Marianne's distorted self-portrait. Compared to the average woman, she is in actuality not short. The problem is that she is not *tall*—a big difference. Marianne was using a very "relative" standard when she labeled herself as short, comparing herself to an older sister who was much taller and to both her parents who were taller. She was more like her grandmother. Clearly, Grandma's genes for average height had skipped a generation and an older sibling and landed plonk on Marianne. The family gene for tallness had swerved around her.

Very early in her teenage years, Marianne had become acutely aware of being shorter than her sister. She became quite self-conscious whenever she was with her sister, a person she both admired and yet resented. The fact that Marianne could never inherit her hand-me-down clothes only accentuated what was to become a grossly distorted self-image. She wasn't testing her self-image against a standard set by the average height for girls her age. Marianne was testing it against a very specific standard—her sister's height. And she came up short!

Marianne's dilemma highlights a serious problem with developing our self-image: it can be distorted, a little or a lot. It does not rationally receive and weigh all the *facts* about itself and form them into a coherent self-image. It receives these facts and processes them through all sorts of emotional and idealistic filters. Those messages which finally get through to the brain to form our self-portrait invariably paint the wrong form in the wrong colors. That usually faulty image determines our feelings about ourselves, which we in turn project back to the world.

How many of us have a distorted self-image? I believe we all suffer from this problem to some extent. I have yet to meet *anyone* who has a totally accurate view of every aspect of himself or herself.

A TRUE IMAGE

We will return later to the issue of how to determine if a self-image is distorted or not, but for now let's move on to the next level. In Figure 5, you can see that self-image splits into two extremes: the *distorted* self-image and the *accurate* self-image. I'm speaking hypothetically, of course. Each of us actually falls somewhere on the *continuum* between these two extremes, at least in terms of our "global" self-portrait. If we break that image up into its different components—how we look, how smart we are, or what we are capable of doing—each trait will be in a different place on the continuum.

Obviously, the further we are to the "accurate" side of the self-image, the healthier will be our self-concept and the less likely we will be to suffer from self-esteem problems. But there is a catch, which will become clear at the next level down.

Before moving on, we need to ask a very pertinent question: by whose standards is the image determined to be "accurate"? We can't always trust our own judgments, which is why we have problems in the first place. So whom do we trust? *God is the only reliable source of data about yourself,* the only one who can tell you whether or not your self-image is distorted. We'll see how we can use the help God provides in forming and reforming our self-image later.

Now let's move down one more level on the diagram. We have these two extremes for the self-image, distorted and accurate. But we also know that the self has the capacity to evaluate, judge, and attribute value to the self-image. We either hate it, or we like it, or fall somewhere in between. Therefore these two images can also be described as having two extremes: the *negative* evaluation and the *positive* evaluation. Again, we fall somewhere between these two extremes on both the distorted and accurate ends of our self-portrait.

As we saw earlier, Marianne's self-image is distorted. But she can fall somewhere between the extremes of negatively or positively evaluating this image. She can like it or dislike it. Her self-image does not have to be accurate to be appraised. A distorted self-image can also be accepted or rejected. Marianne thinks, quite erroneously, that she is too short. Marianne evaluates her distorted perception and her feelings reflect her dislike of her height.

What if Marianne was in fact short, but believed she was tall? Let's imagine that her parents had told her from birth that she was just perfect. Then as she got older, they reflected the perception that Marianne was tall and slender, the ideal physical woman. Such parents certainly exist. This would also be a distorted self-image, but in a positive direction. This young woman would value herself as tall when she was not.

Would this qualify as healthy self-esteem? Not in my book. Neither a *positive* nor a *negative* evaluation of a *distorted* self-image is truthful. A twisted picture can *never* provide an adequate foundation for healthy self-esteem, simply because it is not based on truth. Or to repeat the biblical language of Romans 12:3, it is not a "sober estimate" of ourselves. A distorted self-image will *always* lead to distorted self-esteem. Sooner or later, Marianne will discover that her image of herself is incorrect. If her esteem is based on this mistaken image, she could have a very devastating awakening.

Many parents actually harm their children by unreservedly praising everything they do. These kids grow up believing they're perfect! The constant flattery, compliments, and applause promotes an exaggerated sense of personal competence and importance. They become conceited and pompous, often a real pain to be around. Without having been honestly critiqued, their false sense of confidence overshadows any underlying awareness of weaknesses. Having been fooled into believing they are better than they really are, they like it! Such a self-image feels good! Their self-evaluation is highly positive, but the image they value is false.

Sooner or later such people will experience failure or rejection. Their puffed-up esteem will pop like an overinflated balloon. It is full of air—and hot air at that. Flattery always builds a distorted self-image. Affirmation helps to build an accurate one.

Now let's look at the other side of the diagram, the "accurate" self-image side. Suppose that Marianne is correct in her perception, that she actually *is* short compared to other women in general. Here again, this process of self-evaluation operates in the same two extremes. Her self-image of being short can be valued as negative and thus rejected, or else as positive and thus accepted.

If Marianne *doesn't like* being short, she is still better off than if her self-image was distorted. She has less distance to go in achieving healthy esteem for her self. Perhaps Marianne is *accepting* of her shortness, even if she doesn't actually "like" it. This is the best place of all, the place of healthy self-esteem. Her self-image is honest and truthful and she accepts and values whatever it is.

PUFFED UP WITH CONCEIT

The bottom of the diagram lists the other possible end results of developing our self-image. If we travel along the road of a distorted self-image, there are two outcomes: *self-rejection*, which creates self-hatred or what is typically called "low" self-esteem, or *conceit*, which I would define as too high an estimate of yourself or the acceptance of a positively distorted self-image. We think we're better than we really are and we highly approve that self-image. This causes us to overvalue our abilities and to have an exaggerated opinion of ourselves.

Notice that conceit *must* be based on a distorted self-image. If I claim to be a terrific golfer when I'm really not, I am being conceited. But if I claim to be an accomplished pianist and can point to a string of trophies in my home, am I being conceited? Not if I am stating the facts without gloating over my accomplishments to prove to myself that I'm really not as bad as I think I am.

We can find *low self-esteem* listed in two places in this diagram. The first is under the negative evaluation of a distorted self-image. This is Marianne's problem—the problem of most, if not all, of us. Our overly competitive culture propels us in this direction. Too much preoccupation with appearance and performance leaves most of us feeling like we don't "measure up."

Consequently, we subtly distort our self-image and then place a negative value on our conclusions. Our inability to accurately describe ourselves in all respects is the most frequent cause of low self-esteem or self-hatred. This "epidemic of inferiority" has provoked the self-esteem movement, self-appointed militia which "hunts down negative thoughts with a holy zeal." While only about ten percent of us will openly admit we have low self-esteem, a *Newsweek* Gallup Poll found that more than fifty percent diagnose the condition in someone else in their family.[8]

WHAT'S THE REMEDY?

While many of us do struggle with how we view ourselves, most of the solutions that are being offered—either by psychotherapists or legislative and political action groups—are going to fall far short of solving the problem. Most of the proposed remedies merely encourage us to shift from a *negative* evaluation of a distorted self-image to a *positive* evaluation of the same distorted image. "Just think more positively about yourself." But the best this message can achieve is a growth in either conceit or pride, a shift which does not solve self-esteem problems. A much more drastic move is necessary.

Let me point out one more level of damage on the distorted self-image side of the diagram. *Self-rejection* can lead to either continued rejection—and low self-esteem—or else to greater efforts to "overcompensate" for the perceived deficiency. If Marianne continued to reject her shortness, she could try to overcompensate for her shortness by trying to become a great swimmer. She could devote herself totally to her sport in an effort to prove to herself that she was not inadequate.

But will the accumulation of a lot of trophies succeed in increasing Marianne's self-esteem? All the research shows that such success does *not* help people feel better about themselves at all. The *facts* about being a good swimmer are not that important if Marianne still *feels* short. Her ongoing self-rejection will continue to fuel her low self-esteem.

What if Marianne further tries to augment her esteem by boasting about her trophies? Anyone who shows the least interest is immediately given a tour of trophyville. Then the unhealthy form of *pride* takes hold. Marianne may spend hours polishing and arranging her trophies, talk about them as often as she can, and show them off at every opportunity. These behaviors are her defense against self-rejection. I see pride as a variation in efforts to overcompensate, just a different way to offset the negative evaluation of a distorted self-image. If the image were not distorted to begin with, we wouldn't need pride or conceit.

We often try to move someone from low-esteem by saying "take pride in your accomplishments," or "think positively" about what you can do. Such advice usually only entrenches them further in self-rejection and self-hate. Their primary problem is a distorted self-image. Until they are willing to face who they are honestly and realistically, they can never develop healthier self-esteem. In order to form an accurate picture of the self, we need to journey back up to the self-image and then come down on the *other* side of the diagram.

NO ONE IS PERFECT

Now let's look more carefully at the right side of the diagram depicting the "accurate" self-image. If Marianne rejects a true picture of herself, she will end up with a *second* form of low self-esteem. We may be accurate in assessing that we aren't good-looking, that our intellect is not the greatest, or that we're not good at sports. And if we reject ourselves for any of these facts, we will inevitably suffer from a feeling of inferiority. But we're still closer to health, because at least we're being truthful about our self-image.

The bottom line is that no one can be perfect in all respects. We all have deficiencies and flaws. Those of us who were raised in a healthy environment received feedback about ourselves that honestly reflected *both* our assets and our imperfections. The self-image is thus shaped more *realistically*. When we realize we cannot be totally perfect, we can more easily recognize areas of superiority in others without feeling resentful.

When this accurate and realistic self-image is accompanied by a positive evaluation, it leads to *self-acceptance*. This in turn leads to *healthy self-esteem*, a term I prefer to "high self-esteem." Indeed, this is the *only* road to self-esteem in which we experience intrinsic worthiness, free of a need to compete or overcompensate to prove ourselves. We are able to accept our imperfections with equanimity. Regrettably, other models of self-esteem fail to make this point adequately. They hold to the idea that we should be "positive" about ourselves and ignore or overlook our imperfections. Such an approach is not realistic.

In summary then, the ingredients for healthy self-esteem are:

1. A realistic self-image based on the full and complete knowledge of ourselves, both our strengths and weaknesses, good points and bad. We know who we are.
2. Our complete acceptance of this self-image. This is how God has made us. We don't try to be what we are not. It is sufficient that we exist and that God loves us. Although we might strive for excellence, we do not make this the basis of our self-evaluation.

How does God figure into all of this? Some have said that it is because God loves us unconditionally that we can begin to accept ourselves as we are. Our self-worth comes from being accepted by God as worthy. These are beautiful thoughts, but I'm not so sure that God loves us unconditionally. A lot depends on what we mean by "unconditional." God has set out his *conditions* for salvation which must be met. But no matter how contaminated we are by sin and distorted in our self-image, God longs to fully restore his image in us.

Becoming a "new creation" in Christ makes us acceptable in the sight of God. Experiencing his unconditional love which paid such a price for our salvation revolutionizes how we think about ourselves. No longer do we need to fear rejection. No longer do we need to avoid looking at who we really are. Once this solid foundation for healthy self-esteem is in place, all we have to do is build on it.

12 | Reaching Your Potential in Christ

A BRAHAM MASLOW, who died in 1970, would have turned eighty-four this year. A scrawny child born to Jewish immigrants, Maslow took refuge in the local library from neighborhood gangs and from a cruel mother. At age sixteen he wrote in his diary, "I feel lousy, rotten, bad, sick, nauseated, tired." But this boy was destined to revolutionize psychology and profoundly influence our understanding of the self. His insights, especially concerning "self-actualization" and the self's "hierarchy of needs," are still highly respected.

This man who preached about self-actualization was himself a bundle of paradoxes. He helped to shape the "third force" in psychology, now called "humanism," while repudiating behaviorism and psychoanalysis. He was both gentle and intolerant, timid and arrogant. He bragged about his high I.Q. and refused to attend his mother's funeral. He infuriated his graduate students but could be nauseatingly paternalistic.

Whatever our opinion of his personal life, this tireless thinker was constantly preoccupied with trying to understand the self. Maslow passionately pondered what it meant to reach one's full potential. Later in life, he spent time recuperating from a heart attack quizzing the intensive-care nurses on their motives for working in health care.

I would like to close our examination of the self by tackling the very difficult topic of Maslow's theory of "self-actualization," sometimes referred to as "self-realization." These concepts thundered into our vocabulary as recently as the 1960's through the views of the self popularized by Maslow and Carl Rogers. Both saw the self from a humanistic perspective. They observed that the self has a drive or tendency to grow, develop, mature, and thereby strive to "actualize" or "realize" its full potential. The self is not static. It is always becoming, always searching for a better existence. Maslow and Rogers perceived self-actualization as the sovereign motive for many of our choices and actions.

Of all the notions about the self to come out of psychology, none has been more controversial in the eyes of many Christians. The irony is that many of these critics have enjoyed popularity as seminar speakers and authors of books critical of psychology. By any standard, their careers have been a process and personally demonstrate a high degree of "self-actualization." Even so, they criticize the concept severely.

So what is the real issue here? What is it about the self becoming actualized that is so abhorrent to such critics?

To be "actualized" merely means "to make actual or real." Even Christians want to make the practice of their beliefs real. What believer wouldn't want to make Christ more *real* in his or her own life? Who wouldn't want to be more actualized in his or her marriage or parental responsibilities? Many of us could benefit from being more actual or real in our friendships. The Christian ranks teem with highly actualized individuals, courageous men and women who have overcome tragedy, physical handicaps, and deprived childhoods. Their fight against overwhelming obstacles has allowed them to become outstanding witnesses for Christ, fully "actualized" in the best sense of the word. Yet they give all the glory to God for what they have achieved rather than seek applause for themselves.

No, the idea of actualization does not seem to be the problem. The stumbling block is with the *self* being actualized. Even more specifically, these critics vehemently take issue with actualizing a self that is *outside of Christ.* They find abhorrent the idea that a fallen and corrupt self—whose best before God is no better than dirty rags—can aspire to become actual and real. When we stop to think about exactly *what* is being actualized in such a self, we begin to grasp the reason for their disgust.

But their criticism is rarely balanced. They condemn the whole notion of self-actualization without specifying the exact nature of the problem. All references to self-actualization are roundly slammed as "selfist" and "humanistic." Furthermore, some even contend that the whole idea of self-actualization is "unscientific" and lacks empirical support.[1] A few would even go so far as to label it "satanic."

Paul Vitz argues, "Certainly Jesus Christ neither lived nor advocated a life that would qualify by today's standards as 'self-actualized.'"[2] I can understand why he makes this point, but surely he is referring to the non-believer's quest for actualization—one which is indeed hopelessly inadequate.

So what are we to believe? Should we discourage any form of self-actualization in our children? If so, what is the alternative? The implications of our conclusions can be far reaching indeed, as with so many ideas about the self.

I believe most of the critics are right—up to a point. They have correctly identified the weaknesses or deficiencies in many psychological concepts, but then proceeded to discard the entire idea. While we may take serious issue with the specifics of "self-actualization," we do not dare discard it altogether. How can we make sense of self-actualization from a biblical perspective?

DEFINING THE BEAST

How is self-actualization understood in the secular world? Abraham Maslow proposed the idea that all human needs form a "hierarchy." Starting with basic physiological and safety needs, they proceed up a "ladder" to higher needs, such as belonging, love, self-esteem, and status. Our highest need is called "self-actualization" or "self-realization." These human needs form a sort of pyramid as illustrated in Figure 6.

MASLOW'S HIERARCHY OF NEEDS

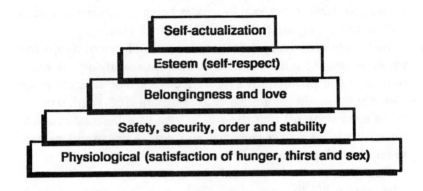

Figure 6

Maslow theorized that we are driven to meet the "lower" needs first. As these more urgent needs are met to ensure our physical survival, we progressively move up the pyramid. The highest need of self-actualization represents a sort of all-encompassing drive for fulfillment, which prompts the self to search for esthetic pleasure, order, and beauty. Once we have reached this pinnacle, we accept ourselves and others and the realities of our existence.

According to Maslow's model, people who are starving are not likely to be concerned about "higher" needs. Preoccupied with survival and security, they would live out their lives searching for food, shelter, and safety. While all of us are motivated to meet the "higher" needs of our being, deprivation and unfavorable social conditions may prevent many of us from ever reaching our full potential. Circumstances beyond our control may leave us stymied in becoming the creative and spontaneous person we were meant to be. For instance, deprived youth brought up in the inner city may be so focused on sheer survival that they never develop a meaningful career. The ever-present threat of drug disputes or rival gangs looms too large.

While merely a theory which cannot be proven experimentally, many psychologists and lay people have accepted Maslow's pyramidal model of human motivation as fact. Being driven to achieve a "higher" order of existence has a certain ring of truth in describing what human life is about. We intuitively nod yes. We certainly know that as soon as our stomach is full or our need for sex satisfied, we no longer focus on meeting these purely physical needs. We move up to "higher" concerns. Art, music, and the other "good things in life" assume greater importance.

What characterizes the fully actualized person who lives at the peak of the pyramid? Chapter ten of this book described the traits of the "healthy" self. Maslow studied many examples of healthy individuals who had made full use of their potential. In many respects, the actualized self embraces all the traits of healthiness, with a few additions:

1. It perceives life realistically and is comfortable with this reality.
2. It has a high acceptance of self and others, with little need to be judgmental or to be rejecting.
3. It is problem-centered instead of self-centered; creative with a philosophical sense of humor.
4. It is spontaneous and able to engage life to the fullest.
5. It is capable of deep and intimate relationships with specially loved people.

Not taboo in Maslow's formulation, religious experiences form a part of his "higher" order of human needs. In this respect he differed from other theorists who tended to see religion as part of the problem rather than the essential solution. Most of the exceptionally actualized persons that he studied reported ego-transcendent or mystical experiences involving feelings of ecstasy, awe, and a loss of fear, anxiety, and inhibition.

Language always seemed inadequate to describe these "peak" moments of happiness and joy, but the aftereffects were always the same: they were therapeutically beneficial. The exposure to beauty, goodness, and truth inherent in the peak experience consistently yielded greater creativity and spontaneity. Maslow believed that many neurotics were even cured by such experiences.

While some have tried to draw parallels between Maslow's

peak experiences and the mystical experiences of Christians, I tend to resist such comparisons. While conversion may be a peak experience in every sense of Maslow's idea, drawing such a parallel reduces conversion merely to a psychological experience. I believe it to be an infinitely more profound spiritual experience: God's work of grace in regenerating the core of the self. While such a renewal may have an explosive impact on the ego- and self-systems, changing some aspects of the personality and producing ecstatic joy or happiness, this peak psychological experience is also accompanied by a profound spiritual transformation.

Furthermore, conversion can occur *without* peak experience. Accompanying emotional manifestations may depend on mere situational factors—what you are doing and feeling at the time, what you ate for dinner, whether you are alone or surrounded by people you love. Just as its absence does not necessarily negate conversion, we should also *never* equate any psychological peak experience, by itself, with conversion. Peak experiences can be too easily mimicked to be of value for spiritual diagnosis.

WHAT ARE THE DEFICIENCIES OF SELF-ACTUALIZATION?

So what is wrong with the idea of self-actualization? Or better yet, what are its limits? The core assertion of this concept is that all humanity is driven by *one* motivational force: the drive to develop our capacities to the fullest in ways that will either maintain or enhance the self's well-being.[3]

Is this true? I wish it were. I know many parents of teenage kids who wish it were true. I know many school drop-outs, drug-addicts and pregnant teenagers for whom it doesn't seem to be true. It may be true for some people, but not for everyone. So the idea that self-actualization is a *natural* tendency is questionable. What we can say is that all humans have been created with the *capacity* to learn how to be self-actualizing. I see a big difference. Becoming the best we can be has to be taught; it doesn't automatically come with the human territory.

Those who preach self-actualization also assume that it hap-

pens at the core of the self and comes out of our innate goodness as human beings. While I am not one of those who asserts
that all humans are totally bad, my model of the self clearly
delineates the influence of sin. Unless our understanding of self-
actualization is divorced from the idea of a sin-free core, it will
not work. I personally know many non-believers who are holistic
and healthy, honest and honorable. But the center of the self
must still be recognized for what it really is outside of Christ:
fallen and alienated from God.

Furthermore, we cannot depend on the unregenerated core
of the self to be a trustworthy source of self-knowledge. Self-actualization demands some sense of direction which the ideal self
should pursue. The inherent subjectivity of all the moral standards that the self can conjure up guarantees that it cannot be
trusted. The blind self needs an external guide for its moral
development.

But what about all the beautiful descriptions we have for what
it means to be a healthy self? If we discard the notion of self-actualization, does it also mean we must discard our pursuit of these
characteristics? I believe not. My issue is not with the *qualities* of
the actualized person, but with the method by which we try to
attain them. Maslow and Rogers believed that once we just
released all that good stuff inside us, we would be sent into a self-
actualizing orbit of our own making like a rocket. I have tried to
show that the self must *first* be repaired at its very core. Only *then*
can the actualization of the new, Christ-centered core become a
reality.

We dare not discount the qualities of the actualized individual. Indeed, we have much to learn from those who have studied
healthiness and what it means to function at one's full potential.
We need to preach these qualities and claim them for all Christian believers. God is the author of the actualizing tendency, not
Maslow or Rogers. Actualization is the realization of our full
potential *when it has been fully restored to God's purpose.*

When we come to faith in Christ, we take upon ourselves the
responsibility to become "good and faithful servants" (Mt 25:21).
In fact, the parable of the talents makes precisely that point (see
Mt 25:14-30). While the preceding parable of the wise and fool-

ish virgins stresses the need for watchful preparation for Christ's coming, the parable of the talents emphasizes the need for faithful service during his absence.

A "talent" was a unit of money of high value, but in the parable it represents the differing responsibilities we exercise in accordance with our abilities (vv. 16-17). The unfaithful servant "hid his talent in the earth" (v. 25) and did nothing with it, whereas the faithful servants put their talents to good use and entered "into the joy of their Lord" (v. 21). Obviously this parable is not about making a financial profit, but about being responsible for developing the gifts God gives us. He wants us to be available to God so that he can "multiply" these gifts.

MAKING CHRIST REAL

Every believer should strive to develop his or her unique gifts. What is actualized or made real is not that part of the self that is hedonistic, self-seeking, self-indulging, or self-serving. We actualize our redeemed self, making it over in Christ. The core, which has already been renewed, must now be made real in every part of our being.

What we seek to fulfill is not the fallen self, but the redeemed self. This self has not only a new direction but also the power to become whole, healthy, and real because it is grounded in Christ. It seeks the best that God can offer for itself, yearning for every opportunity to reflect the purity of God. "Christian self-actualization" means making Christ real in every part of the self.

Since God is the author of all health, every characteristic of the healthy self as identified by psychology is potentially available to the believer. But God is not only the *author* but also the *enabler*. He empowers each of us to be the healthiest person we can be. He gives us the ability to be cohesive, vigorous, balanced, vulnerable, honest, controlled, spontaneous, and trustful. All the qualities of a fully actualized person are ours for the taking as believers. Sadly, many never bother to "stretch" themselves to be all that God calls them to be.

Should anything further distinguish a Christian who is fully actualized? I am saddened not so much by what *is* on the list of wonderful characteristics that distinguish a fully actualized person, as I am by what *is not.* God's additional prescription for the actualized Christian self includes:

- commitment
- confession
- contemplation
- compassion
- consecration

Commitment. First, we are committed to Christ. This is essential. But beyond this lies a commitment to our fellow believers, to our spouse and family, and even to the larger social community. By fostering preoccupation with the self even at the expense of community, secular self-actualization often omits this commitment.

Confession. Every actualized Christian should be a confessing person, willing to own up to shortcomings and to confess sins to God. A Christian is constantly aware of the fallen nature of the self and the influence of this fall on the ego and self-system. The self doesn't just need *therapy* to heal itself. Even more basic is our need for confession and forgiveness. Repentance helps us to shed the contamination of sin as we are cleansed by the blood of Christ.

Contemplation. By contemplation I mean two things. First, the contemplation that should accompany worship in all its forms: church worship, personal worship, prayer, Scripture reading, and all the spiritual disciplines. Second, the contemplation that Paul refers to when he instructs us to "examine ourselves" (1 Cor 11:28 and 2 Cor 13:5). Actualized believers do not hide from themselves. They are open to discovering the inadequacies of their inner selves so that they can change and become more complete.

A lot of psychotherapy is nothing more than forced self-contemplation. It provides an opportunity to look within and discover the places where God's Holy Spirit can become more fully realized.

Compassion. I often fail to find compassion in the highly self-actualized non-Christians I know. Their ability to love, and especially to forgive, seems to lack a certain quality. I doubt if anyone who has not personally experienced God's overwhelming love and forgiveness can be fully compassionate. We need to be touched with such compassion ourselves before we know what it is to give it.

Paul tells us, "Who comforteth us in all our tribulation [troubles], that we may be able to comfort them which are in any trouble, by the comfort wherewith we ourselves are comforted of God" (2 Cor 1:4). I strongly suspect that pure compassion and comfort are not indigenous to the secular self. They must be learned from encounters with compassionate others. Knowing God's compassion and comfort makes it possible for us to pass it on to others.

Love is also an important element of compassion. If there is one major divide between a selfist actualization and a Christian actualization, it is probably about the nature of love. Maslow only addressed love between the sexes in his writings; Carl Rogers never discusses love in any depth. He focuses on self-acceptance and "unconditional positive regard," not love as we understand it. Yet Scripture is filled with it, starting with God's love in creation and ending with God's calling and empowering us to love as he loves. No Christian is "actualizing Christ" who is not manifesting this love.

Consecration. Every Christian who is making Christ real in his or her own life has to be "consecrated" or "set apart to be holy." I don't mean this in a sacramental sense, but rather in the sense of self-sacrifice. We are to present our bodies as a "living sacrifice," holy, acceptable unto God, which is our "reasonable service" (Rom 12:1). To be consecrated is to be radical in our obedience, submissive to the will of God, dependent upon the Holy Spirit, and able to transcend the petty and mundane issues of life to understand God's eternal purposes.

These qualities of actualization are often unknown to the world. They may understand the human side of the actualizing formula, while ignoring the divine side. As Christian believers we need to know *both* sides. Integrating the spiritual and psychological dimensions of our wholeness requires hard work.

STRATEGIES FOR GROWTH

Self-actualization for a Christian is a process of realizing our own unique individuality, capabilities, gifts, and potential for continued growth and development. This goal is carried out in the context of discovering God's will for our lives and depending upon his resources—especially prayer, Scripture, and the Holy Spirit.

But to become what we are capable of becoming, we must begin with a greater awareness of who and what we already are. Then we try to discern the direction God would have us go. To be as practical as I can here, let me describe a few strategies that you can use in this process of making Christ real in your life.

Strategy number one: review your growth history. Write down how you have grown over the past few years in the following areas. "Externalizing" your answers will help you to get a clearer picture of where you are coming from than if you just tried to think about it in your head. Reflect on and pray about this history of growth. Try to identify obstacles which have prevented you from making the progress you would have liked.

- Spiritual life (prayer, Scripture study, spiritual reading, etc.)
- Psychological and emotional life
- Achieving your aspirations
- Self-understanding
- Understanding God's will for your life
- Accepting your appearance
- Accepting your weaknesses
- Owning your strengths
- Accepting your personality

- Changing aspects of yourself that can be changed
- Overcoming bad habits that are eating away at your life

Strategy number two: evaluate your present needs. We all have a particular set of needs at any given time in our lives that require urgent attention. It varies according to the stages of life (e.g., adolescence, early adulthood, or advanced years), but even within a given stage our needs change from time to time. Try to describe some of the more important and urgent needs you currently experience. Try to identify and set down your three most critical needs and write them down in order of importance.

- Friendship or particular relationships
- Success at school or work
- Improved relationship with parents, spouse, or children
- Improved social life
- Recognition
- Control of habits
- Spiritual hungers
- Being more congruent or spontaneous

Strategy number three: evaluate your present communion with God. Secular self-actualization emphasizes the importance of "communion with the self"—whatever that means. Christians emphasize communion with God as central because he is our source of strength, wisdom, self-control, and purpose. Write down your evaluation of this communion in your own life. Try not to give yourself a specific grade. You probably could not give an accurate rating anyway, and might use it as an opportunity to be self-punishing. Write your evaluation in descriptive words about the following areas:

- Prayer
- Scripture reading and study
- Participation in public worship
- Private worship
- Fellowship with other believers

Strategy number four: evaluate your values. We all hold to a specific set of values, beliefs we hold about many things, whether they are "good" or "bad," "right" or "wrong," "satisfying" or "unsatisfy-ing." At one time secular psychologists believed that all therapy had to be "value-free." No one believes this any more. *All* therapy is guided by a set of values. The values that guide a Christian's actualization should be derived from God, through the Scrip-tures, not just from humanistic philosophy or psychology. In evaluating your values, write down how you feel about the follow-ing areas. Try to determine which are important for you and which are not. How would you prioritize them? Do you want to change their ranking? Are there any of these values that are not on your list that you would like to enhance in yourself?

- Money
- Status and power
- Work and play
- Success and failure
- Relationships and family

Strategy number five: develop some general goals for your life. These goals should be concordant with what you sense God's goals are for you. Reflect and pray over your evaluation thus far. Try to ascertain what it is God has in mind for you. If you seek this guid-ance God will give it to you. Then write down several general goals for yourself for the immediate future, and some for the long term. Try to be realistic. State your goals in single sen-tences. Here are some examples:

- I would like to spend more time in prayer.
- I want to regain my health by being more diligent in exer-cise and eating habits.
- I need to get a new job where I can be more fulfilled.
- I intend to develop closer friendships or work at being more intimate with my spouse.
- I will seek out a competent Christian counselor and work through issues of pain from my past.
- I would like to work at finishing projects I start.
- I will hold myself accountable to a friend for implementing these goals.

You could move to even greater specificity, as in the following examples:

- Next summer I will take a two-week vacation.
- I will learn to type (swim, play tennis, write poetry).
- I will seek therapy to overcome my fear of flying (heights, closed places, crowds).
- I will pray and ask God to help me control my temper with my children.
- I will work at losing ten pounds before my birthday.
- I will take a Bible study course.

Now rank these goals, in order of priority for *immediate* implementation. Remember, if your goals are consistent with God's purposes, he will have a vital interest in helping you fulfill them.

Strategy number six: identify painful aspects of your life. Up to now we have focused on positive changes in building Christian actualization. But each of us also needs to identify painful aspects of life that need to be eradicated or healed. Emotional pain robs us of vitality and keeps us in a constant state of deprivation. Write down your thoughts about the following areas in as much detail as possible:

- What is the status of your marriage?
- How well have you adjusted to singleness?
- Do you carry a lot of resentment?
- Are you alienated from friends or parents?
- Are you angry with someone?

Now set out a strategy for dealing with your sources of pain. Forgiveness will be a major component in your healing, so pray for a better understanding of how to forgive. It may be that the "unfinished business" of your past will need outside help. Seek out this help as soon as possible. You will never be able to actualize your Christian self while you continue to fight ancient emotional battles or harbor grudges from your past.

Strategy number seven: maintain your renewal as a self. One of the most important distinguishing principles about Christian self-actualization is that it readily acknowledges our need for renewal *from without.* True, we can and should do some nurturing for ourselves, but *there is a limit* to what the self can do for itself. We especially need help from God. He can renew our vitality when we feel drained of all strength. He can recreate our ideals when we feel demoralized or downcast. He can refresh our staleness, repair our brokenness, and give vision to our lost dreams when we feel hopeless. Write down your answers to the following questions:

- Do you devote enough time and effort to seeking God's revitalizing strength?
- Do you obtain regular rest, adequate sleep, and relaxation to not abuse your body, which is the "temple of the Holy Spirit"?
- Do you exercise on a regular basis, control your eating, and attend to physical needs?
- Do you have any hobbies or non-stressful creative activities in your life?
- How often do you use a spiritual discipline (prayer, Scripture, fellowship) to renew your Christian self?
- Do you pause every now and again to celebrate your life in Christ and enjoy the reality of his presence?
- Do you always turn to him in times of personal crisis or difficulty?
- Are you willing to place yourself on the receiving end of compassion and comfort from others, including your pastor, friends, spouse, relatives, counselor, or spiritual advisor?

THE UNFINISHED SELF

No examination of self-actualization would be complete without reference to the biblical idea of the "unfinished" or "incomplete self." You will recall the words of Paul in Philippians 3:12: "Not as though I had already attained, either were already perfect: but I follow after...." The New English Bible translates this

Scripture more understandably: "All I care for is to know Christ and to experience the power of his resurrection.... It is not to be thought that I have already achieved all this. I have not yet reached perfection, but I press on..." (Phil 3:10-12).

Very few persons ever become fully self-actualized in the sense that they achieve the absolute peak of their unique potentialities. How can one even know when they have reached the maximum?

Our limits are a mystery known only to God. We all have the capacity to become more actualized than we are now, in the spiritual, physical, and emotional aspects of our being. But we must never become so preoccupied with our onward and upward striving that we forget our limits and fail to be satisfied with and celebrate what God has helped us achieve. One of the most subtle traps of a purely humanistic approach to self-actualization is its tendency to breed discontent. We can constantly strive to be better but not always for the right reasons. We can fail to ever celebrate our achieving anything.

I personally take great comfort in Paul's words, "It is not to be thought that I have already achieved...." As the years go by, I find myself being less driven to be the best. I have become more content to just "be" in Christ. We need to accept the fact that we will always remain "unfinished." I think this is God's plan, until we go home to be with him forever. If we ever achieved perfection in the body, we would think we no longer needed God!

So be content to be "in process." Be content to be imperfect. Be content to be unfinished. Not that we should ever stop striving for greater Christlikeness, but we should value the *journey* toward wholeness more than the *goal* itself. I want to be pressing "toward the mark for the prize of the high calling of God in Christ Jesus" up to the very last moment (Phil 3:14). There is no final point of arrival. May God keep us all faithful to the end.

Epilogue

EVERY BOOK HAS CERTAIN LIMITATIONS and this one is no exception. In a practical sense, I have confined myself to addressing only two of the primary implications of what it means to be a healthy self: that of self-esteem and self-actualization. But what I have written in this book has far-reaching implications for a host of areas which bridge the concerns of psychology and Christian faith. The need for "integrating" psychology and faith is urgent. People are being stranded in a vast wasteland of confusion, not knowing how to integrate their emotional and spiritual lives.

I have tried to lay a foundation that clearly builds on the importance of regeneration and that recognizes the work of God, through his Holy Spirit, in the whole life of the believer. Such a foundation has implications for how Christian psychotherapy should be practiced as well as for how spiritual counseling and direction should be integrated into the process of emotional growth. Regrettably, the paths of psychotherapy and spiritual direction have often diverged rather than converged.

I am left with one strong residual concern as I close this book. It is this: the modern church, especially its evangelical wing, places an excessive focus on issues of salvation rather than sanctification. I am not suggesting that we be less concerned for evangelism. Quite the contrary. But I am suggesting that scores of believers are bogged down just inside what John Bunyan in *Pilgrim's Progress* calls the "Gate." They have been delivered of their guilt and the burden of sin by the death and blood of Christ. But now they need to know how to gird up their loins and embark on their "journey," a journey of personal and spiritual growth. They need help on this journey. They need companions like Faithful and Piety, Goodwill and Hopeful. They need wise counsel. But much preaching and teaching today seems only to focus on salvation. It keeps believers hanging around the gate rather than moving on in the upward call to become like Christ. These Christians need help in moving forward—in making real the promises of God and in reclaiming the promised land called the "self," for God. God grant us the wisdom and power to point all those who are redeemed toward sanctification, showing them how to "be guided by the Spirit" so that they may become all they were created to be in Christ.

Notes

ONE
Sick of Our Selves?

1. Dave Hunt, *Beyond Seduction: A Return to Biblical Christianity* (Eugene, OR: Harvest House, 1987).
2. John MacArthur, Jr., *Our Sufficiency in Christ* (Dallas, TX: Word Publishing, 1991).
3. Hunt, 128.
4. Hunt, 151.
5. Hunt, 165.
6. MacArthur, 58.
7. MacArthur, 61.
8. MacArthur, 67.
9. MacArthur, 94.
10. Paul C. Vitz, *Psychology as Religion: The Cult of Self-Worship* (Grand Rapids, MI: Wm. B. Eerdmans, 1977), 73.
11. Vitz, 10.
12. Vitz, 13.
13. Vitz, 91.
14. Oswald Chambers, *Biblical Psychology* (London: Marshall, Morgan, and Scott, 1962), 152.
15. Ian Kent and William Nicholls, *I AMness: The Discovery of the Self Beyond the Ego* (Indianapolis, IN: The Bobbs-Merrill Company, 1972), x.

TWO
Stuck with Our Selves

1. Quoted in *The Concept of Self* by Kenneth J. Gergen (New York: Holt, Rinehart and Winston, 1971), 4.
2. J. Bronowski, *The Identity of Man* (New York: American Museum Science Books, 1965), 6.
3. Gerald E. Myers, *Self: An Introduction to Philosophical Psychology* (New York: Pegasus, 1969), 14.
4. Gregory Hamilton, *Self and Others: Object Relations Theory in Practice* (Northvale, NJ: Jason Aronson, Inc., 1988), 21.
5. Hamilton, 29.

THREE
Four Mistakes Christians Make about the Self

1. Lewis B. Smedes, *Love Within Limits* (Grand Rapids, MI: Wm. B. Eerdmans, 1979), 58.
2. Matthew Henry, *Matthew Henry's Commentary* (Grand Rapids, MI: Zondervan Publishing House, 1961), 1289.
3. Don Browning, "Psychology in the Service of the Church," unpublished paper presented to the Rech Conference, Wheaton, IL, October 25, 1990.

FOUR
Beneath the Tip of the Iceberg

1. Seymour Fishback and Bernard Weiner, *Personality* (Lexington, MA: D.C. Heath and Co., 1991), 161.
2. Fishback and Weiner, 193.
3. James F. Masterson, *The Search for the Real Self* (New York: The Free Press, 1988), 23.

FIVE
The Damage-Prone Self

1. Archibald D. Hart, *Healing Adult Children of Divorce* (Ann Arbor, MI: Servant Publications, Vine Books, 1991).
2. Philip Cushman, "Why the Self is Empty," *American Psychologist* (Washington, DC, May 1990), 599-611.
3. Cushman, 599.
4. Cushman, 605.
5. Nathaniel Branden, *The Psychology of Self-Esteem* (New York: Bantam Books, 1969), 144.
6. Christopher Lasch, *The Culture of Narcissism* (New York: Womer Books, 1979), 36.
7. Lasch, 96.
8. Lasch, *The Minimal Self* (New York: W.W. Norton & Company, 1984), 15.
9. Lasch, *The Minimal Self,* 57.

SIX
The Disordered Self

1. Ernest S. Wolf, *Treating the Self: Elements of Clinical Self Psychology* (New York: Guilford Press, 1988), 24.
2. Erik H. Erikson, quoted in *Dictionary of Pastoral Care and Counseling*, Rodney J. Hunter, ed. (Nashville, TN: Abingdon Press, 1990), 565.
3. American Psychiatric Association, *Diagnostic and Statistical Manual of Mental Disorders*, Third Edition, (Washington, DC: 1980), 321.
4. David Benner, ed., *Baker Encyclopedia of Psychology* (Grand Rapids, MI: Baker Book House, 1985), 736.
5. Flora Rheta Schreiber, *Sybil* (New York: Warner Books, 1973), 440.

SEVEN
Sin Leads to Dysfunction

1. Ray S. Anderson, *On Being Human: Essays in Theological Anthropology* (Grand Rapids, MI: Wm. B. Eerdmans, 1982), 6-7.
2. Augustus Hopkins Strong, *Systematic Theology* (Old Tappan, NJ: Fleming H. Revell, 1976), 484.
3. Scott M. Peck, *People of the Lie: The Hope for Healing Human Evil* (New York: Simon and Schuster, Touchstone Book, 1983), 269.
4. Peck, 36.
5. Strong, 549.
6. Strong, 562.
7. Dallas Willard, *The Spirit of the Disciplines: Understanding How God Changes Lives* (San Francisco, CA: Harper San Francisco, 1988), 91.
8. Ernest Becker, *Denial of Death* (New York: MacMillan Publishing Co., The Free Press, 1973).
9. Becker, 271.
10. Becker, 270.

EIGHT
Made in the Image of God

1. Willard, 67.
2. Indra Finch, "The Effect of Religion on Clinical Psychologist's Attitudes Toward Suicide" (Pasadena, CA: unpublished Ph.D. dissertation, February 1992).
3. Archibald D. Hart, *Unlocking the Mystery of Your Emotions* (Dallas, TX: Word Publishing, 1989).
4. Willard, 67.
5. Archibald D. Hart, *Healing Life's Hidden Addictions* (Ann Arbor, MI: Servant Publications, Vine Books, 1990).
6. Anderson, 215.
7. Anderson, 219.
8. E. Stanley Jones, *Victory Through Surrender* (Nashville, TN: Abingdon, 1966), 12.

NINE
Grace Heals the Evil Within

1. Helmut Burkhart, *The Biblical Doctrine of Regeneration* (Downers Grove, IL: Intervarsity Press, 1978), 7.
2. Lawrence M. Brammer and Everett L. Shostrum, *Therapeutic Psychology* (Englewood Cliffs, NJ: Prentice-Hall, 1960), 447.
3. Brammer and Shostrum, 60.
4. Becker, 271.
5. Becker, 69.
6. Peck, 269.
7. Peck, 37.
8. Peck, 40.

TEN
The Healthy Self

1. Stanton L. Jones and Richard E. Butman, *Modern Psychotherapies* (Downers Grove, IL: Intervarsity Press, 1991), 71.
2. Jones and Butman, 125.
3. Jerome Cramer, "Why Children Lie in Court," *Time Magazine*, March 4, 1991, B14.

ELEVEN
The Gospel of Self-Esteem

1. *Newsweek*, "Hey, I'm Terrific," February 17, 1992, 3.
2. *Newsweek*, "Hey, I'm Terrific," 46.
3. Hunt,, 163.
4. *Newsweek*, "Hey, I'm Terrific," 46.
5. *Self Esteem*, (Washington, DC: American Psychological Association, 1989), 4.
6. *Newsweek*, "Hey, I'm Terrific," 46.
7. *Self Esteem*, 12-14.
8. *Newsweek*, "Hey, I'm Terrific," 46.

TWELVE
Reaching Your Potential in Christ

1. Vitz, 23.
2. Vitz, 91.
3. Jones and Butman, 257.

Other Books of Interest
by Dr. Archibald Hart

Healing Life's Hidden Addictions

One out of every four Americans exhibits regular compulsive behaviors which can predispose him or her toward hidden addictions—the obsessive desire for food, sex, exercise, entertainment, relationships, shopping, and a host of seemingly innocent attachments.

Healing Life's Hidden Addictions includes self-tests to help readers determine whether they are at risk. *$8.99*

Healing Adult Children of Divorce
Taking Care of Unfinished Business
So You Can Be Whole Again

Healing Adult Children of Divorce examines the long-term effects of this traumatic event, the damaging consequences that follow children of divorce, and ways to resolve past hurts that have shaped their lives.

If you are an adult child of divorce, you probably struggle with fear, shame, anxiety, anger, and disillusionment. You may fear failure, suffer low self-esteem, and avoid risks in love and work. This book will help you find the road to healing, wholeness, and freedom. *$16.99*

Available at your Christian bookstore or from:
Servant Publications • Dept. 209 • P.O. Box 7455
Ann Arbor, Michigan 48107
Please include payment plus $1.25 per book
for postage and handling.
Send for our FREE catalog of Christian
books, music, and cassettes.